Wanted

Wanted

The Outlaw Lives

of

Billy the Kid

& Ned Kelly

ROBERT M. UTLEY

Yale

UNIVERSITY PRESS

New Haven and London

Yale University Press books may be purchased in
quantity for educational, business, or promotional
use. For information, please e-mail sales.press@yale.
edu (US office) or sales@yaleup.co.uk (UK office).

Designed by Nancy Ovedovitz. Set in Century
Schoolbook type by Integrated Publishing Solutions.
Printed in the United States of America.

Library of Congress Control Number: 2015944117
ISBN 978-0-300-20455-1
A catalogue record for this book is available from the
British Library.

This paper meets the requirements of ANSI/NISO
Z39.48–1992 (Permanence of Paper).

10 9 8 7 6 5 4 3 2 1

CONTENTS

Preface, vii

Billy the Kid

1 Billy the Kid Named Captain of Outlaw Gang, 3
2 The Making of an "Outlaw," 7
3 A Genuine Outlaw?, 13
4 Ranch Cowboy and Hired Gunman, 22
5 A Warrior in McSween's Army, 34
6 Blazer's Mill, 42
7 Billy Indicted for Murder, 47
8 "The Big Killing," 54
9 Drifter, 62
10 The Governor and the Kid, 67
11 The Kid Turns Outlaw, 75
12 Stinking Springs, 81
13 Tried for Murder, 87
14 Escaping the Hangman's Noose, 90

15 Pete Maxwell's Bedroom, 97

16 Legend and Myth, 101

Ned Kelly

17 Father and Son, 111

18 The Larrikin Years, 121

19 Stringybark, 130

20 Euroa, 140

21 Jerilderie, 147

22 A Republic?, 155

23 Glenrowan, 161

24 Path to the Gallows, 171

25 Australian Icon, 183

Conclusion, 191

Bibliographic Essay, 211

Index, 213

Illustrations follow pages 46
and 146

PREFACE

In February and March 1998, my wife, Melody Webb, and I toured New Zealand and Australia. In Beechworth, Australia, we spent the night and visited the Ned Kelly sites. That was my introduction to Ned Kelly. In driving south to Melbourne, we stopped briefly at Glenrowan. Melody pointed to a statue of Ned Kelly in armor and remarked that he was Australia's Billy the Kid. Even though I had written a biography of Billy the Kid a decade earlier, I brushed it off without further thought. At the Old Melbourne Gaol, however, as we stood next to the trapdoor where Ned was hanged and examined the adjacent suit of armor and an interpretive panel that explained who Ned Kelly was and what he had done, it dawned on me that Ned was indeed Australia's Billy the Kid. Melody made the suggestion in Glenrowan, but I failed to take it seriously until the Old Melbourne Gaol. Thereafter my goal was to write a book comparing the two. In subsequent trips to Australia, especially one in 2004, we visited the major Kelly sites and accumulated a photographic record.

Other books intervened, and the project did not get under way until Chris Rogers, my editor at Yale University Press, which had just published my biography of Geronimo, became interested in Ned and encouraged me to undertake the project. That was in 2013, and

I soon resumed the study of Ned from the stack of books I had acquired during our 2004 visit. I already had the basis for Billy the Kid
in my biography published in 1989 and its predecessor, *High Noon
in Lincoln,* published in 1987. Chris Rogers sent a contract, which
spurred the work that resulted in this book.

After that 1998 revelation in Melbourne, I sensed that enough
similarities link Billy the Kid and Ned Kelly to warrant comparison
of the two, even though they lived and operated in countries so far
distant from each other—the United States and Australia—that one
is hard-pressed to think of two places on earth farther apart.

Both lived and died at roughly the same time: Billy from 1859
to 1881; Ned from 1854 to 1880. Both died at the hands of the law,
Billy at age twenty-one, Ned at age twenty-five. Both were outlaws
who lived by the gun. Both became legends in their own time and
remain so. Both created a trail of motion pictures and television productions that continues to appear in modern times. Both have been
the subject of books, articles, and other printed material, as well as
art. Both have their own modern followers: the Billy the Kid Outlaw
Gang and the Ned Kelly Fan Club. Both spawned conspiracy theories: Billy lived until 1950 under the name of Brushy Bill Roberts.
The charred bodies pulled from the fire at Glenrowan were not Steve
Hart and Ned's brother Dan, and the two later turned up in South
Africa to fight in the First Boer War. Both Ned and Billy became
tourist attractions: you can travel the Billy the Kid National Scenic
Highway and the Ned Kelly Trail.

Neither Billy nor Ned seems to qualify as an outstanding outlaw.
Billy rustled cattle, fought in the Lincoln County War, and used his
guns on the enemy. Ned stole cattle and sheep, killed three policemen, robbed two banks, and always endured harassment from the
police. Neither, however, systematically pursued outlawry.

Australia and the United States are very different places, and
readers in both countries may find themselves confused by language, culture, politics, geography, economics, social relationships,
and ways of thinking. I have tried to remedy the confusion, not always successfully. One striking example is the position of North

America above the equator and Australia below. That means that winter in Australia is summer in the United States. The reader is left to bear in mind this distinction and, when a date in December is mentioned, keep in mind that the season is winter in North America and summer in Australia.

* * *

In expressing appreciation for assistance, I must place Ian Jones at the head of the list. I have never met him. But his biography of Ned Kelly forms the solid base for the Australian part of my story. I have relied heavily on his account and interpretations in dealing with Ned Kelly. His is widely acclaimed the best biography of Ned Kelly, which I discovered to be true. A hearty thanks, Ian; may we meet some day.

In the United States, my thanks are due first to my wife, Melody Webb. I have never published a book without her critique chapter by chapter. Almost all her comments have been honored. I owe a debt of gratitude to Professor Emeritus Richard W. Etulain of the University of New Mexico, who generously agreed to read the manuscript and provide his interpretive insights.

Last, my friend and editor at Yale University Press provided the same thoughtful counsel he did in steering my biography of Geronimo through publication. Chris is a master at the editorial business, and my praise for his indispensable role in shaping the draft of Billy and Ned into a publishable book falls short of the reality.

Billy the Kid

CHAPTER 1

Billy the Kid Named
Captain of Outlaw Gang

Las Vegas, New Mexico, defined the northern edge of Billy the Kid country. A transcontinental railroad, the Atchison, Topeka and Santa Fe, had reached Las Vegas in 1879, turning a sleepy little Hispanic village into a city of regional economic growth and domination. (Las Vegas, Nevada, did not exist at that time.) W. S. Koogler edited the city's newspaper, the *Las Vegas Gazette,* which also exerted regional influence. Koogler took great interest in the country south of Las Vegas, a huge grassland cut by the trough of the Pecos River, rimmed on the east by the caprock rising to the Staked Plain of the Texas Panhandle. The caprock defined the western edge of a tableland of grass covering about 37,000 square miles. West of the Pecos, mountains defined the landscape. The Sierra Blanca and Guadalupe Mountains were the most formidable, the Sierra Blanca rising to twelve thousand feet, the Guadalupes to almost nine thousand. Both ranges were rugged and well timbered.

Not only did Koogler's newspaper command great influence in eastern New Mexico, but the editor enjoyed a close relationship with the territorial governor, Lew Wallace, who resided in the ancient Palace of the Governors in Santa Fe. A general during the Civil War, he enjoyed enough influence with President Rutherford B. Hayes to be appointed governor. He took less interest in governing, however, than in writing a massive novel he would title *Ben-Hur*.

The newspaper article Koogler published on December 3, 1880, therefore, caught the attention not only of Governor Wallace but of sensation-seeking newspapers throughout the United States, as far east as New York and as far west as San Francisco.

Koogler had just returned from a journey down the Pecos River and discovered "a powerful gang of outlaws harassing the stockmen of the Pecos and Panhandle country, and terrorizing the people of Fort Sumner and vicinity." The gang numbered "from forty to fifty men, all hard characters, the offscourings of society, fugitives from justice, and desperados by profession." This gang of outlaws, Koogler concluded, "is under the leadership of 'Billy the Kid,' a desperate cuss, who is eligible for the post of captain of any crowd, no matter how mean and lawless."

The young man Koogler described—he may have just turned twenty-one—was known throughout the territory, but never under this name. The closest newspapers had come, and only recently, was "Billy, the Kid." Throughout his short life, he had called himself by various names, among them Henry McCarty, Billy Bonney, Kid Antrim, and just plain Kid, but never Billy the Kid. The most fitting was simply Kid because that is what he was, had been, and would remain until his death seven months later.

Nor was he "captain" of an outlaw gang. The Pecos country did harbor numerous outlaws, more properly defined as rustlers because they preyed on cattle herds. The Kid himself had joined with these men to rustle Texas cattle on the Staked Plains and drive them west to various destinations, even as far as Arizona, to sell to men who made that their business. But he "captained" no group of outlaws: these rough men did not lend themselves to organization or leadership of any kind.

Nevertheless, Koogler had created and named an outlaw guilty of ferocious deeds. The name quickly buried all the other names by which he had called himself. He was now "Billy the Kid," and that name lodged itself in the public imagination, where it has remained ever since.

* * *

The country drained by the Pecos River made up only half of Billy the Kid country. The other half extended west from the Sierra Blanca and Capitan Mountains, including the town of Lincoln, along the foot of the Guadalupe Mountains, and across the White Sands and Organ Mountains to the Rio Grande. The Kid had ranged all this country, thirty thousand square miles, from the Rio Grande to the Staked Plains of Texas—but not as the notorious outlaw depicted by Editor Koogler.

Aside from his widely admired skill and dexterity with rifle and pistol, Billy's principal claim to notoriety was his role in the celebrated Lincoln County War of 1877–78. Based in the town of Lincoln, seat of the county that covered all southeastern New Mexico, the war pitted rival commercial enterprises in a contest for monopoly control of the county and for lucrative government contracts to furnish beef and other goods to the army at nearby Fort Stanton and the Indian Bureau at the Mescalero Apache Indian Agency. Neither side won; in fact, each succeeded in destroying the other. But Billy played a conspicuous part in the confusing, violent maneuvering of the combatants and emerged under indictment for a murder he shared with others and in which he may not even have fired a fatal round.

Nor was he the "desperate cuss" of Koogler's portrait. Quite the opposite. He was a vivacious, smart, good-humored, likable youth. He enjoyed gambling, became an expert at monte, but also loved to sing and dance with the county's bevy of young Hispanic women, who found him adorable. The Hispanic sheepmen and cattlemen scattered around the country venerated him as a true friend.

In later years one of the Hispanic women recalled Billy: "He was a tall slim boy, he was an attractive, handsome, smart, active boy that always stood erect. Everyone liked 'The Keed,' because he was brave, and not afraid of anyone. Billy was a blonde with laughing blue eyes, who was a deadly enemy to those he was against, and a real friend to his friends. He never had a mexican for an enemy, they all loved him, and would do anything for him."

This was hardly the youth created by Editor Koogler in December 1880 and given national exposure in newspapers and magazines everywhere. Yet Koogler's Billy the Kid, now with a price on his head, spent the rest of his short life trying to elude officers of the law pursuing him. The episodes of these months, featuring bloodshed, gunfights, murders, and other adventures, descended to posterity as often-recounted events of his short and violent life. They also laid a firm base for the growth of the legend of Billy the Kid.

❄ CHAPTER 2 ❄

The Making of an "Outlaw"

Sixteen years before Las Vegas editor W. S. Koogler coined the name "Billy the Kid" to describe a "desperate cuss" who captained an outlaw gang, young Henry McCarty, now also named Henry Antrim, took his first short step toward crime. The date was September 23, 1875, the place Silver City, New Mexico, his age fifteen. He had begun to associate with a town drunk called "Sombrero Jack." When clothing from a Chinese laundry disappeared, Grant County sheriff Harvey Whitehill quickly identified the culprits and arrested Henry. As the local newspaper recounted, "It is believed that Henry was simply the tool of 'Sombrero Jack,' who done the stealing whilst Henry done the hiding. Jack has skinned out." Henry sat in jail, ostensibly to await the action of a grand jury on the charge of theft. Sheriff Whitehill in fact simply intended to frighten the youth into abandoning petty thievery before releasing him. In Henry's mind, however, he had broken the law, and he did not want to live in a jail cell. Allowed in the sheriff's absence to exercise in the jail corridor, he put his slim, wiry, athletic frame and quick mind into play by climbing up the chimney and escaping.

* * *

Many elusive questions spot the fifteen years before this escapade. Most notably, where and to whom was he born and when?
A handful of avid researchers have pored over census records, city
directories, baptismal and marriage records, newspapers, and other
sources seeking the answers. Many thought they had the solution
when they identified the parents of Henry and his younger (or
older) brother, Joe, as Catherine McCarty and an unnamed husband (she later said Michael), Irish immigrants living in New York
City. Henry was born in November 1859. Widowed in New York,
Catherine gathered her two sons and headed for Indianapolis, Indiana. Here she teamed up with a much younger man, William Henry
Harrison Antrim, a Union veteran of the Civil War.

Such has remained the dominant consensus for years. However,
historian Frederick Nolan has demonstrated that not a shred of
credible evidence supports this or any other story. His conclusion:
we simply do not know and probably never will. Even so, Henry's
age, dating from November 1859, will be accepted in this book—
placing his age when first arrested at almost fifteen and his age
when killed at twenty-one.

After Indiana the record brightens. In 1870, both the widow Mc-
Carty and "Uncle Bill" Antrim are recorded in Wichita, Kansas,
where Catherine operated a laundry, and both acquired land under
the Homestead Act. They lived in Wichita only until the summer of
1871, when they abruptly headed for Denver and then turned south
to Santa Fe. The explanation lay in Catherine's worsening tuberculosis. On March 1, 1873, the pastor of the First Presbyterian Church
in Santa Fe united Catherine McCarty and William H. H. Antrim
in marriage, with Henry and his brother, Joe, signing as witnesses.
Shortly afterward, the family turned south, down the Rio Grande,
and then west to the mining town of Silver City. Bill wanted to strike
it rich in the mines.

As they eked out a living, Catherine's tuberculosis worsened.
On September 16, 1874, she died. William exercised little discipline
over the two motherless boys. They did as they pleased.

During these youthful years after his mother's death, Henry

styled himself both Henry McCarty and Henry Antrim. Later he would acquire the alias of William H. Bonney, or simply Billy. Therefore, people who recalled him in his early years usually named him "Billy," even though they were remembering Henry.

Nothing in the recollections of Henry's pals in Silver City (after he became known as "Billy") foreshadowed a life of crime, even the petty crime that got him in trouble a year after his mother's death. "Billy was one of the best boys in town," remembered one. "He was very slender. He was undersized and was really girlish looking." "I never remember Billy doing anything out of the way any more than the rest of us." "He was quiet, I remember," said another, "and never swore or tried to act bad like the other kids." His schoolteacher later declared him "a scrawny little fellow with delicate hands and an artistic nature, always willing to help with the chores around the school house," "no more of a problem in school than any other boy growing up in a mining camp."

Not only did the youth learn to read and write, but he joined a minstrel troupe that put on performances for local audiences. One member of the cast recalled him as "Head Man in the show." Here Henry acquired his lifelong love of singing and dancing. He also read obsessively, often in the *Police Gazette*.

"He was a good kid," declared another friend, "but he got in the wrong company." And that "wrong company" led him to flee west, into Arizona, a fugitive from justice—in his own mind.

* * *

Henry Antrim's sprightly mind, which had led to his imaginative escape up the chimney of the Silver City jail, combined with his agile physique, equipped him to survive even in a land of deserts and mountains in which he was a stranger. The center of his world was the army's Camp Grant, located at the southwestern base of Mount Graham, 150 miles west of Silver City. Along the southern boundary of the military reservation a hotel, saloons, a general store, and other civilian enterprises had taken root. Sprawling south into the Sulphur Springs Valley lay a rich grassland occupied by the huge cattle ranch of Henry C. Hooker, a pioneer who preferred to dress like an eastern gentleman. He sold beef to the army and the Indian agencies.

Although unversed in handling cattle, Henry persuaded the ranch foreman to hire him. During his brief employment, he learned the basic skills of horseback riding, herding cattle, roping steers, handling a wagon and team, and the other chores required to operate a ranch. He also learned how to use a rifle and pistol. All these abilities would stand him in good stead in future years. Hooker's foreman, however, judged Henry not man enough for the job and fired him.

Believing himself an outlaw, Henry teamed up with a discharged soldier named John R. Mackie. Their specialty was stealing saddles, blankets, ropes, and other horse equipment, occasionally even a horse. Twice arrested, twice Henry escaped.

Although he rarely drank, Henry enjoyed socializing with the men who gathered in the saloons on the edge of the Camp Grant reservation. So did a hulking blacksmith from the post. His name was Francis P. Cahill; saloon patrons knew him as "Windy" Cahill. Windy liked to bully young Henry. A Hooker cowboy remembered that Windy "would throw Billy [Henry] to the floor, ruffle his hair, slap his face and humiliate him before the men in the saloon."

Windy Cahill bullied Henry once too often. On the night of August 17, 1877, in George Atkins's saloon, Cahill slapped Henry and called him a pimp. Henry replied by calling Cahill a son-of-a-bitch. The two began to fight, an uneven contest in which Windy landed on top of Henry. As they struggled, Henry managed to reach into his pocket and pull out a revolver, which he jammed into Windy's paunch and fired. Cahill died the next day.

A coroner's jury convened and concluded that the killing was "criminal and unjustifiable, and that Henry Antrim alias Kid is guilty thereof." A territorial grand jury would consider the evidence and decide whether to indict Henry and try him for murder.

But Henry quickly put himself beyond the reach of an Arizona grand jury. By early in September he had ridden east, back to old friends near Silver City, New Mexico.

Henry Antrim, not yet seventeen, lacked the experience to understand all the implications of his present predicament. To be sure, he was a fugitive from the law—in Arizona. He now resided in New Mexico. Arizona authorities would not trouble to pursue him beyond Arizona's boundary. Even had he stood trial for murder in Arizona, youth and a plea of self-defense would have been adequate to free him from the murder charge. No New Mexico officer would apprehend him for escaping the Silver City jail. In his own mind, he may have thought himself an outlaw. Technically, he was. In reality, he hardly deserves the term.

Yet scarcely more than three years later he was Billy the Kid, captain of a fierce outlaw band.

* * *

Henry Antrim may not have returned from Arizona a real outlaw, but he came back changed in many ways. At sixteen, he was still an adolescent, a faint fuzz on his upper lip hinting of approaching manhood. He possessed a new set of skills, especially those acquired on Henry Hooker's ranch. He stood erect at a little over five and a half feet, about 140 pounds, with body toughened and muscles developing. Wavy brown hair topped a smooth, oval face with sparkling blue eyes and a mouth almost always smiling and verging on laughter at the slightest excuse. Two front teeth protruded slightly, but people did not find them disfiguring. His mind remained as quick and versatile as when he had climbed up the chimney of Sheriff Whitehill's jail. His cheerful demeanor covered a bold, even risky disposition as well as a dormant rage that could explode violently if provoked. Windy Cahill's death demonstrated his flammable temper and its potential results.

Camp Grant and the Hooker ranch had introduced the youth to a new culture, that of America's western frontier. It emphasized mastery of horse and gun. Guns especially fascinated Henry, so much so that for the rest of his life he constantly practiced marksmanship and dexterity in handling both rifle and pistol. Like most frontiersmen, he frequented saloons. He liked the saloon camaraderie and found it a congenial place to sing and dance.

Henry sported none of the gaudy attire that adorned many frontiersmen. He dressed neatly and conservatively, his only affectation a broad Mexican sombrero that warded off the southwestern sun. The sombrero may indicate that he spent some time in Mexico because he now spoke Spanish fluently.

He was still Henry Antrim, but increasingly he accepted Kid Antrim and then, the most common in the usage of his associates, simply Kid. In the two months following his return to New Mexico, emulating the men he now rode with, he chose an alias: William H. Bonney, or simply Billy Bonney. Reams of speculation have sought to identify the origin of Bonney, but without success.

Although Henry was still an adolescent, his Arizona experiences had endowed him with a new identity. It fueled no long-range ambitions, however, and he tended to act on the impulse of the moment. Throughout his remaining years seldom did he consider the consequences of his actions. Whether moral or immoral, lawful or unlawful, he cared little, if at all. This trait stamped him as a self-centered young man blind to the effect of his deeds on his fellow man.

❀ CHAPTER 3 ❀
A Genuine Outlaw?

What prompted the Kid to ride east from Silver City early in October 1877? Newfound associates, though hardly friends, played a role. These were all indeed real outlaws who stole nine horses near Silver City and turned back east. The Kid rode with them—recognized by a horseman who met them on the road and who named him to the editor of the *Mesilla Valley Independent*. Though they numbered only nine, they made up part of an outlaw gang fluctuating between ten and thirty. They called themselves "The Boys," and often they behaved like boys. But they were tough men, owing fealty to New Mexico's prime outlaw, Jesse Evans.

About twenty-five in 1877, at five feet six and 140 to 150 pounds, Evans was hardly of an imposing physical stature, but he was endowed with arrogance, ruthlessness, and devotion to any form of crime. In 1872, he had drifted up from Texas, where he had been a wrangler at several ranches. On the Pecos, he signed on with cattle baron John Simpson Chisum, ostensibly as a cowboy but actually to plunder the herds of the Mescalero Apaches in retaliation for their plundering of Chisum herds. Joined by other Chisum cowboys, he stole enough cattle to earn his wages.

Ever since leaving Chisum, Evans and his gang had been plundering, robbing, and killing, often in tandem with another outlaw, John Kinney, who owned a ranch near Las Cruces. Across the Rio Grande from Las Cruces, largely an Anglo town, lay the old Mexican village of Mesilla, which had rested on the west bank of the river for more than a century. In the neighborhood of these two communities, Evans had constant run-ins with law, killed three men, and was known by everyone simply as mean. The depredations of his gang inspired a series of articles in the *Mesilla Valley Independent.* Through the columns of his paper, Albert Jennings Fountain crusaded against crime in general and Evans in particular. The columns, naming The Boys as "banditti," infuriated Evans.

Evans either took on the Kid as an apprentice outlaw or simply tolerated his presence. Sources track the banditti but not the Kid, who became the subject of many a ridiculous story to account for his time with The Boys. The Kid had his first opportunity as the outlaws headed for Mesilla. They rode east from Silver City on the barren trail that led toward the Rio Grande through Cooke's Canyon on the southern edge of the Mogollon Mountains. Three more men joined Evans, making twelve in all, counting the Kid. The three had stolen two horses at the village of Santa Barbara, thirty-three miles up the Rio Grande from Mesilla. A six-man posse pursued. Armed only with six-shooters, they proved no match for the fusillade loosed by the gang's Winchester rifles. Driven into a canyon, they gave up the pursuit.

Seven miles east of abandoned Fort Cummings, the gang stopped a stagecoach. The driver assured the bandits that he carried no gold. "Well, we'll let you pass this time," Evans retorted, but insisted that they have a drink together first. The stage driver described each man as armed with two revolvers and a Winchester rifle and with two belts full of cartridges draped over his chest. That such an arsenal included the Kid is doubtful.

The Boys stopped at three roadhouses on the ride down the Rio Grande to Mesilla. At each they ate and drank copiously, then told the innkeeper to "chalk it up." Editor Fountain wrote in the *Independent,* "They desired to have it distinctly understood that they were 'gentlemen' and did not propose to be insulted by having beg-garly tavern keepers thrust bills under their nose." Spotting a copy of the *Independent,* Evans read one of Fountain's editorials and an-nounced that he intended to present him with "a free pass to hell."

Reaching Mesilla, The Boys forded the Rio Grande, climbed San Augustine Pass through the jagged peaks of the Organ Mountains, and descended to the sandy desert at the base of the Guadalupes, entering Lincoln County. On October 9, they reached Tularosa, an-other small Mexican village that lay at the base of the road climbing the Sierra Blanca. Here, as the Kid watched, the gang got drunk and shot up the town. At the home of a man named Sylvester, who had testified against one of the gang, they shot his dog and riddled his house with bullets as Sylvester pleaded for them to spare his wife and children.

The Boys continued up the mountains to a store near the sum-mit. They stopped for provisions and further raucous partying. They voted Evans the title of colonel and captain for all the rest, presum-ably even the Kid. The festivities continued with the adoption of a resolution. It proclaimed "that the public is our oyster, and that having the power, we claim the right to appropriate any property we may take a fancy to." The gang built a huge bonfire and consigned a copy of the *Independent* to the flames. They then followed "Colonel" Evans in a rogues' march around the "funeral pyre."

Afterward, the gang topped the summit and turned down the val-leys on the east side of the Sierra Blanca leading to the Pecos.

The Kid is unlikely to have joined in the shootout with the posse or participated in the drunken behavior and its consequences for the Hispanic citizens of Tularosa. But he saw it all and had a chance to observe the life of the men he had cast his lot with. They were real outlaws, and he probably began to wonder if this was the life he wanted to live.

When The Boys reached the lower Pecos at Seven Rivers, they bunked with the leader of the cowboys at the town of Seven Riv-ers while the Kid bunked at the nearby home of Heiskell Jones, who provided him with bed and board cooked by the widely known

Barbara Jones—"Ma'm Jones" of the Pecos. The Joneses were the first American settlers on the Pecos, and Barbara Jones was a good woman and a good mother who kept a family Bible in the trunk and taught her children to be good citizens. As more people settled, especially the cowboys at Seven Rivers, Barbara cooked splendid meals for any traveler while Heiskell provided a bunk for them. Such was their relationship with the Kid.

The Kid, however, had not entirely broken with The Boys. While he was living with the Joneses, Evans and three of his men were seized after a shootout with a posse out of Lincoln. Charged with horse theft, they were thrown in Lincoln's primitive jail, a hole in the ground with bars on top. With about thirty of The Boys, the Kid was observed riding toward Lincoln to free Evans and his compadres from the jail, which they accomplished shortly before dawn on November 17, 1877. The task was simple because their way had been prepared by men who wanted the prisoners freed. They were some of Lincoln's business and political elite who believed that Evans and his followers might play a useful role in the brewing Lincoln County War.

When Evans and The Boys who had liberated him rode back down to the Pecos, the Kid followed. But he obviously harbored second thoughts because he soon turned back, toward the mountain valley of the Río Ruidoso. Evans and The Boys would remain an occasional part of the Kid's life, although not as fellow outlaws. Rather, the association would usually be hostile and even violent.

Although the Kid did not remain long with The Boys, their country became his country—the vast expanse reaching from the Rio Grande east beyond the Pecos to Texas, marked on the north by Las Vegas, New Mexico, at the southern base of the Sangre de Cristo Mountains, and on the south by the Mexican boundary.

The town of Lincoln emerged as the center of the Kid's universe. It was the seat of Lincoln County, which embraced all southeastern New Mexico, nearly thirty thousand square miles. Lincoln County consisted of two worlds, the mountain world on the west and the plains world on the east. Lincoln lay in the mountain world.

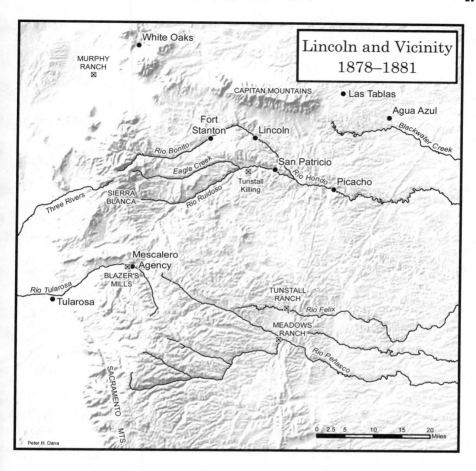

Lincoln and Vicinity 1878–1881

A tiny town with fewer than five hundred residents, Lincoln was a scattering of flat-roofed adobe dwellings of varying size that rambled along a single dirt street extending less than a mile next to the Río Bonito, a small stream lined with tall cottonwoods. To the north, beyond the creek, slopes dotted with piñon and juniper rose to the Capitan Mountains. To the south, a steep, timbered bluff crowded the town against the stream.

The most imposing structure rose to two stories south of the street on the western edge of Lincoln. Lawrence G. Murphy's big store, known simply as "The House," dominated the street as well as the economy. Across the street a long, one-story adobe housed a modest hotel operated by Sam Wortley. He kept a few sleeping rooms and served meals. In the center of town, north of the street, rose the round stone *torreon,* twice the height of the adobes, erected years earlier as a defense against Indians but now crumbling in ruin. Across the street stood a large, one-room adobe, the domain of "Squire" John B. Wilson, who at times served as justice of the peace. His adobe provided space for the district judge, based in Mesilla, to hold court when he came to Lincoln twice a year. Squire Wilson's "courthouse" also found use as a dance hall and a meeting place for community events.

Hispanics, commonly called "Mexicans," lived in the village and the valleys draining east into the Pecos, some for generations. With primitive but time-honored methods, they tilled the soil and, in the canyons and on the mesas, herded sheep and goats. Anglos, many Civil War veterans, began arriving after the war. They, too, took up farming and cattle-raising. Most took Hispanic wives or, in the absence of clergy and to avoid the license fee, "partners."

Ten miles west of Lincoln stood Fort Stanton, a US Army post perched on a low rise of ground south of the Bonito. About thirty miles to the south and west of Fort Stanton, across a pass in the Sierra Blanca, Blazer's Mill provided a site and building for the Mescalero Apache Indian Agency. The Kid would intimately know all these buildings, and more.

On the east, fifteen miles down the Bonito, San Patricio marked the creek's union with the Río Ruidoso to form the Río Hondo, which flowed down to the Pecos. San Patricio would also figure in the Kid's life.

The plains world stood in stark contrast to the mountain world. A huge sea of grass bisected by the Pecos River, it was mainly the domain of cattle king John Simpson Chisum, a skilled manager of cattle who had brought his herd up from Texas in 1867. Along the southern edge of his range, sixty miles from his ranch headquarters, lesser cowmen came up from Texas. Based at the village of Seven Rivers, their small herds grew rapidly, mainly through their skill at stealing Chisum cattle and altering the Chisum brand of a long rail into a hatchet, a pitchfork, or other shape of brand. Gunfights were not necessary; rustling was easy, given the enormity of the Chisum range. Nor was rustling considered a serious offense. Most of the public regarded it simply as part of frontier life. In 1875, Chisum decided to dampen the conflict by selling his herds to a Saint Louis commission house, but he agreed to manage them until they were all disposed of. So the hostility of Chisum cowboys and the Seven Rivers cowboys continued.

The residents of the plains were mostly Texas cowmen who had moved north to sell beef to the army at Fort Sumner. But the army closed Fort Sumner in 1868 when the Navajo exiles it guarded were allowed to return to their homes to the west. Fort Sumner transformed itself into a community when purchased by Pete Maxwell, heir to the Maxwell land grant, the 1.7-million-acre expanse of territory granted to Lucien Maxwell and a partner by the Mexican governor in 1841. A few Anglo cattlemen established themselves in the area, but most of the occupants were Hispanic sheepmen.

The plains world and the mountain world would soon interact, violently. And Kid Antrim, increasingly known as Billy Bonney, would play a starring role in the action.

*   *   *

How Billy impressed others at this critical juncture in his career tells much about the youth who had decided not to be one of The Boys. While still at Seven Rivers, he tried to persuade a widow pushing a herd of cattle into Texas to let him go, too. She refused, but her daughter watched the Kid: "The Kid was as active and graceful as a cat. At Seven Rivers he practiced continually with pistol or rifle, often riding at a run and dodging behind the side of his mount to fire, as the Apaches did. He was very proud of his ability to pick up a handkerchief or other object from the ground while riding at a run."

Arizona had introduced the Kid to horses and guns, about which he knew virtually nothing. Now, scarcely two years later, he had developed remarkable skills with both. Guns, at least, became an obsession that others would describe in similar terms for the rest of his life. That he could display the feats observed by the young woman on the lower Pecos suggests that he developed a self-confidence in tandem with his self-esteem.

Making his way back to the high country from Seven Rivers up the Hondo and Ruidoso, the Kid first met the two cousins Frank and George Coe at Frank's ranch just below the junction of the Ruidoso and Bonito. Part of a big family of Missourians, they had first settled in northeastern New Mexico, then moved to the Hondo and Ruidoso to escape the Colfax County War, another feud that erupted in gunplay.

His outlaw life behind him, the Kid was looking for work. Frank liked the boy but thought him too young for ranch work. Even so, he took the Kid in as a guest. "We became staunch friends [recalled Frank]. I never enjoyed better company. He was humorous and told me many interesting stories. He always found a touch of humor in everything, being naturally full of fun and jollity. Though he was often serious in emergencies, his humor was often apparent even in such situations. He drank very little and smoked in moderation. His disposition was remarkably kind; but he rarely thought of his own comfort first."

Coe also noted his skill with firearms: "The first trip out [hunting] I saw that the Kid was a fine shot with a rifle; he was very handy in camp, a good cook and good-natured and jolly. He spent all his spare time cleaning his six-shooter and practicing shooting."

The Coes had proved friendly and hospitable, and Billy would have occasion to associate with them in the future. As Billy worked his way up the Ruidoso from Frank Coe's ranch, however, he sought the stable employment that Frank had withheld. He soon found it and made more friends, some of whom left a record of their impressions as had Frank Coe. The stable employment involved the Kid in the Lincoln County War, the next chapter in his life.

* * *

The Kid had rejected the kind of outlaw life led by The Boys. That did not necessarily mean he intended to become a law-abiding citizen. Few men in Lincoln County could claim that distinction. But he had ridden with The Boys for two months and had a good opportunity to observe them and their excesses, such as drunken revelry and shooting up Tularosa. This life did not appeal to him.

When seeking work on the Ruidoso, Billy Bonney had demonstrated an identity different in some ways from the youth who had fled Arizona and teamed up with Jesse Evans. The new Billy did not evolve naturally; it was actively sought. Most notably, his good humor impressed everyone; people liked him. He had grown even more skillful with rifle and pistol, as Frank Coe noted. He cultivated friends with whom he could associate on an amicable basis. And he wanted to find employment that earned an income and allowed him to practice the abilities he had begun to acquire in Arizona and had developed ever since, particularly with guns. He would find that opportunity as a warrior in the Lincoln County War—which gave him another new identity.

❋ CHAPTER 4 ❋
Ranch Cowboy and Hired Gunman

On the Ruidoso, after leaving the Coes, Billy met with Richard Brewer, who had his own ranch and also managed another ranch twenty miles to the south, on the Río Feliz. This spread belonged to an Englishman, John H. Tunstall, who lived in Lincoln. Brewer, a large, handsome man in his mid-twenties, was a masterful horseman and skilled with rifle and pistol as well as a competent ranch manager. Tunstall described Brewer "as a very fine specimen of humanity both physically and morally." Early in December 1877, Brewer hired Billy to work on the Tunstall ranch.

At the ranch, in a small adobe constructed to house the men, Billy joined with a few others Brewer had engaged. The most prominent was John Middleton, twenty-three, a muscular veteran of cattle work in Texas, a deadly shot with a pistol, and endowed with black eyes, black hair, and a huge black mustache that gave him a fearsome appearance. Tunstall characterized Middleton as "about the most desperate looking man I ever set eyes on." Desperate he was not; soft-spoken yet stalwart in a fight he was.

Billy's convivial disposition equipped him well to make friends with the rest of the cowboys. But his special friend, who returned the friendship in equal measure, was Frederick T. Waite. At twenty-five,

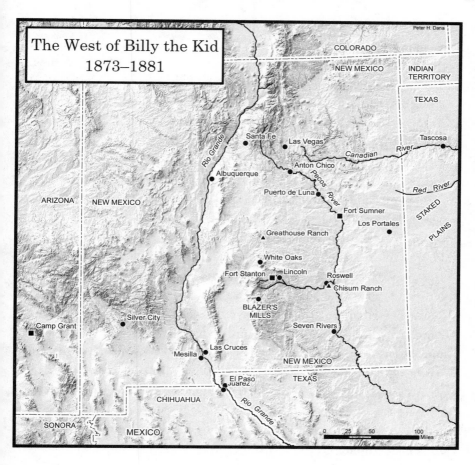

The West of Billy the Kid
1873–1881

he was seven years older than Bonney, an adventurous young man of Chickasaw Indian heritage, and schooling that included some college work. Waite was slender, dressed neatly, and sported a thin, light-colored mustache. "An OK lad," opined Frank Coe. Despite the differences, Billy and Fred became inseparable companions.

Indeed, so close did they grow that in February 1878 they formed plans for a future partnership. In a rare show of looking beyond the immediate moment, Billy agreed with Fred that when opportunity offered they would acquire land on the Río Peñasco, the next river south of the Feliz, and establish their own ranch.

Two others with whom Billy formed lasting friendships were

Charley Bowdre and Doc Scurlock. Charley was twenty-nine, a Mississippian who teamed up with Doc Scurlock to operate a ranch on the Ruidoso. Charley sported a neat mustache, liked fancy clothes, and wore them when he could afford it. An Alabaman who studied medicine in his youth, the same age as Bowdre, Scurlock married Antonia Herrerra and began a large family. But in 1877, Scurlock and Bowdre drank copiously and made a lot of trouble in Lincoln. They then abandoned ranching and went to work for Brewer. Both formed a lasting attachment with Billy. Like Scurlock, Bowdre took a Hispanic wife. With his command of Spanish, Billy could talk with Manuela Bowdre better than Charley.

Another of the hands on the Tunstall ranch destined to have a lasting relationship with Billy was Henry N. Brown. At nineteen he was only a year older than Billy. Sandy hair and mustache and a slim and wiry build characterized Henry. He had hunted buffalo in Texas before coming to New Mexico to work on Lawrence Murphy's ranch thirty miles west of Lincoln. A dispute interrupted his work, and he quit to hire on with Tunstall. Like the rest of the Tunstall cowboys, he could use a gun and had even killed a man in Texas. Frank Coe thought him "nervy, but not smart like the Kid."

As Dick Brewer knew, and the Tunstall cowboys doubtless suspected, they had been hired not only as cowboys but, if the need arose, as gunmen in the Lincoln County War. The war had already begun when the Kid parted with the Jesse Evans gang in November 1877. The Kid's exploits in the Lincoln County War not only demonstrated a growing power of leadership but are vividly remembered in history.

The Lincoln County War pitted two men and two institutions against each other. The characters changed as the conflict developed, but in the fall of 1877 there were four. On the one side was a twenty-four-year-old Englishman, John H. Tunstall, and his ally, attorney Alexander McSween; on the other an Irishman, Lawrence G. Murphy—Major Murphy, signifying service in the New Mexico Volunteers during the Civil War—and his store clerk, James J. Dolan. Tunstall operated a general store in the middle of Lincoln, its purpose to challenge the economic domination of the county and control of government contracts by "The House," Murphy's two-story mercantile concern at the western edge of Lincoln.

Neither side harbored any business scruples. Murphy had achieved his monopoly by fraudulent manipulation of government contracts for beef and other supplies at Fort Stanton and the Mescalero Apache Indian Agency. He falsified vouchers, overcounted Indians, and elevated the true weight of beef. Some of the cattle he bought at reduced rates from rustlers and included them in contract beef at much higher prices. In turn, Murphy locked the citizens to The House by setting high prices for buying House merchandise and low prices for acquiring their produce. In this cashless economy, everyone dealt on credit extended by Murphy, a system that lent itself to fraud. Murphy also sold land to newcomers and provided them with titles, but the titles were worthless because all the land was public domain. As one of Murphy's victims recounted, "They done as they pleased. They intimidated, oppressed and crushed people who were obliged to deal with them. They were a gigantic monopoly."

With Murphy declining because of excessive indulgence in whiskey, he elevated his clerk, James J. Dolan, to the post of manager. Discharged from the army in 1869, Dolan had worked for Murphy ever since and learned his ways well. Slender, short, and with a beardless face that looked evil, Dolan liked expensive, fashionable clothes. He drank heavily and caroused easily with the other men attached to The House but was mean enough to shoot anyone who crossed him. As manager, Dolan supplied the youth, drive, and lack of scruples that kept The House ascendant.

Twenty-three-year-old John Henry Tunstall stood in stark contrast to Dolan and Murphy. A well-educated London patrician, he spoke several languages. He liked horses and dogs. Tunstall was tall at five feet eleven, and weighed 138 pounds. An accident had cost him the sight of his right eye.

Bankrolled by his London father, Tunstall had failed in a Canadian business venture before turning to New Mexico in 1876. In Santa Fe, he immediately attracted public attention. His sandy

hair and thin mustache with side-whiskers, slender form, fashionable tweeds, and English accent charmed the Anglo citizens. For his
part, he held the Hispanic population in contempt and distrusted
the Anglos. "All the men have a great 'six shooter' slung on their hip,
& knife on the other as counter poise," Tunstall wrote his parents.
He acquired his own weapon: "I have contracted the habit of keeping
my hands on my 'shooting iron.' It carries a fearful ball & shoots
quick, but I don't calculate to have to use it."

Noting Tunstall's interest in acquiring land, several Santa Fe
stockmen advised him to investigate Lincoln County. When a Lincoln resident checked into his hotel, Tunstall hastened to meet him.
The man happened to be Lincoln's only lawyer, Alexander McSween.
Thus, owing to McSween's persuasion, Tunstall established himself
in Lincoln.

McSween was a mild-mannered Scotsman, thirty-four, a man of
peace. A long mustache fell below his chin. A Hispanic woman, resident of Lincoln, remembered the lawyer: "Mr. McSween was a very
refined gentleman and never could believe that the guns should rule
like they did, and could never be convinced that he should carry a
gun. . . . Mrs. McSween was a beautiful lady, and understood the
ways of the world much better than his that was an idealist."

Tunstall promptly set forth to earn a fortune by whatever means
it took. His intent, he wrote his father, was "to get the half of every
dollar that is made in the county by *anyone*." In addition to his cattle enterprise, with lawyer McSween he founded a store in Lincoln
to oppose the economic supremacy of The House. Tunstall's youth,
geniality, English accent and clothing, good nature, and challenge to
The House endeared him to many of Lincoln's citizens.

Alexander McSween wanted to get rich as much as Tunstall, and
he enthusiastically joined in building and stocking the store, although they were not legal partners. McSween failed to understand
the ruthlessness of Jimmy Dolan. Susan McSween had more sense.
"I told Tunstall and Mr. McSween they would be murdered if they
went into the store business. I did my best to keep McSween from
entering the business, but he went in against my will."

As part of his store, Tunstall set up the Lincoln County Bank. McSween had introduced Tunstall to cowman John Chisum, who agreed to serve as president of the bank. Chisum's apparent alliance with Tunstall and McSween brought the plains world into contact with the mountain world. Chisum favored the Tunstall-McSween side, offered refuge at his ranch, and sometimes provided beef, but he took no active part in the conflict.

Murphy's decline continued, and he sold out to Jimmy Dolan. The House now became Dolan & Co. Dolan owned a cow camp near Seven Rivers, south of the Chisum ranges. He began with stock acquired when Murphy retired and placed the camp under Murphy's foreman, William S. "Billy" Morton. They intended to enlarge their herd by the same method employed by the Seven Rivers cowboys, who at once became their allies. According to Sue McSween, "Morton laughed and told me he could steal from Chisum. He said he could change the rail [the Chisum brand] into a hatchet."

In The House, Tunstall was taking on a formidable adversary, now more formidable than ever with Dolan in control. The House dominated the county's political establishment as well as the county's economy. Sheriff William Brady was a generally effective lawman, but his longtime friendship with Murphy made him a tool of The House. The district judge, Warren Bristol, was a timid, easily frightened man who usually did The House's bidding. The district attorney, William L. Rynerson, based in Mesilla, a veteran of vicious political wars in Santa Fe, shamelessly favored The House and advanced Dolan's cause in every way he could, legal or not.

Nor did Murphy and Dolan hesitate to use hired guns if it became necessary—Jesse Evans and The Boys furnished not only the guns but the stolen cattle for the beef contracts. Although the Evans gang fluctuated in number and owed loyalty to no one, a core group appears in many of the escapades involving The House. These men, besides Evans, were Tom Hill, George Davis, and Frank Baker—all as thuggish as Evans. Although not on the payroll, they found that association with The House opened possibilities for profitable criminal deeds.

Tunstall in turn felt the need for gunmen to protect his interests. He had Dick Brewer hire cowboys who were also experts with rifle and pistol. Billy Bonney's expertise was well known, and Brewer quickly put him on the payroll.

A complicated legal imbroglio brought the conflict to a violent phase. McSween had been engaged to collect the life insurance of Murphy's partner, Emil Fritz, who had died in Germany in 1874. McSween succeeded, but refused to turn over the proceeds until guaranteed his fee. Urged on by The House, the Fritz heirs sued McSween for embezzlement. In Mesilla, with Tunstall and Dolan present, McSween appeared before Judge Warren Bristol.

Bristol served as both federal and territorial judge for the district. Although frightened by guns, he nevertheless owed fealty to The House, as he would demonstrate as the Lincoln County War unfolded.

Judge Bristol postponed McSween's case until April 1878, when the court would sit in Lincoln. But as bail he insisted that McSween's property be attached in the amount of eight thousand dollars (that is, removed from McSween's ownership). Tunstall had probably accompanied McSween because everyone understood that he and McSween were partners in the store. They were not, but Dolan had already singled out Tunstall as the true enemy.

Jimmy Dolan hurried back to Lincoln to get the attachment process started before McSween and Tunstall returned from Mesilla. Attachment offered an opportunity to strike a mighty blow at his adversary. The House was now Dolan & Co. Dolan had learned well from Murphy the ways of The House, but he was smarter, more ruthless, a cunning schemer, and determined to lift the power of The House to even greater heights. First, that meant brushing aside McSween and getting rid of Tunstall.

Dolan raced into Lincoln on February 8 and began the attachment at once, thus avoiding any interference by McSween and Tunstall, who arrived two days later.

This task fell to Sheriff William Brady—like Murphy, "Major" Brady. The two were Irishmen, had served together during the Civil

War, and had been friends and collaborators ever since. Although not entirely lacking integrity, he could be counted on to carry out any mission in behalf of The House. The attachment process was such a mission.

Sheriff Brady zealously set about this task at once, employing a tactic that unscrupulously favored Dolan and The House. Legally, the contents of McSween's house more than satisfied the bail. But Dolan probably pushed Brady to consider McSween a partner of Tunstall, which would make Tunstall's property McSween's also, and by so doing he was able to attach every item in the Tunstall store—totaling four times the amount of the bail.

Tunstall reached Lincoln on February 10, finding Brady and a posse inside the store, along with an angry fellow named Rob Widenmann. Tunstall had met this officious young man in Santa Fe and invited him to come to Lincoln. Widenmann was not on Tunstall's payroll but acted in his behalf. Tunstall had left him in charge of the store during his absence in Mesilla. Billy Bonney and Fred Waite had ridden to Lincoln several days earlier and stayed to watch the scene unfold. Tunstall summoned them and headed for the store. Inside he joined Widenmann in confronting Brady and his posse, berating them for occupying his store day and night and inventorying the contents when the judge's order applied only to McSween. As the shouting match continued, Bonney and Waite stood menacingly on the porch brandishing Winchesters and pistols. The Kid had instantly stepped into his role as hired gunman. But guns proved unnecessary. Brady and his men continued with their task, and Tunstall withdrew.

Dolan plotted his next move: to prod the sheriff to attach all the cattle and horses at the Tunstall ranch. Brady deputized Jacob B. Mathews to form a four-man posse of House employees and carry out the mission. Mathews had no special qualifications for this assignment, in fact was a hesitant sort of fellow. On the way south, four more men joined the posse, although not as members—Jesse Evans and his three closest sidekicks, Hill, Baker, and Davis. Evans explained that he wanted to reclaim a horse borrowed by Billy Bonney. Whether or not true, it excused his presence. Mathews did not argue and probably did not care.

During breakfast on February 13, 1878, the men in the ranch house saw the posse approaching. Dick Brewer and the blustery Rob Widenmann stepped out on the porch and commanded the men to halt. Billy, Fred, and the other Tunstall cowboys remained inside as backup. Mathews rode forward and declared that the posse had come to attach McSween's cattle. Informed that McSween owned no cattle here, a confused Mathews responded that he would have to return to Lincoln and get new instructions. Bonney, Widenmann, and Waite rode with Mathews, presumably to get their own instructions from Tunstall. Evans and his Boys remained at the ranch to await the next move.

Mathews got his instructions—emphatic orders from Sheriff Brady to return and attach Tunstall's livestock—and began to assemble a larger posse. Dolan sent a rider down to his Seven Rivers cow camp, where his foreman, Billy Morton, formed another posse of nine Seven Rivers cowboys. Dolan fixed a place of rendezvous at a ranch on the Peñasco eight miles south of the Tunstall ranch. Dolan himself headed for the Peñasco, leaving little doubt who actually controlled the Mathews posse. With the advent of Morton and the Seven Rivers men, the posse numbered twenty-three men. Jesse Evans and his three Boys unofficially augmented the number.

In Lincoln, Tunstall had resolved to defend the ranch with his hired guns and gave those instructions to Bonney, Waite, and Widenmann. On February 14 they rode back to the ranch and with the others prepared it for defense. They punched firing ports in the adobe walls and piled sacks of grain as barricades.

Tunstall himself arrived on the night of February 17. He had decided not to fight and risk the lives of his men. He sent a courier to inform Mathews that he could impound the cattle. At daybreak of February 18, trailing nine horses, Tunstall took the road north toward the junction of the Ruidoso and the Bonito. Fred Waite drove a buckboard, although what it carried is unrecorded. The rest, including Tunstall, were mounted. Of the nine horses, Sheriff Brady had released six to Tunstall; two belonged to Dick Brewer and one to Bonney (or Jesse Evans).

Back at the ranch, Dolan and Mathews decided that the horses with Tunstall also had to be attached. Since Billy Morton from Seven Rivers worked for Dolan, he was deputized to lead a subposse of fourteen men and take the horses. Morton demonstrated that he knew exactly what Dolan wanted by shouting, "Hurry up boys, my knife is sharp and I feel like scalping someone." Although uninvited, Jesse Evans and his men brought up the rear, ostensibly to reclaim the horse lent by Bonney to Evans. Probably none of the posse objected to the presence of Evans and his Boys. After all, they were House allies.

By the evening of February 18, Tunstall and his party had reached the head of a trail that descended a tortuous canyon and offered a shortcut down to the Ruidoso. Fred Waite was sent to drive their buckboard on the longer road, while Brewer and Widenmann helped Tunstall drive the horses down the trail. Billy Bonney and mustachioed John Middleton rode several hundred yards in the rear. As Tunstall and his two companions, Brewer and Widenmann, started down the canyon trail, they spooked a flock of wild turkeys. Leaving Tunstall alone with the horses, the two rode up the bare hillside to bag some of the turkeys. Behind, Bonney and Middleton spotted some of the posse riding fast and firing. The two spurred their horses, Bonney turning to the left to join Brewer and Widenmann on the hillside, Middleton racing to reach Tunstall. When Morton's men cleared the crest, they spotted Bonney, Brewer, and Widenmann. Some turned to attack the three men, who scrambled up the bare slope to some scrub timber that offered a defensible position. The others continued on the trail to seize the horses.

Middleton reached Tunstall and shouted for him join him in fleeing up the hillside to take cover with the others. As Middleton later explained, "I sung out to Tunstall to follow me. He was on a good horse. He appeared to be very much excited and confused. I kept singing out to him for God's sake to follow me. His last words were 'What John! What John!'"

Morton, Jesse Evans, and Tom Hill pushed down the trail ahead of the rest of the posse, which was busy rounding up the horses. About one hundred yards down the trail, Morton, Evans, and Hill turned up the slope, supposedly to join their other men in exchanging fire with the turkey hunters but probably to follow Tunstall into a brush thicket halfway up the hillside. A burst of gunfire followed. At the top of the hill, Middleton remarked, "They've killed Tunstall."

The posse had gathered the horses and waited for Morton to appear. He emerged from the thicket to explain what had happened. He and the two Boys had confronted Tunstall. Morton had begun reading him the writ of attachment when Evans shouted for Tunstall to throw down his arms. Tunstall had then drawn his pistol and fired two shots. The three men instantly shouldered their Winchesters and loosed a fusillade at Tunstall, one bullet hitting him the chest, another in the head. He dropped to the ground, along with his fatally shot horse.

No one else had seen the encounter. Tunstall's pistol showed two shots fired. Morton's explanation became the official version. Tunstall had died resisting arrest by a deputy and two men who had no right to be there. Few doubted, however, that Tom Hill had fired two shots from Tunstall's revolver to back the story. Nor did few doubt that Tunstall had been murdered.

Perhaps these events happened so rapidly that Bonney, Brewer, and Middleton had failed to grasp their primary responsibility. They had been hired by Tunstall in large part because of their guns. Their duty was to protect him rather than shoot at turkeys. Instead, they left him alone to Morton's scalping knife.

* * *

Even before word of Tunstall's murder reached Lincoln during the night of February 18, his followers had gathered at McSween's home, next to the Tunstall store, to help him in the spiraling conflict. That night Bonney and his comrades had ridden down to the Ruidoso and arranged for men to retrieve Tunstall's body the next day and bring it to Lincoln. They then continued to Lincoln and told their story to the men in the McSween house.

Now Tunstall's friends had even more reason to war against The

House. McSween was not a warrior. As a lawyer, he favored legal means rather than violent. But the law belonged to The House—beginning with Sheriff Brady and his friends down the street in The House. Nevertheless, McSween was now the leader.

Lincoln, however, claimed another arm of the law, hardly a match for Brady's arm, but the law nonetheless. "Squire" John B. Wilson served as justice of the peace. He was an indecisive old man, virtually illiterate, and easily manipulated. But like Judge Bristol, he could issue arrest warrants, and Constable Atanacio Martínez could execute them. Judge Bristol could call on Sheriff Brady to assemble a posse and execute his warrants. Justice Wilson could have Constable Martínez call on the men in the McSween house to form a posse and execute his warrants.

McSween quickly seized on this alternative. The morning after Tunstall's men arrived with word of Tunstall's death, February 19, Billy Bonney, Dick Brewer, and John Middleton swore affidavits attesting to the murder of Tunstall. McSween persuaded Squire Wilson to issue arrest warrants charging Dolan, Morton, and the entire Mathews posse with Tunstall's murder.

The next stage of the Lincoln County War featured the lawfully empowered sheriff and his followers facing off against the lawfully empowered enemies of The House operating under the authority of the justice of the peace.

* * *

From the time Billy Bonney had been employed as a Tunstall hand by Dick Brewer until this February morning when he swore an affidavit against the posse, Bonney had been little more than a hired hand. Tunstall, Brewer, and even Widenmann made the decisions. Bonney did as he was expected, but not boldly or prominently. Most notably, together with Brewer and Middleton, he had failed to use his guns to safeguard Tunstall. All three let down their employer.

How Billy Bonney comported himself in McSween's army and the events that followed would mark another chapter in his evolution.

❀ CHAPTER 5 ❀
A Warrior in McSween's Army

Billy Bonney had no more than a casual relationship to John H. Tunstall, that of employer and employee, a hired gun if needed in the conflict with Jimmy Dolan. According to Frank Coe, however, as Tunstall's body lay in the back room of his store, Billy approached, looked down at his dead boss, and declared, "I'll get some of them before I die."

Perhaps his vow reflected a degree of remorse for shooting at turkeys rather than the posse that killed Tunstall. Remorse, however, was not part of his character. Even so, the murder of Tunstall changed Billy from simply a hired hand into a daring and effective warrior in the army taking shape under Alexander McSween's leadership. He would indeed "get some of them"—and long before he died.

* * *

McSween wanted Squire Wilson's warrant served. About forty of the McSween followers stood ready to avenge Tunstall's death, including Bonney and Waite. Constable Martínez balked at serving warrants on Sheriff Brady and his entire posse, even with McSween's little army. That would be certain to set off a gun battle. But Billy stepped forward and told the constable to do as he was told or be killed.

Before Martínez could act, however, Rob Widenmann appeared. Somehow he had wangled a commission as deputy US marshal, and he carried a warrant for the arrest of Jesse Evans. Widenmann had obtained a contingent of cavalry at Fort Stanton to back up his search for Evans in the Dolan and Tunstall stores. As the soldiers entered the Dolan store, Martínez and about a dozen possemen slipped in with them. Jesse Evans was not there. So the cavalrymen and posse went to the Tunstall store, still held by Brady's deputies. Again they failed to find Evans, but they found Brady himself and arrested him, not for the Tunstall murder but for authorizing the troopers to feed their horses with hay stored behind the Tunstall store. The hay belonged to the Tunstall estate, so the sheriff had stolen the hay. Neither Brady nor his deputies were willing to resist US soldiers. Brady tamely submitted and stood before Justice Wilson charged with larceny. Wilson released the sheriff and his deputies but made Brady post bond to ensure his appearance at the spring term of court. Brady and his men returned to the Dolan store, presumably in a foul mood.

* * *

Martínez still had the murder warrant in his pocket, so he deputized Billy Bonney and Fred Waite to join him in serving it.

The three pushed open the door of the Dolan store. Inside they confronted Brady and many of his posse, Winchesters trained on the chests of the intruders. Martínez began reading the warrant, but Brady stopped him. He declared that these men were *his* posse, and no one was going to arrest them. Moreover, he did not recognize the authority of Squire Wilson. Relieved of their arms, Martínez, Bonney, and Waite had failed in their mission and been made prisoners. Brady soon released Martínez, but he held Bonney and Waite for thirty-six hours before freeing them—without their arms.

Probably the only factor that prevented either side from drawing their six-shooters was the presence in Lincoln of a platoon of US cavalrymen.

Billy's rationale for what could have turned into a suicidal task almost certainly sprang from a naive understanding of the legal complexities of the brewing conflict. In his mind, he had a legally issued warrant that fully empowered him to arrest those named in the warrant. Backed by a phalanx of Winchesters, Sheriff Brady destroyed that notion. Although Brady represented the other and more substantial arm of the law, he later avoided that explanation by declaring that he had acted as he did simply because he had the power.

* * *

McSween had been an ineffective leader. Worse, he faced the criminal charge of embezzlement, personalized in District Attorney William L. Rynerson. Long an aggressive partisan in New Mexico's political wars, an unflinching ally of The House, Rynerson resorted to any means to achieve his purpose. In particular, he intended to destroy McSween and Tunstall on behalf of The House. Several of Lincoln's most prosperous citizens posted bond to guarantee McSween's appearance at the next session of Judge Bristol's court. Rynerson refused to accept the bondsmen, which meant McSween would have to spend six weeks in Brady's cellar jail. Rather than face the prospect that Jesse Evans might, as Dolan put it, "do his part," McSween vanished from Lincoln.

McSween's following, with a core group of about a dozen that fluctuated over time and ultimately included some Hispanics, sought a new leader. Squire Wilson made out a new warrant, then appointed Dick Brewer "special constable," empowered to arrest all those named in the first warrant. Brewer had earned Tunstall's admiration by his competent management of the Tunstall ranch and had proved a constructive citizen in the affairs of Lincoln. Brewer's followers styled themselves the "Regulators," a term at least a century old that meant setting right an intolerable wrong.

Most of Tunstall's former cowboys, including Bonney and Waite, numbered themselves among the Regulators, as did many of Tunstall's supporters who had remained faithful to McSween. As instruments of the law, the Regulators now faced off against Sheriff Brady and his instruments of the law—largely influenced by Jimmy Dolan.

William B. "Buck" Morton headed the list of men to be arrested.

Morton was foreman of Dolan's cow camp at Seven Rivers, on the lower Pecos. Morton also headed the subposse that, with Jesse Evans and Tom Hill, had entered the thicket where Tunstall had taken refuge and murdered him.

Brewer led eleven Regulators to the lower Pecos to search for Morton. On March 6 they discovered five horsemen and gave chase. A gallop of five miles, with shots exchanged, caused three to veer off from the other two, whom Brewer followed. They were Morton and Frank Baker, one of Jesse Evans's sidekicks. The pursuit continued until the horses of the two gave out, and they took cover in a natural depression. Brewer promised to ensure their safety if they surrendered. They gave up their arms, although Morton had his doubts. Before heading for Lincoln, Morton had a chance to write and post a letter to a friend back East expressing his fears: "There was one man in the party who wanted to kill me after I had surrendered and was restrained with the greatest difficulty by others of the party." Billy Bonney was likely that one man. As he had vowed, he would get some of them before he died.

In fact, killing Morton was the simplest solution. In Lincoln, Brewer would have to turn over his prisoners to Sheriff Brady, who could hardly be expected to hold Morton until court convened, especially since he denied the authority of Justice Wilson.

Before turning toward Lincoln, the posse took on another member, William McCloskey, who had been one of Tunstall's hands but was also a friend of Morton's. The riders took a back road to Lincoln. What happened en route, as Brewer described it, resembled the fate of Tunstall. Morton had reached over, grabbed his friend McCloskey's pistol and shot him dead, then with Frank Baker made a break for safety. Brewer and his men pursued and quickly shot the two from their horses. Casting doubt on the story was the fact that each body bore eleven bullet holes, one for each member of the posse. As surely as Tunstall, Morton had been murdered. Billy Bonney was later named as the man who first shot Morton. Whether that statement was true or not, one of the eleven bullets came from Billy's pistol.

When Brewer and his men reached Lincoln, they discovered their cause a shambles. Territorial governor Samuel B. Axtell had been in Lincoln that day investigating the turmoil. An ally of The House and its friends in Santa Fe, the governor had signed a proclamation declaring Justice Wilson to be occupying his office illegally and Judge Bristol and Sheriff Brady the only law enforcement authority in Lincoln County. To complicate affairs even more, McSween, tiring of fugitive life, had returned to face Sheriff Brady.

As lawyer McSween understood, the Regulators themselves were now outlaws. If Justice Wilson had been holding office illegally—as the governor had officially ruled—Wilson lacked the authority to issue warrants and appoint Dick Brewer special constable. The activities of the Regulators had been unlawful, and Dolan had already moved to have Sheriff Brady round them up and hold them on charges of making false arrests and murdering Morton and Hill.

McSween reasoned that he and the Regulators had only one option: flee Lincoln and hide in the tangled landscape until district court convened on April 1 and resolved the issue. In fact, the Regulators simply disbanded and for the last three weeks in March kept to their homes or otherwise remained out of sight. Billy Bonney and Fred Waite took refuge among Billy's Hispanic friends in the village of San Patricio, fifteen miles down the Bonito at its union with the Ruidoso.

With Sue McSween absent in the East, Alex McSween had been living at John Chisum's South Spring Ranch. Chisum favored the Regulators but, other than holding the Lincoln bank presidency, took no active role in the war. When Sue McSween returned late in March, McSween summoned the Regulators to a strategy meeting. The strong-minded Sue probably prompted her husband. With other Regulators, Billy and Fred heeded the call. Some were Hispanics, with a weak command of English. Their memory is the only surviving evidence of what occurred. In this meeting, McSween may have stated or implied or at least left the impression that he wanted Sheriff Brady assassinated. As Francisco Trujillo recalled years later, "Macky Swin [McSween] then asked us to meet him the following Monday in Lincoln because said he 'As soon as I arrive, Brady is going to try and arrest me and you should not let him get away with it. If I am arrested I will surely be hung and I don't want to die, while if you kill Brady you shall earn a reward.'" In any event, the Regulators headed back for Lincoln with the belief that McSween wanted Brady removed from the equation.

Six Regulators formed the execution squad. Among them, the most prominent were Billy Bonney, Fred Waite, and John Middleton, all of whom had shot turkeys while Tunstall was killed. A recent Regulator recruit was "Big Jim" French, who enthusiastically joined the group.

With court expected to open on April 1, 1878, during the night of March 31 the six gunmen gathered in the corral behind the Tunstall store. A shoulder-high adobe wall, with a gate in the center, extended east from the front of the store. This formed a rampart from behind which the men planned to carry out their mission.

About 9:00 a.m. on April 1 they watched the sheriff and four deputies stroll down the street from the Dolan store toward the courthouse. One was Billy Mathews, who had headed the posse sent to impound the stock at the Tunstall ranch. The others had played significant roles in the attachment process. Brady paused to talk to a woman while the rest continued, thus avoiding a burst of fire.

The assassins would have a second chance, however, because Brady intended only to post a notice at the courthouse that a clerical error had stated the wrong date for the judge to convene court. It was April 8, not April 1. So the sheriff and his deputies walked back toward the Dolan store.

When the sheriff reached the front of the adobe wall, the six gunmen rose, leveled their Winchesters, and swept the street with a deadly fusillade. Sheriff Brady dropped with a dozen or more bullets in him. Another deputy died, but the rest took cover in the buildings across the street.

As the smoked cleared, Billy Bonney vaulted over the adobe wall, followed by Jim French, and ran to the sheriff's body. He picked up Brady's Winchester rifle. At this moment, however, Billy Matthews fired from a window across the street. The bullet pierced the Kid's thigh and also the thigh of Jim French. Billy dropped the rifle, and the two hobbled back through the gate to safety behind the wall.

What motivated Billy to take such a reckless risk when he knew armed deputies were posted across the street? Aside from his usual daring, he followed his habit of respecting authority—McSween. Also, the humiliation inflicted by Brady when he, Fred Waite, and Constable Martínez entered the Dolan store to serve Justice Wilson's warrant still haunted him. Moreover, he sought to retrieve the Winchester Brady had seized from him, if not his at least a replacement. And there was the ever-present desire to avenge Tunstall's death.

As likely as any of these reasons, as Frank Coe observed, he intended to rifle Brady's pockets for the warrant for McSween's arrest and the writ of attachment. In both he failed, for the documents remained on the sheriff's body and the rifle fell to the ground when Mathews put a bullet into his thigh.

Neither side seemed anxious to engage in a gun battle. Jim French was too badly wounded to leave and took refuge in the home of the Reverend Taylor Ealy. But the rest made their way leisurely out of town, followed in a leisurely way by the deputies. They exchanged long-range fire. In fact, John Middleton dismounted, sat with his rifle propped on his knee, and fired an occasional round.

One of Brady's deputies, George Peppin, took over. He tried to arrest McSween, hiding in Isaac Ellis's store at the east end of town, but McSween argued that Brady's death deprived Peppin of such authority. Peppin called for help from Fort Stanton. A detachment arrived to back Peppin. But the lieutenant in command knew that if held in civilian custody McSween was unlikely to survive the week until court met. Resolving the issue, McSween agreed to put himself in custody of the army.

Sheriff Brady, who lived with his wife on a farm east of Lincoln, was generally respected as a substantial citizen and effective lawman despite his ties to Dolan. His assassination by what people regarded as foul play lost McSween and the Regulators much public support. But the Regulators, under Dick Brewer, considered their mission unfinished. Even though invalidated by Governor Axtell, former Justice Wilson's warrants remained in their pockets. Brewer intended to serve them.

Such a course seems strange for men who believed in a cause grounded in an idealism totally lacking in the Dolan camp. In four days, five men had been killed: McCloskey, Morton, Evans's hench-man Frank Baker, Sheriff Brady, and a deputy. The explanation lies in the reality that both sides considered the conflict *war*—a just war—rather than simply legal sparring backed by guns.

For his role, especially in the murder of the sheriff, Billy Bonney gained prominence among the Regulators. But his youth and lack of maturity kept him from rising to the stature of the older Regulators. Nevertheless, he rode with them; he was one of them, and he enjoyed their camaraderie. Even more distinction awaited in the next episode of the Regulators.

CHAPTER 6
Blazer's Mill

Andrew L. Roberts, "Buckshot" Roberts, herded some cattle on the upper Ruidoso and worked part time in Dolan's branch store near Blazer's Mill. As a Dolan employee, he had been recruited as part of the Mathews posse charged with attaching Tunstall's stock. Thus his name appeared on the arrest warrant carried by Dick Brewer, although it no longer held any validity. A short, stocky, tough man, Roberts carried a load of buckshot in his right shoulder, origin unknown. This prevented him from raising his right arm above the hip, so in firing a Winchester or six-shooter he had to shoot from the waist.

Roberts favored neither side in the Lincoln County War. Indeed, he simply wanted to escape from all the turmoil, so much so that he had put his ranch up for sale and only awaited the payment until leaving the country altogether. He lingered in the vicinity of Blazer's Mill waiting for the mail to bring his money.

Blazer's Mill was the domain of former dentist Joseph H. Blazer, who after the Civil War had established himself at the head of the Tularosa River, here a mere rivulet. On the north slope of the canyon, overlooking the stream, he built a sawmill and a gristmill, as well as a two-story house. His enterprise prospered. Lumber from his sawmill, for example, was hauled to Lincoln and used in the construction of Lawrence Murphy's "big store." A sizable community grew in the vicinity. Blazer served as postmaster, which explains the presence of Buckshot Roberts.

Later, the government established the Mescalero Apache Indian Reservation surrounding his property. Blazer leased his house to the Mescalero Apache Indian agent, Frederick C. Godfroy, for use as a residence and agency headquarters. Godfroy's wife cooked meals for travelers and occasionally took in lodgers. Blazer and his family lived in a smaller house a short distance farther upstream, although Blazer kept an office in the big house.

Late on the morning of April 4, 1878, only three days after the slaying of Sheriff Brady, Dick Brewer and fourteen Regulators appeared at Blazer's Mill. Included in the group were Billy Bonney and Jim French—sitting on their horses gingerly after taking a bullet in the thigh—Fred Waite, John Middleton, Charley Bowdre, and Frank and George Coe.

The men unsaddled and placed their horses in a corral across the stream from the big house. A high board fence surrounded the corral and therefore hid the horses from view. Entering the house, they asked Mrs. Godfroy to fix dinner for them. Outside, descending the canyon rather than wait longer for his check, Roberts spotted the mail carrier riding up the trail across the river. He turned around and rode back to see if the mail brought his payment.

Roberts tied his pack mule to a tree across from the big house, above the corral, and surveyed the surroundings. With the Regulators' horses hidden by the plank wall around the corral, all seemed quiet. He crossed the stream and tied his mule to the southwest corner of the house. Blazer had a rule that all visitors had to drape their pistol belts on their saddle horns before entering. Roberts complied with the rule, then grasping his Winchester carbine, he headed for the porch.

Meanwhile, John Middleton had been keeping watch on the porch. When he saw Roberts coming up the trail, he went inside and reported to Brewer. He added that he had heard the man tell one of Blazer's sons that his name was Roberts. Brewer at once declared that the name appeared on his warrant and that Roberts had to be arrested. Frank Coe, a neighbor and friend of Roberts on the Ruidoso, persuaded Brewer to delay while he tried to convince Buckshot to surrender. Outside, Coe met Roberts approaching the front door. They shook hands, then returned to the west porch to sit in front of the door to Blazer's office. Despite Coe's assurance that he would guarantee Roberts's safety if he gave up his carbine, he stubbornly resisted. "No," replied Roberts, according to Coe, "never alive. The Kid is with you and he will kill me on sight." "I'll stand by you," promised Coe, to no avail. "We talked for half an hour," recounted Coe, "but the answer was no, no, no."

With unseemly haste, Brewer would wait no longer. With the rest of the men, he emerged from the house and turned to the west porch. Pistol in hand, Charley Bowdre confronted Roberts and Coe. John Middleton and George Coe stood behind Bowdre.

"Roberts, throw up your hands," shouted Bowdre.

"No," replied Roberts as he rose from the bench and brought his carbine to his hip. Both fired at the same time. Roberts's bullet struck Bowdre's belt buckle and dropped his belt and holster to the ground. It then ricocheted into George Coe's hand, smashing his thumb and finger. Bowdre's bullet punched into Roberts's stomach. As the other of Brewer's men ran to the fight, Roberts rapidly levered his Winchester, hitting John Middleton in the chest, grazing another man's leg, and narrowly missing Billy Bonney. As Coe related, "The Kid slipped in between the wall and a wagon. Roberts took a shot at him, just shaved his arm. Kid backed out as it was too hot there for him." Billy knew how many rounds Roberts's carbine held. When it had been emptied, the Kid ran to the door, aimed his own carbine at Roberts, and pulled the trigger. At that moment Roberts thrust the muzzle of his empty carbine into his opponent's stomach, deflecting his aim and causing the bullet to smash the door frame. Again, Billy retreated.

Roberts, mortally wounded, dragged himself through the door into Blazer's office. Mounted on the wall, he saw an army Springfield rifle and a box of cartridges. Retrieving the rifle, he pulled a mattress from the bed to form a barricade at the door, then lay down and prepared to defend himself. A few shots from the heavy Springfield persuaded the Regulators to give Roberts a wide berth. Not so Dick Brewer, whose agitated determination to get Roberts ran counter to his usually rational disposition. If none of the other Regulators would end the shootout, he himself would. Hopping the creek, he made his way two hundred yards down the trail to the sawmill and gristmill. Recrossing the stream, he took station behind a stack of logs with a commanding view of Blazer's office door. Raising his Winchester above the logs, he took aim at Roberts and fired.

Alerted by the bullet punching into the wall behind him, Roberts looked out and saw a residue of gun smoke drift from the top of the woodpile. Sighting his rifle on the logs, he waited until Brewer's head rose from behind the rampart. At the same instant he squeezed the trigger. The blast sent the bullet into Brewer's left eye and blew out the back of his skull.

After that, said Frank Coe, "No one tried to get Roberts." They knew he would die, and the risk was not worth pursuing Brewer's relentless quest.

And die he did, the next day.

* * *

As with the assassination of Sheriff Brady, the killing of Buckshot Roberts lost the McSween cause even more public sympathy. Killing two men from ambush and ganging up on a mortally wounded man violated the sense of fair play that prevailed in the culture of guns and violence. All Lincoln County subscribed to this point of view, mainly imported by Texans moving north during the aftermath of the Civil War. "I'll die before I'll run" was their creed. Although dominated by guns and violence, however, the culture did include a code of fair play, and the Regulators had twice violated it. Moreover, the courage and determination of Roberts in defending himself against fourteen gunmen appealed to people steeped in that culture.

Still, this was war. Roberts was an enemy. He had sold his life dearly. So had Brewer. War offers the only sensible explanation of why Brewer, "one of nature's noblemen," according to Tunstall, proved so fanatical in his resolve to take Roberts. After trying to get Blazer, Godfroy, and another man to evict Roberts, even threatening to burn the house down, he took on the task himself. Soldiers get killed in war. Brewer's life proved a casualty of war.

Billy Bonney's mind probably had not sharpened on the concept of these troubles as war. Both in the assassination of Brady and in rushing Roberts's door, he had shown courage and recklessness. Although a kid of eighteen, Billy had graduated to the role of a full-fledged Regulator and a full-time soldier in war even if not grasped in his own mind.

*Billy the Kid, aka William H. Bonney, aka Kid, aka Henry McCarty, aka
Henry Antrim. This is the only known likeness of Billy, one of two tintypes
taken at Fort Sumner in 1880. The original of the first disappeared long
ago. This is taken from the original of the second, which surfaced in 1986.
Tintypes were reversed images, showing Billy holding his Winchester with
his right hand and his pistol hanging from his left side. In this picture,
the reversed image has been reversed to show him as he actually appeared.
(Courtesy Special Collections, University of Arizona Library.)*

Now exposed as a fake, this photograph was long thought to be Catherine McCarty Antrim, Billy the Kid's mother. She died of tuberculosis in 1874, when Billy was fifteen. Before tuberculosis forced her to her bed, she exerted enough influence on her son that he was a popular lad whose prospects appeared promising. After her death, he was on his own, untutored by his stepfather. (Courtesy Robert N. Mullin Collection at the Haley Memorial Library and History Center, Midland, Texas.)

Aerial view of Lincoln in the 1920s. The Murphy-Dolan store, later the county courthouse, is at the lower left, across from the Wortley Hotel, partly obscured by trees. The site of the McSween house is occupied by later structures. The Tunstall store is the long building in the upper center of the picture. The torreon rises above surrounding walls just beyond the Tunstall store. The Ellis store is the next to last building in the upper right. The Río Bonito winds across the upper left half of the picture. (Courtesy Special Collections, University of Arizona Library.)

Richard Brewer. Prominent rancher with his own ranch and manager of the Tunstall ranch, Dick Brewer hired Billy the Kid as a cowboy and gunman in the Lincoln County War. He was the first chief of the Regulators but was killed by Buckshot Roberts in the shootout at Blazer's Mill. (Courtesy Special Collections, University of Arizona Library.)

John Henry Tunstall, the Englishman who took on the economic domination of the county by the Murphy-Dolan store. His murder changed the conflict into war. (Courtesy Special Collections, University of Arizona Library.)

Alexander McSween, Lincoln's peace-loving lawyer who had to lead the armed Regulators in their war against the Murphy-Dolan gunmen after the murder of Tunstall. McSween and Tunstall joined in building and stocking the Tunstall store. (Courtesy Special Collections, University of Arizona Library.)

James J. Dolan and Lawrence G. Murphy. Murphy founded "The House" but yielded leadership to Dolan after alcoholism forced his retirement. Dolan thus played the major role in The House's conflict with McSween's Regulators. (Courtesy Robert N. Mullin Collection at the Haley Memorial Library and History Center, Midland, Texas.)

(right) *William Brady, sheriff of Lincoln County and protagonist of The House in the Lincoln County War. He was assassinated by a group of six Regulators, including Billy the Kid. (Courtesy Special Collections, University of Arizona Library.)*

(left) *Jacob B. Mathews. A House acolyte, Mathews led the posse that tried to attach Tunstall's cattle, then led the posse whose subposse killed Tunstall. At the Brady assassination, Mathews shot Billy the Kid through the thigh. (Courtesy Special Collections, University of Arizona Library.)*

Fred Waite, Billy's closest comrade at the Tunstall ranch and then in the Lincoln County War. They talked about partnering in a ranch of their own, but the idea expired almost as soon as it was born. Billy could not form long-range goals, much less carry them out. (Courtesy Special Collections, University of Arizona Library.)

Lieutenant Colonel Nathan Augustus Monroe Dudley, commander of Fort Stanton. He led a checkered army career that kept him in trouble most of the time. He intervened in the five-day battle for Lincoln that ended in McSween's death. A court of inquiry later exonerated him in what was essentially a whitewash. (Massachusetts Commandery Military Order of the Loyal Legion, courtesy US Army Military History Institute.)

Lew Wallace, territorial governor of New Mexico, who promised Billy a pardon if he testified in a murder trial. Billy met his part of the bargain, but Wallace did not. Billy's subsequent turn to outlawry made it politically impossible for Wallace to extend any form of clemency. (Courtesy Palace of the Governors Photo Archives [NMHM/DCA], negative 13123.)

Robert Olinger, "Pecos Bob," bullied Billy after his conviction of murder and pending his hanging. When Billy escaped, Olinger hastened from across the street at the Wortley Hotel and was blasted in the face and chest by Billy with Olinger's own shotgun. (Courtesy Special Collections, University of Arizona Library.)

(above) *The Lincoln County Court-house, formerly the Murphy-Dolan store in the 1880s. In escaping the forthcoming hanging, Billy blasted Bob Olinger from the second-floor window on the side. He then spoke to the townspeople from the balcony in the front before riding out of Lincoln to freedom. (Courtesy Palace of the Governors Photo Archives [NMHM/DCA], negative 5441.)*

(left) *Tom O'Folliard, Billy's worshipful companion. Tom accompanied Billy everywhere and waited on him hand and foot. In an ambush set up by Sheriff Pat Garrett at Fort Sumner, Tom was shot in the chest and soon died. (Courtesy Palace of the Governors Photo Archives [NMHM/DCA], negative 105046.)*

(left) *Charley and Manuela Bowdre. Charley rode with the Regulators and was especially close to Billy. Charley died in the shootout at Stinking Springs where Billy was taken prisoner. (Courtesy Palace of the Governors Photo Archives [NMHM/DCA], negative 105048.)*

(below) *The Maxwell House at Fort Sumner. Billy was shot and killed in Pete Maxwell's bedroom, in the corner room facing the camera. (Courtesy Robert N. Mullin Collection at the Haley Memorial Library and History Center, Midland, Texas.)*

Sheriff Pat Garrett (sitting left) with his two deputies, Jim Brent (standing) and John Poe, taken in 1881 shortly after Garrett shot Billy the Kid. (Courtesy Robert N. Mullin Collection at the Haley Memorial Library and History Center, Midland, Texas.)

❋ CHAPTER 7 ❋

Billy Indicted for Murder

The killing of Buckshot Roberts only added to the confusion and turmoil roiling Lincoln County. When district court at last convened in Lincoln on April 8, 1878, confusion and turmoil still roiled. Judge Bristol failed to appear. He finally claimed the bench on April 10. Selection of grand and petit juries proved almost impossible. Brady's replacement as sheriff was John N. Copeland, appointed by the county commissioners. Copeland called the names of the grand jury panel. District Attorney Rynerson challenged the entire panel on the grounds that the justice of the peace, Squire Wilson, had no authority to select jurors. Judge Bristol dismissed them all. When a petit jury was summoned, Rynerson challenged them all on the same grounds. Bristol instructed Copeland to select fifteen men to serve as grand jurors and twenty-four as petit jurors. At last, on April 13, a grand jury was empaneled. The foreman was Joseph H. Blazer, owner of Blazer's Mill, while nine Hispanics and six Anglos rounded out the jury.

Not an auspicious beginning. Not until April 24 could the court adjourn. Most witnesses had chosen sides in the conflict, so delivered questionable testimony to a jury composed of men who had also chosen sides—McSween's.

After listening to hours of largely spurious testimony, the grand jury began returning indictments almost indiscriminately on both sides of the conflict. Although exonerating McSween of the embezzlement charge, among others they indicted Dolan and Mathews in the Tunstall killing; Billy Bonney, Fred Waite, and John Middleton in the Brady killing; and Charley Bowdre for the murder of Buckshot Roberts. Overlooked was the murder of Morton and Hill. Many of the cases were postponed to the next year's court session, when some were further postponed. The April 1878 district court session in Lincoln proved more chaotic than orderly.

Meanwhile, Jimmy Dolan faced further catastrophe: bankruptcy. In January he had mortgaged his property to Thomas B. Catron, US district attorney for New Mexico. Catron was a political powerhouse in Santa Fe, reputed to head the shadowy "Santa Fe Ring." Catron took possession of Dolan's property and sent his brother-in-law to Lincoln to manage Dolan's assets.

Another setback for Dolan was the county commissioners' appointment of John Copeland to succeed Brady as county sheriff. A big man with a small intellect, he served the interests of McSween. He carried the arrest warrants for the Kid and other Regulators but failed to serve them. Instead, he caroused with the Regulators in McSween's house, now the Regulator headquarters.

As the Reverend Ealy's wife recalled, they loved to sing, none more than Billy. Mary Ealy played Sue McSween's piano as the men gathered around her to sing. "And how they did sing," she remembered. "They stood behind me with their guns and belts full of cartridges; I suppose I was off tune as often as on it as I felt very nervous, though they were very nice and polite."

Dick Brewer's death had not disorganized the Regulators. They elected one of their own, Frank McNab, as the new chief. A Scotsman, about twenty-seven, McNab was a "cattle detective" employed by the commission house that now was disposing of John Chisum's cattle to protect them from rustlers.

With Sheriff Copeland on their side, the Regulators felt confident of prevailing. Dolan had not given up, however. George Peppin and Billy Mathews still claimed to be deputies by virtue of Brady's appointment. Dolan convinced them that Sheriff Copeland needed help in understanding his duty. Peppin and Mathews rode down to Seven Rivers and organized a posse of about thirty men consisting of Seven Rivers cowmen; all were Dolanites and some had been part of the posse that killed Tunstall. On the night of April 29 they were on their way back to Lincoln when they encountered Frank McNab en route to his station on the Pecos. George Coe and his brother-in-law Ab Saunders accompanied McNab.

The posse set up an ambush that killed McNab, wounded Saunders, and made a prisoner of Coe.

The murder of McNab served as a prelude to what became known as the "Battle of Lincoln." The next morning a messenger brought word to the McSween house that the Peppin-Mathews deputies had come to help Copeland arrest the Kid and others for whom he held warrants. The Regulators quickly scattered themselves around the town and took up firing positions on top of the flat-topped roofs, some of which had parapets in which the gunmen punched firing ports. All day the two sides exchanged fire without doing any damage.

Copeland, however, sent to Fort Stanton for military help. Twenty troopers under a lieutenant responded. Copeland led them to the lower end of town and confronted the Seven Rivers posse, about thirty men. Asked which men he wanted to arrest, Copeland responded, "I want the whole damn business." None would surrender to Copeland without a fight, however, so the lieutenant accepted their surrender and escorted them to Fort Stanton to remain under military protection until the issue was resolved.

What Billy Bonney did during the Battle of Lincoln is unrecorded. He distinguished himself with none of the bravado that had characterized the death of Brady and Buckshot Roberts. He probably still hurt from the bullet that grazed his arm during the exchange of fire with Roberts. Presumably, Billy did what the others did: fired at the Peppin-Mathews posse from the top of a building. With Charley Bowdre and John Middleton, still recovering from the wound sustained at Blazer's Mill, the Kid then rode to his favorite haunt of San Patricio.

Meanwhile, Sheriff Copeland appeared at Fort Stanton, where "the whole damn business" was under military protection. There he encountered a new actor in the Lincoln County War. Nathan Augustus Monroe Dudley, lieutenant colonel of the Ninth Cavalry, had taken command of the fort on April 4, the same day as the shootout at Blazer's Mill. His erect form, prominent forehead and nose, sweeping dragoon mustache, and bushy white eyebrows gave him the appearance of a model cavalry officer of twenty-three years' service. It failed to conceal a striking ineptitude, however, as well as a weak intellect, pompous conceit, despotism, bluster, and an aptitude for contention. He carried on a feud with his district commander, Colonel Edward Hatch, that kept him constantly in trouble wherever he was stationed. A fondness for whiskey marked a trail of courts-martial, the latest at Fort Union. The court convicted him of disobedience of orders, drunkenness, and conduct to the prejudice of good order. Colonel Hatch reassigned him to command Fort Stanton.

Dudley formed an instant dislike of McSween and his followers, but on April 30 he confronted Sheriff Copeland and the men who surrendered to the army instead of Copeland at Lincoln. They had never been formally arrested because they had never been in Copeland's possession. McSween quickly appeared, however, and produced a warrant for the arrest of the posse for murdering McNab. McSween obtained the warrant from the justice of the peace at San Patricio, where Billy and his pals had resided since the Battle of Lincoln. After presenting the warrant to Dudley, McSween returned to San Patricio.

Not to be outdone, Dudley countered McSween by obtaining an arrest warrant from the justice of the peace at Blazer's Mill charging McSween and the Regulators with "riot." So Dudley held two warrants, one for the thirty possemen from Seven Rivers, the other for all the Regulators. He then dispatched Copeland, with a cavalry detachment, to serve the warrant on McSween as head of the Regulators.

In San Patricio on May 2, McSween had just bought dinner for Billy Bonney, Charley Bowdre, and John Middleton when Copeland

and the cavalry rode into town. Bonney, Bowdre, and Middleton promptly took to the hills as the lieutenant ordered Copeland to serve the warrants for "riot" on McSween.

Back at Fort Stanton, where the thirty men Copeland had tried to arrest in Lincoln for the murder of McNab remained under Dudley's protection, Copeland asked the colonel to release them to him. Dudley readily complied. Copeland had no idea what to do with them. Confused as usual, he simply turned them loose and told them to go home and quit feuding.

With Dudley's help, the Lincoln County War had begun to look more like a comic opera than a war.

*   *   *

In Lincoln, the Regulators once more reorganized. They elected a new captain, Josiah "Doc" Scurlock. Deputized by Copeland, Scurlock gathered his men, including Billy Bonney, and headed for Seven Rivers to arrest men whose names appeared on the warrant issued by Justice Wilson in February. In a shrewd move, Scurlock also included a group of Hispanics led by their own deputy, Josefita Chavez. The posse now numbered more than twenty.

On May 15, near Seven Rivers, the posse stormed the Dolan cow camp, seized the horses and mules, and scattered the cattle. The camp cook, Manuel Segovia (usually known as "Indian"), had fought vigorously for the Dolan side and was believed to have been the killer of Frank McNab. Quickly taken into custody, he broke free and rode to escape. As Francisco Trujillo recalled, "Billy the Kid and Jose[fita] Chavez took after him and began to shoot at him until they got him." Thus Billy Bonney scored another kill or possible kill.

The raid on Dolan's cow camp proved a serious mistake. The horses and cattle belonged not to Dolan but to Thomas B. Catron, who held the mortgage on all of Dolan's assets. When that Santa Fe potentate learned the fate of his cattle, he went at once to Governor Axtell. Prompted by Dolan, Catron pointed to a technicality that invalidated Sheriff Copeland's commission. Axtell promptly removed Copeland and substituted George Peppin as sheriff.

"Dad" Peppin hardly represented an improvement on Copeland. In fact, he embodied the same flaws as Copeland. The law, however, now shifted from McSween to Dolan and his allies. Dolan easily manipulated Peppin. The conflict would soon resume as a genuine war.

* * *

Sheriff Peppin carried a second arrest warrant. Doubtless prompted by Dolan, Rynerson, and Catron, the US marshal for New Mexico issued federal warrants for Billy and his friends—federal indictments stemming from the reasoning that the killing of Buckshot Roberts took place on a federal Indian reservation. Billy now stood indicted by the territorial government for the murder of Sheriff Brady and the federal government for the murder of Buckshot Roberts.

At San Patricio, the Regulators spent their days in town consorting with the Hispanics and their nights hiding in the mountains. Besides Billy, Fred Waite, Charley Bowdre, and their chief, Doc Scurlock, McSween and former sheriff Copeland had joined the group.

Peppin placed his posse under a big-mouthed, ostentatious Dolanite named Jack Long, once a follower of Jesse Evans. Early on June 27, the two sides stumbled into each other accidentally as the Regulators rode down a mountainside. The Regulators took positions and easily drove off the attackers.

Long legally summoned fifteen Hispanics and forced them to join his posse. They rode under their own deputy, José Chavez y Baca. Dolan himself accompanied the aggressors. They had learned that the Regulator stronghold was in San Patricio. Before dawn on July 3, the enlarged posse rode into the town. They found the Regulators waiting, posted on top of the houses. As George Coe recalled, "We were scattered all over town. Three or four of us got on top of every house. It was too dark to see to shoot accurately, but we killed a horse or two and think we wounded a man." The attackers backed off.

Heading down the Hondo, Scurlock found Peppin's posse trailing behind. Scurlock spread his men along a ridge crest and loosed a volley that drove the posse off. He then led his men on down the Hondo and settled in at John Chisum's ranch for a Fourth of July celebration. Chisum was absent, but his hands prepared a fine spread. A handful of Seven Rivers cowboys interrupted the festivities, but the Regulators' fire drove them off.

For the Kid, another interruption proved more congenial: Chisum's niece Sallie, a petite sixteen-year-old blonde. Billy bought her candy and otherwise courted her. She returned his affection. This marked the blossoming of a long-distance romance.

In addition, sometime during June, before the fights of early July, Billy had partnered with a new comrade, one to whom he grew even closer than Fred Waite. Tom O'Folliard, a tall, strapping youth from Texas, idolized his new friend, especially after Billy taught him how to shoot. As recounted by Frank Coe, "He was the Kid's inseparable companion and always went along and held his horses. He held his horses when the Kid would pay his attentions to some Mexican girl. It mattered not that he was gone thirty minutes or half the night. Tom was there when he came out."

In the fights at San Patricio and the skirmish at Chisum's ranch, Sheriff Peppin had shown himself no more effective than his predecessor. After the exchange of fire at the Chisum ranch on July 4, Peppin and his posse returned to Lincoln.

McSween had resolved to quit leading a fugitive life, dashing from place to place to elude Peppin's posse. He led the Regulators into Lincoln on July 14, 1878, ready to fight if Peppin tried to arrest him again. The two sides had set the stage for the final confrontation of the Lincoln County War, one that shrank the first Battle of Lincoln to a tame irrelevance.

Throughout these events, Billy Bonney had performed as one of the Regulators, prominent, to be sure, but not outstanding. Reinforcing his membership were the camaraderie of the older men; the pleasure of dancing, singing, and charming the *señoritas* at San Patricio; teaching marksmanship to his new comrade Tom O'Folliard; and finally the prospect of romance with Sallie Chisum. Billy remained the "kid," lacking any long-term goal other than his talk with Fred Waite about establishing a ranch; scarcely remembered, it had fallen victim to current events.

CHAPTER 8

"The Big Killing"

The Regulators slipped quietly into Lincoln on the night of July 14, 1878, while most of Peppin's men were absent searching for them. Peppin's deputy Jack Long and five men held the torreon while Dolan, Peppin, and a few deputies had set up headquarters at the Wortley Hotel. None challenged the Regulators, who took firing positions at the Isaac Ellis store on the east end of town, the Montaño store and the home of Juan Patrón in the center of town opposite the torreon, and the McSween house itself on the west, next to the Tunstall store and only a short distance east of the Wortley. Billy Bonney joined those at the Montaño store.

The Regulator army had grown to almost sixty men, including a newly recruited contingent of Hispanics under Martín Chavez of San Patricio. Sheriff Peppin's force numbered forty when the absent members rode into town the next day. Peppin's gunmen included some hard cases, such as the Seven Rivers warriors, Jesse Evans and his henchmen, and veterans of the Mathews posse.

Although outnumbered sixty to forty, Peppin enjoyed an advantage that favored his smaller force. Except for Jack Long at the torreon, the sheriff's gunmen concentrated in one place, the Wortley. The Regulators, holding four positions, could not safely communicate with one another without exposing themselves to the posse's fire.

When the remaining posse dismounted at the Wortley on the afternoon of July 15, they loosed a fusillade at the McSween house, splintering the window shutters. The firing brought Billy and about a dozen others in the Montaño store running up the street to the McSween house, exchanging fire with Jack Long in the torreon as they ran. From the McSween house, the reinforcements sent a blast of gunfire back at the Wortley, scattering the men in the corral into the hotel.

McSween's U-shaped adobe housed two families. McSween and Susan occupied the west half. The family of David Shield, McSween's law partner, lived in the east half. Shield himself was in Las Vegas, New Mexico, but his wife, who was Susan McSween's sister, and five children resided in the east half. Beginning with a kitchen in the back, the rooms in each half opened one onto the next until reaching the street. Each half had its own kitchen, the west kitchen of the McSweens and the east kitchen of the Shields. Both opened on the backyard, fenced in the rear by an adobe wall and on the east by another, less substantial wall.

Fifteen staunch gunmen stood at the ready in the house. Among them were the Kid and his buddy Tom O'Folliard, Jim French, and other veterans. Also present were seven of the San Patricio Hispanics.

George Coe and two others had crept into the Tunstall store and taken positions commanding the McSween house. At the Ellis store, about a dozen Regulators under Doc Scurlock held that strongpoint, along with Charley Bowdre and John Middleton.

The stalemate continued for several days, until July 19, with both sides taking random shots at each other. On the morning of the nineteenth the two sides witnessed Colonel Dudley riding down the street in front of eleven black cavalrymen and twenty-four white infantrymen. In the rear trailed a small twelve-pounder mountain howitzer and a rapid-fire Gatling gun.

Disobeying his orders from above to stay out of Lincoln's civic feud, Dudley reasoned that the conflict put women and children at risk and justified his intervention. Although he sympathized with

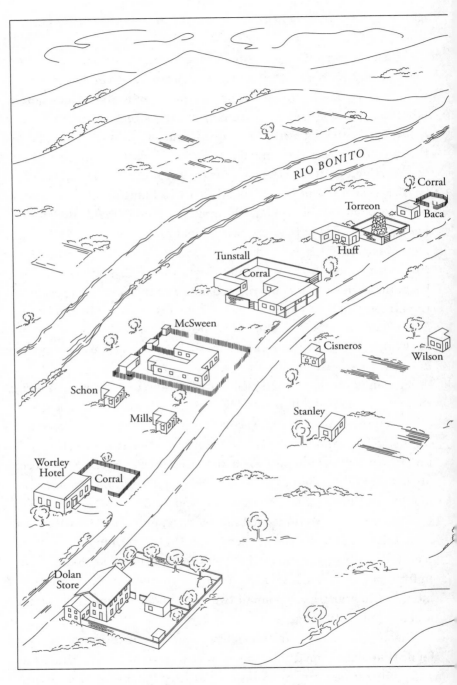

Drawing by Bill Nelson based on a drawing in the Mullin Collection,
Haley History Center, Midland, Texas.

Ellis

Dudley
Camp Site

Jail

Brady

Montaño
Store

Ike
Stockton's
Saloon

Patron

Court House

Aguayo

LINCOLN
NEW MEXICO
1878
PRINCIPAL LOCATIONS

the Peppin side, Dudley made a big show of impartiality. He would fire on neither side unless fired on himself.

Dudley's presence, supposedly impartial, proved detrimental to the Regulators. The posse could fire on any of the Regulator strongholds without fear of a return fire. That would have endangered Dudley's soldiers, however, and brought him into the fight.

"We all became alarmed," said Susan McSween, because they all assumed that the army had come to help Peppin. They also were frightened by the sight of artillery. McSween scrawled a note to Dudley, handed it to the Kid to read, then sent it with the Shields' young daughter to Dudley. It was phrased so ambiguously that Dudley could interpret it as he wished. It read: "Would you have the kindness to let me know why soldiers surround my house. Before blowing up my property I would like to know the reason. The constable is here and has warrants for the arrest of Sheriff Peppin and posse for murder and larceny. Respectfully. A. A. McSween."

McSween must have been referring to the cannon, but Dudley chose to believe that he intended to blow up his own house. Moreover, the warrants meant nothing to Dudley. Peppin had a pocket full of warrants, too, and Dudley's orders forbade him to interfere in civil affairs.

The reply came back signed by Dudley's adjutant: "I am directed by the Commanding Officer to inform you that no troops have surrounded your house, and that he desires to hold no further correspondence with you. He directed me to say that if you desire to blow up your house he has no objections provided you do not injure any of his command by so doing."

As a matter of fact, no troops surrounded McSween's house. They camped with Dudley in the middle of town, their cannon trained on the Montaño store across the street. Although McSween clearly had no intent to blow up his house, the Regulators in the Montaño store and the Patrón house feared Dudley might blow them up. They ran down to the street to the Ellis store. Dudley promptly swung the artillery to point at the Ellis store. He also trained his Gatling gun on the hills across the river, the most likely escape route for the men in the Ellis store. Such was the colonel's neutrality.

Meanwhile, Sheriff Peppin, who had taken station on the top of the torreon, ordered the McSween house set on fire. As Deputy Jack Long entered the east kitchen and began to pile kindling on the floor, Sue McSween marched down the street intent on a conversation with Dudley. At the torreon she encountered Peppin, who told her that if she wanted to save her house from flames she had to induce the men inside to surrender. At the army camp, she tried to persuade the colonel to intervene, but he again proclaimed his neutrality. After a nasty exchange of shouts, Sue retreated to her home.

Back in her home, Sue found Long engaged in trying to fire the east kitchen while her sister was moving her belongings out. Billy helped her. Probably worried about the danger to the Shield family if he shot at Long in the kitchen, Billy allowed him to set the fire. Either it sputtered out or Billy put it out.

Another attempt had more success. A deputy piled planks on the roof of the west kitchen, the McSweens', and fired the roof. Flames and smoke filled the kitchen below and during the afternoon moved slowly forward room by room in the west wing toward the street. The occupants had to move, too. Sue McSween offers a revealing glimpse of Billy Bonney during the crucial late afternoon hours: "The boys talked to each other and McSween and I were sitting in one corner. The boys decided I should leave. McSween said he guessed that was better. The Kid was lively and McSween was sad. McSween sat with his head down, and the Kid shook him and told him to get up, that they were going to make a break."

McSween had lost any control he had exercised. Billy had suddenly risen to the role of leadership. He tried to energize McSween, without success. And he decided that the only escape from the flames was a break. Billy must have made that decision himself and the others went along. In those moments when certain death approached, a new Billy Bonney emerged: a leader whom men respected and followed. It proved permanent.

Sue McSween had slipped out the front door and reached safety. So had all the Shield family. Only Regulators remained in the house, and they could escape only by making their way through the debris left by Long in the east kitchen, descending steps to the backyard, crossing the yard to a gate in the wall facing the Tunstall store, and sprinting across the open space to the shadows behind the Tunstall store. This was perilous because deputies were posted behind the back wall and at the street corner of the Tunstall store from which they could bring the open space under fire. George Coe and the two Regulators in the back room of the Tunstall store could not help. They could neither see the gunmen at the front corner of the store nor fire at the deputies at the back wall of the house without endangering the escapees.

About 9:00 p.m., the men left the kitchen and filed slowly into the darkened yard. Five succeeded in reaching the gate in the wall facing the Tunstall store without alerting the deputies. Led by Jim French, with Tom O'Folliard in the center, and the Kid bringing up the rear, they burst through the gate and began racing across the open space toward the Tunstall store. Not until they emerged from the gate into the light cast by the flames did the posse see them. From behind the back wall and the street at the corner of the Tunstall store, they opened a heavy fire on the running men, dropping one but missing the others as they dodged back and forth. The four safely reached the shadows along the Bonito behind the Tunstall store.

McSween and the others had followed into the backyard, but the fire of the deputies blocked the escape route. The men crouched against the wall of the house and remained in the shadows. After ten minutes McSween called out that he would surrender. Deputy Bob Beckwith from Seven Rivers advanced across the yard to where McSween stood. "I am a deputy sheriff and I have got a warrant for you," asserted Beckwith. Suddenly McSween shouted, "I shall never surrender."

That triggered what one of the deputies termed "the big killing." Both sides fired wildly, unable to see well enough to fix on a target. A bullet hit Deputy Beckwith in the face and killed him. Five bullets killed McSween. Two Hispanics crumpled next to McSween, dead, while another, young Yginio Salazar, took two bullets but managed to crawl to safety. The three remaining Hispanics succeeded in es-

caping in the confusion. How the several other men in the house fared
is not recorded, although one had been killed by a random shot.

As Billy and his three companions made their way down the
Bonito to the Ellis store, George Coe and his two companions left
the Tunstall store, vaulted over the back wall, and joined the Kid's
group. Scurlock and the rest of the Regulators had remained at the
Ellis store. They had made one hesitant foray to relieve the McSween
house, but fell back when a scattering of rifle fire came their way
from Peppin on top of the torreon. They probably also feared the
Gatling that Dudley had trained on this area.

Obtaining dinner from an apprehensive Isaac Ellis and spending
the night in the hills, the Kid, Jim French, Tom O'Folliard, José
Chavez y Baca, and George Coe traveled on down the Bonito, taking
time to steal horses and remount themselves.

The "big killing" had ended. No one emerged with much glory.
Peppin, Dudley, McSween, and Scurlock exercised almost no leadership. Peppin's only decision, a decisive one, was to order the
McSween house set afire. Dolan hovered about the battle scene but
took no active role in the strategy. He left that to Peppin.

Although the five-day battle left both sides with nothing more to
fight about, the Regulators remained an organized force. The Kid was
now a much more prominent member. Doc Scurlock may have been
the captain, but the Kid's performance in the burning McSween
house brought him new stature. Men listened to him, and he did not
hesitate to speak his mind.

* * *

The five-day battle in Lincoln in July 1878 began with Billy
Bonney simply a soldier in the Regulator army, a proven one, to be
sure, but no more than distinctive for his role in the assassination
of Sheriff Brady and his courageous act in the shootout at Blazer's
Mill. The battle ended in the blazing McSween house with Billy virtually taking command of those trapped by the flames. When no one
else took the lead in organizing an escape, he rose to the challenge.
His motivation probably began with concern for his own safety, but
it ended with Billy as leader of men.

❋ CHAPTER 9 ❋

Drifter

After stealing enough horses to mount themselves, the Regulators returned to Lincoln. For the Kid, if not the others, the purpose was revenge. But they found none of the Dolanites on whom they wanted take revenge. Sheriff Peppin had wisely taken refuge at Fort Stanton. Numerous citizens, even those who had not been members of the posse, felt threatened, especially as the Regulators rode about Lincoln vowing revenge.

At Blazer's Mill, Mescalero agent Frederick Godfroy believed himself targeted for assassination by the Kid, though why is not apparent. His fear ran so deep that he asked Colonel Dudley for an escort between Fort Stanton and the agency.

Seeming to confirm Godfroy's apprehension, on August 5, 1878, Regulators showed up at the Mescalero agency. Ostensibly, the purpose was to visit Dick Brewer's grave. More likely, the purpose was Indian horses. Included in the twenty Regulators were the Kid, Doc Scurlock, John Middleton, Fred Waite, Charley Bowdre, George Coe, and Jim French, all veterans of the Lincoln County War. Also riding with them were ten Hispanics.

Nearing the agency, the Anglos left the road and headed down a slope to a spring. Dismounting to drink, they heard gunfire on the road behind them. The Hispanics had encountered a party of Indians. Firing had erupted at once. Godfroy and his clerk, Morris Bernstein, mounted and hastened to the scene, Bernstein in advance. A bullet knocked him off his horse, dead. Godfroy promptly turned and retreated.

At the agency, Godfroy called on a few soldiers there and galloped back. Spotting the men at the spring, they joined the Apaches in firing on them. Startled, Billy's horse reared and bolted. As the men turned to race back to the road, George Coe hoisted the Kid on the back of his own horse and joined the others. Under heavy fire, they made it into the timber north of the road.

Picking their way through the woods toward the agency, the men came to the agency corral. Besides the Kid, three others had lost their horses. The Regulators opened the gate and herded the horses out. Billy roped one and rode bareback all the way to Frank Coe's ranch.

Although the collision was accidental, it lost even more public sympathy for the Regulators. Bernstein had been shot four times, his arms and cartridge belt taken, and his pockets turned inside out and emptied of their contents. Whether inflicted by Hispanic Regulators or Mescalero Apaches remains unknown. Either way, the blame fell on Billy Bonney, who was absent at the spring in the valley. Fueling public sentiment, Colonel Dudley declared that "this wanton and cowardly affair excels the killing of Sheriff Brady." The fight had occurred on an Indian reservation, which Dudley concluded justified him in fielding cavalry to pursue the culprits. The Regulators easily lost them.

The Regulators abandoned the war zone entirely and rode down to the Pecos River at Bosque Grande, site of John Chisum's first ranch. Chisum was absent, but they met his brothers, Jim and Pitzer, preparing a herd to drive north from the war zone. Present also was Sallie Chisum, who recorded the Regulators' arrival on August 13 but identified them as "Bonney and friends."

The war had not interrupted the association of the two. They had exchanged letters, and the Kid had even mailed one from the house fated to burn. As the Chisum party moved out, "Bonney and friends" went, too. Billy continued to court Sallie, as recorded in her diary.

At Fort Sumner the two groups parted, Billy and friends continuing up the Pecos, the Chisum party turning toward Texas. At Puerto de Luna, the men danced and partied for several nights, then continued on up to Anton Chico. Here, word came that a posse from Las Vegas under Sheriff Desiderio Romera of San Miguel County was at Manuel Sanchez's saloon looking for the "Lincoln County War party." Billy led his men down to the saloon to confront the posse. As Frank Coe recalled, "about eight big burly Mexicans" lined the bar, draped with rifles, pistols, and belts of cartridges. Billy asked the sheriff what he wanted. Sheriff Romero replied, "The Lincoln County War party." Billy told him he had found the party. "Now is the time and you'll never get us in a better place to settle it than right here." The sheriff eyed the group's firepower and called off the conversation. Billy said, "Come up here and take another drink on the house, and then we want you to leave town right now." The posse quickly did as ordered and hastened back up the Pecos to Las Vegas.

Several days later the group rode back down the Pecos and made camp for a talk. The time had come for a talk because the Regulators were dissolving. Frank and George Coe announced that for them the adventure was all over; they were going to Colorado. "Well, it's not all over for me," replied the Kid, "I'm going to get revenged." Walking away from the group, he asked, "Who wants to go with me?" All but the Coes joined the Kid. Billy Bonney was the new chief of the Regulators, or what was left of them.

The Kid led his followers on a horse-stealing foray back to Lincoln. Colonel Dudley announced the return to Lincoln of the "McSween ring. Stock stealing is a daily matter, the animals being taken toward the Pecos and Seven Rivers."

Indeed they were. Billy intended to herd them into Texas and sell them to the cowmen on the Staked Plains. But even under his leadership the Regulators had fallen apart. Doc Scurlock and Charley Bowdre had taken up residence at Fort Sumner. Others went home. Remaining with the Kid as he moved up the trail to the Panhandle in late September were Tom O'Folliard, Henry Brown, Fred Waite, and John Middleton.

En route, they overtook the Chisum party. "Regulators came up with us at Red River Springs on 25 Sept 1878," Sallie Chisum wrote in her diary. Given the Kid's robust libido among the señoritas, one is left to speculate if it ever connected with Sallie. Her diary indicates an intense mutual attraction. She was a strong young woman and did what she pleased. Whatever the relationship, here they parted for the last time.

In the Panhandle boomtown of Tascosa, the Kid easily disposed of his horses to the Texas cowmen. He also made friends with a young doctor who later became a distinguished physician. He remembered Billy Bonney as "a handsome youth with smooth face, wavy brown hair, an athletic and symmetrical figure, and clear blue eyes that could look one through and through. Unless angry, he always seemed to have a pleasant expression with a ready smile. His head was well shaped, his features regular, his nose aquiline, his most notable characteristic a slight projection of his two upper front teeth. He spoke Spanish like a native, and although only a beardless boy, was nevertheless a natural leader of men."

Billy's natural leadership failed to halt the dissolution of the Regulators. Middleton, Waite, and Brown wanted to continue east, away from the dangers of New Mexico. Billy refused. He and Tom O'Folliard headed back for the dangers of New Mexico.

Billy and Tom returned to Lincoln in December 1878, not as drifters, but with a purpose. Billy was tired of the fugitive life. He had been indicted for murder. He wanted to put that behind him. He may have recalled his bargain with Fred Waite nearly a year earlier to acquire a spread on the Río Peñasco and relax into the quiet life of a rancher.

He found that much had changed in Lincoln. It had not settled into a sleepy town untroubled by a factional war. One cause of discord was the return in November of Susan McSween, accompanied by a blustery one-armed lawyer named Huston Chapman. "He was a 'rule or ruin' sort of fellow," according to Isaac Ellis's son, "whom nobody liked." Sue and Chapman came to rule or ruin the man whom Sue regarded as the murderer of her husband: Colonel Dudley.

In Santa Fe, a new governor had taken office with the mission of restoring peace and order to Lincoln County. He was Lew Wallace, a Civil War general with literary ambitions who was focused on finishing a novel he would title *Ben-Hur*. Wallace adopted a simple approach to his assignment: proclaim the war ended and offer a "general pardon" to all combatants who had not been indicted by a grand jury.

Billy Bonney, of course, failed to qualify for the "general pardon." He labored under two indictments, territorial for the murder of Sheriff Brady and federal for the murder of Buckshot Roberts. Moreover, Sue McSween and the loud-mouthed Huston Chapman roiled the town, loudly damning Dudley and demanding his trial for murder. Dolanites, backed by Jesse Evans, turned belligerent once more. Billy and Tom had ridden into a hornet's nest that put to rest all thought of a quiet life on the Peñasco.

❉ CHAPTER 10 ❉

The Governor and the Kid

Billy Bonney still wanted to be at peace, with the law and with his longtime Dolanite enemies, especially the aggressive Jesse Evans. In the November elections, Dad Peppin had been replaced as sheriff by George Kimball, an honest, conscientious man intent on doing his duty. Since he carried a warrant for Billy's arrest, the Kid had to be careful not to run into him personally. The other danger lay in the men who hung around Fort Stanton: Dolan, Billy Mathews, Jesse Evans, and a newly arrived thug, Billy Campbell. A Texas cowboy, Campbell looked ferocious with a huge brown mustache and manifested a temperament as ferocious as his looks.

On February 18, 1879, a year after the day John H. Tunstall met his death, the Kid sent a message to Fort Stanton asking whether the Dolan bunch intended war or peace. An answer came back at once: they would come to Lincoln that night and talk it over.

The parley hardly began auspiciously. Billy had enlisted several former Regulators, who joined the Kid and Tom O'Folliard behind an adobe wall. Across the street, behind another adobe wall, stood Dolan, Mathews, Jesse Evans, and Billy Campbell. Evans began the "negotiations" by shouting that the Kid could not be dealt with and had to be killed on the spot. Billy replied that they had come to talk

peace, and a shooting was not the way to begin peace talks. Talk
peace they did and made peace without much talk.

Both sides gathered in the street, and a few words readily produced an agreement. Neither side would kill or testify against anyone. Withdrawal from the "treaty" could be accomplished with prior
notification. Violation of any of these terms carried the penalty of
death. They set the terms to paper, and everyone signed it.

Peace made, the men set forth on a drunken debauch, moving
unsteadily from one saloon to another. The Kid and Tom O'Folliard
went along, but stood back and merely watched the antics of the
others. About 10:30 p.m. the crowd encountered Huston Chapman
in the street. Campbell challenged him, asking his name. "My name
is Chapman." "Then you dance," demanded Campbell, thrusting
his pistol into Chapman's chest. Chapman declared that he did not
intend to dance, then asked, "Am I talking to Mr. Dolan?" "No,"
said Evans, "but you are talking to a damn good friend of his." The
drunken Dolan, standing about ten feet behind Campbell, drew his
pistol and fired a shot into the street. The blast startled Campbell
into jerking his trigger finger. The bullet plowed into Chapman's
chest, set his shirt on fire, and dropped him onto the street, dead.

Leaving Chapman's body blazing in the street, the group mer-
rily continued their party, staggering to another place and ordering
an oyster supper. One of the men had the wit to remember that
Chapman was unarmed; he suggested that someone return and
place a pistol in his hand. The Kid quickly volunteered. He ran out,
mounted, and galloped out of town. He wanted to distance himself
from the scene. So did Tom O'Folliard, who went with Billy.

An added reason for leaving town was that Sheriff Kimball
had seen Billy in town and ridden to Fort Stanton for a military
posse. Dudley furnished a lieutenant and twenty cavalrymen. They
searched in vain for the Kid, but they did find the body of Huston
Chapman, shirtless and with a charred breast. They carried it into
the courthouse and went about their failed mission.

Lew Wallace had been territorial governor for five months, and
he had not, as promised, visited Lincoln. The murder of Huston Chap-

man brought him at last to town, accompanied by the district military commander, Colonel Edward Hatch. They arrived on March 5, 1879, and lodged at the Montaño store.

As a first move, Wallace asked Colonel Hatch to relieve Colonel Dudley of command of Fort Stanton. He had become so tangled in Lincoln's rivalries that he could not restrain his partisanship. Hatch reluctantly complied, slipping the command from a furious Dudley to the senior captain, Henry Carroll. Carroll concentrated on deploying his soldiers to find 135 men whose names Justice Wilson provided. Most of those they caught simply pleaded the "general pardon" and went free.

For Wallace, the objective shifted to the murder of Huston Chapman, which occurred after the general pardon and could be prosecuted; the governor wanted to restore the people's confidence in the system of justice. He needed to assemble the group present when Chapman met his death. Rumor placed the Kid and Tom O'Folliard in the Capitan Mountains at Las Tablas and Dolan, Evans, and Campbell at Lawrence Murphy's former ranch farther west. Army detachments discovered Dolan, Evans, and Campbell and jailed them at Fort Stanton. Billy and Tom could not be found; they hid with a friend at San Patricio.

At San Patricio in March 1879, Billy Bonney was no longer the innocent youth who had climbed up Sheriff Whitehill's chimney. In the four years since, at the age of nineteen, he had acquired a wide range of skills and, more important, a robust self-confidence, an extraordinary ability to lead, and an even sharper mind.

Those qualities, combined with boldness, enabled him on March 13 to address Governor Wallace himself:

> I have heard that you will give one thousand ($) for my
> body, which as I can understand it, means alive as a wit-
> ness. I know it is as a witness against those who murdered
> Mr. Chapman. If it was so [arranged] that I could appear
> in court, I could give the desired information, but I have
> indictments against me for things that happened in the late

Lincoln County War and I am afraid to give myself up because my enemies would kill me. The day Mr. Chapman was
murdered I was in Lincoln at the request of the good citizens
to meet Mr. J. J. Dolan, to meet as a friend so as to lay aside
our arms and go to work. I was present when Mr. Chapman
was murdered and know who did it, and if it were not for
those indictments I would have made it clear before now. If it
is in your power to annul those indictments, I hope you will
do so as to give me a chance to explain. Please send me an
answer telling me what you can do. You can send answer by
bearer. I have no wish to fight any more, indeed I have not
raised an arm since your proclamation. As to my character,
I refer to any of the citizens, for the majority of them are my
friends and have been helping me all they could. I am called
Kid Antrim, but Antrim was my stepfather's name.

He signed the letter W. H. Bonney.

Two days later, Saturday, March 15, the governor replied:

Come to the house of old Squire Wilson (not the lawyer) at
nine (9) o'clock next Monday night alone. I don't mean his office, but his residence. Follow along the foot of the mountains
south of the town, come in on that side, and knock on the
east door. I have authority to exempt you from prosecution if
you will testify to what you say you know. The object of the
meeting at Squire Wilson's is to arrange the matter in a way
to make your life safe. To do that the utmost secrecy is to be
used. *So come alone.* Don't tell anybody—not a living soul—
where you are coming or the object. If you could trust Jesse
Evans, you can trust me.

In fact, Billy never trusted Jesse Evans or any of his comrades.
By agreeing to testify, he broke the treaty that the two sides had
signed, which meant execution. The other parties to the treaty, how-

ever, were locked up at Fort Stanton. The governor's letter, moreover, contained another error, a vital one. He did not have the authority to exempt anyone from prosecution. That was the sole prerogative of District Attorney William L. Rynerson, who would not be swayed from prosecuting the Kid for murder.

Even so, the meeting occurred as planned. At the appointed time Billy knocked and entered the east door of Squire Wilson's home, Winchester in one hand and pistol in the other. The three sat around a table lit by a candle. Governor Wallace explained his plan: "Testify before the grand jury and the trial court and convict the murderer of Chapman, and I will let you go scott-free with a pardon in your pocket for all your own misdeeds." Billy protested that compliance meant his death. But the governor countered with a promise to arrange a fake arrest and hold the Kid in protective custody.

In this exchange, Wallace switched from exemption from prosecution to a pardon, which he did have the authority to issue. Billy accepted this scheme, although he knew he exposed himself to killing. Furthermore, any comfort derived from the imprisonment of his enemies at Fort Stanton vanished the day after the meeting. Evans and Campbell persuaded their guard to desert and free them from the lockup. They took to the mountains and eventually, unknown to Billy, headed for Texas.

As arranged by Governor Wallace, on March 21, Sheriff Kimball led a posse to San Patricio and arrested Billy Bonney and Tom O'Folliard, who as always had clung to Billy throughout the night of Chapman's murder. They were placed under guard in the Patrón house next to Wallace's rooms at the Montaño store. Joining them soon was Doc Scurlock, who had been arrested at Fort Sumner.

In a letter to the secretary of the interior, Wallace described a scene that revealed his contempt for Billy and Lincoln in general. Unwittingly, he confirmed Billy's assurance that he had many friends in Lincoln: "A precious specimen nicknamed 'The Kid,' whom the Sheriff is holding here in the Plaza, as it is called, is an object of tender regard. I heard singing and music the other night; going to the door, I found the minstrels of the village actually serenading the fellow in his prison."

Holding such an opinion of the Kid foreshadowed the way Wallace would honor the promise of the night-time meeting with the "precious specimen." He could have issued a pardon at any time, before or after the approaching term of court. Instead, he hastened back to Santa Fe, doubtless to resume his work on *Ben-Hur*.

Judge Bristol convened district court on April 24. Honoring his promise, Billy took the stand and described the killing. So did Tom O'Folliard. Based on their testimony, the grand jury indicted Dolan and Campbell for murder and Evans as an accessory.

District Attorney Rynerson did not, as Wallace had predicted, drop the charge against Billy in exchange for his testimony. On the contrary, he intended to see the Kid hanged for the murder of Sheriff Brady. As a first move, he obtained from Judge Bristol a change of venue to Doña Ana County, distant from Billy's Lincoln friends.

The grand jury had indicted a large number of participants on both sides in the Lincoln County War, including Colonel Dudley, on the charge of arson. With Campbell and Evans long gone to Texas, that left Dolan as the most prominent of those indicted. None of the others were even brought to trial.

Long before the outbreak of the Lincoln County War, District Attorney Rynerson, living up to his stormy role in New Mexico politics, had allied himself closely with the Dolan faction. He stood ready to serve Dolan's interests in any way Dolan desired. Now, however, his duty was to prosecute Dolan for murder. Not surprisingly, Dolan was acquitted. By testifying against Dolan and his friends, however, Billy had so infuriated Rynerson that his only objective was to convict Billy Bonney for murder.

In Lincoln, Sheriff Kimball knew the circumstances of the Kid's detention, so he let him wander around town at his leisure. Billy could simply have ridden away, but he delayed to help Susan McSween pursue her vendetta against Colonel Dudley. In fact, the army had decided to investigate Dudley, and throughout June a court of inquiry examined his conduct in Lincoln. Billy testified, but

Dudley's defense attorney contemptuously shredded his evidence. Dudley easily won a whitewashed decision of the court.

Billy felt betrayed by Governor Wallace. He knew the outcome of any trial prosecuted by Rynerson. On the night of June 17, 1879, he and Doc Scurlock rode out of Lincoln. They spent the rest of June and all of July enjoying the attractions of Las Vegas, New Mexico. Probably facing the prospect of a tolerant Sheriff Kimball, Billy came back to Lincoln early in August. But Kimball had lost his tolerance. He summoned an officer and fifteen men from Fort Stanton and followed Billy down the Bonito to a cabin in which he was spending the night. The troopers surrounded the cabin to wait for daylight. But Billy discovered their presence and, repeating his long-ago experience in Silver City, climbed up the chimney and made good his escape.

That experience convinced the Kid that the time was past due to look for a new, safer place. As he later explained, "I went up to Lincoln to stand my trial on the warrant that was out for me, but the territory took a change of venue to Doña Ana, and I knew I had no show, and so I skinned out."

* * *

Governor Lew Wallace had left Billy Bonney with little choice but to skin out. The night-time talks between the two lifted Billy's morale because it promised a way out of his troubles. But did the governor intend a pardon or an attempt to persuade District Attorney Rynerson not to prosecute the Kid for murder? He phrased it both ways, or at least implied that he could have the charges dropped. If he had the least knowledge of Rynerson, he had to know that approach would fail. The only source for the conversation in Squire Wilson's home lies in a newspaper interview Wallace gave in 1901. No clue is to be found in his papers. How sharp was his memory in 1901? How much did the fame of the dead Billy the Kid lead him to embroider the story? The exact nature of his promise remains a mystery. In Billy's mind as he left the meeting, however, "pardon" was the operative word. Subsequent events convict the governor of betraying his "precious specimen."

The Kid's other adventures in Lincoln, such as the "treaty" with Dolan and Jesse Evans, lack much significance when compared with the meeting between Billy and Governor Wallace. In Billy's mind, Wallace's promise remained central to his actions until events persuaded him to skin out of Lincoln.

CHAPTER 11

The Kid Turns Outlaw

The destination to which Billy Bonney "skinned out" was Fort Sumner, the domain of Pete Maxwell. Maxwell lived in one of the houses of the abandoned fort, and the other buildings were occupied by residents or used for storage.

Fort Sumner stood on the Pecos River one hundred miles south of Las Vegas, New Mexico, and eighty miles north of Roswell. For Billy, this meant an almost complete absence of lawmen. A crime had to be a public spectacle to entice the sheriff of San Miguel County to ride down from Las Vegas.

For Billy, Fort Sumner offered a lively social scene. Doc Scurlock had gone home to Texas and his family, now numbering ten; but Charley Bowdre remained, and of course the ever-present Tom O'Folliard had skinned out of Lincoln with Billy. Others with whom Billy associated regularly were Dave Rudabaugh, Tom Pickett, and Billy Wilson.

Rudabaugh was the fiercest of the three, long a successful outlaw. He was also the oldest of the three, about forty. He sported a big mustache and a beard. He had stolen cattle in Texas, robbed trains and stagecoaches in Kansas, and in New Mexico terrorized

Las Vegas. Killing a Las Vegas deputy prompted him to flee to Fort Sumner, where he arrived in the spring of 1880.

Tom Pickett, a rugged Texan not much older than the Kid, had teamed up with Rudabaugh in Kansas and went to Las Vegas with him. As a Las Vegas policeman, he made himself so disliked by the citizens that, fearing a bullet, he too took refuge in Fort Sumner.

Billy Wilson came west from Ohio to Lincoln, then to Fort Sumner. Although two years younger than the Kid, he was huskier. He formed a member of the trio that joined with the Kid and Tom in the Fort Sumner scene.

The saloons of Beaver Smith and Bob Hargrove provided congenial settings for cowboys, sheepmen, rustlers, and outlaws to drink and gamble. Billy, an expert at monte, plied his hobby for many hours in both watering holes.

A potent attraction lay in the frequent *bailes,* or dances. As always, Billy charmed the señoritas. As one of them recalled:

> Fort Sumner was a gay little place. The weekly dance was
> an event, and pretty girls from Santa Rosa, Puerto de Luna,
> Anton Chico, and from towns and ranches fifty miles away
> drove in to attend it. Billy the Kid cut quite a gallant figure
> at these affairs. He was not handsome but he had a cer-
> tain sort of boyish good looks. He was always smiling and
> good-natured and very polite and danced remarkably well,
> and the little Mexican beauties made eyes at him from be-
> hind their fans and used all their coquetries to capture him
> and were very vain of his attentions.

And capture him they did. He is known to have fathered two children, who died of diphtheria. In every village on the Pecos, "some little señorita was proud to be known as his *querida* [or lover]," recalled one who probably was herself one of his queridas. How many other children Billy fathered with his queridas of course is unknown, but it could have been more than a few.

As he had done for four years, Billy maintained his skill with firearms, constantly practicing with rifle and pistol. He was a superb gunman, although his only certain kill was Windy Cahill at Fort Grant. The other killings, such as Sheriff Brady and Billy Morton, he shared with others and may or may not have fired the fatal round. At Fort Sumner, on January 10, 1880, he alone fired the fatal round.

In Bob Hargrove's saloon, a beefy Texas bully, Joe Grant, drunkenly wagered Billy twenty-five dollars that he would kill someone today before him. Grant spotted a fine revolver in the holster of a Chisum hand, pulled it out, and replaced it with his own. Billy walked over to Grant and said, "That's a mighty nice looking six-shooter you got." Lifting it from Grant's holster, Billy admiringly twirled the cylinder, noting that three rounds had been fired. He returned the weapon to Grant with one of the empty chambers positioned in front of the hammer. Grant grew louder and more violent, smashing whiskey bottles on the bar and shouting his intent to shoot someone. When John Chisum's brother Jim entered, Grant declared that he intended to kill John Chisum. "Hold on," said Billy, "you got the wrong sow by the ear." The man was not John but Jim Chisum. "That's a lie," yelled Grant. Aware that the hammer of Grant's pistol would fall on an empty chamber, Billy simply turned to walk out the door. As Jim's son Will Chisum described what happened next: "Grant squared off at Billy, who when he heard the click whirled around and 'bang, bang, bang.' Right in the chin—could cover all [three] of them with a half a dollar."

"Joe," said Billy, "I've been there too often for you."

Actually, he had not been there since Windy Cahill. The remark, however, suggested a growing cockiness, a tendency to make wisecracks and put himself on display. Asked later about the motive for the shooting, Billy tossed it off with, "Oh, nothing; it was a game of two and I got there first." Another who watched accurately observed that "the daring young rascal seemed to enjoy the telling as well as the killing."

Such a trait would increasingly characterize Billy Bonney.

Earnings from dealing monte at the saloons hardly sustained the lifestyle to which the Kid was becoming accustomed at Fort Sumner. Panhandle beef did. White Oaks, a new mining boomtown fifty miles northwest of Lincoln, housed a middleman for a dealer in stolen cattle at Tularosa. In May 1880, Billy joined with Charley Bowdre and Tom O'Folliard to steal a herd of cattle and drive it to White Oaks to sell. How many other such expeditions he made is unrecorded, but by May he had become a well-known name in White Oaks and had been identified by the Panhandle Stockman's Association as a leading rustler.

The association hired a detective, Frank Stewart, to investigate. In White Oaks he discovered cattle hides draped over a fence bearing Panhandle brands and heard from citizens who identified the Kid as the culprit. The cowmen determined to organize an expedition to New Mexico to recover their cattle and if possible capture the Kid.

Billy's increasing notoriety was not limited to rustling cattle. At White Oaks he had become involved on the fringes of a counterfeiting ring, which brought a Secret Service agent to New Mexico. Also, he held up a buckboard carrying US mail. Both were federal offenses.

Finally, in November 1880 the citizens of Lincoln County, prodded by John Chisum and other town leaders in Roswell, elected a sheriff with a mandate to clean up the county. He was Patrick F. Garrett, a tall, slim Texan who had been a buffalo hunter and had gravitated to Fort Sumner and then moved to Roswell to run for sheriff. He possessed the requisite qualities of a lawman—rugged, resourceful, relentless in pursuit of lawbreakers.

By November 1880, Billy Bonney still maintained his popularity in Fort Sumner, with its bevy of queridas. In White Oaks, however, he had alienated the citizens by his repeated presence with stolen cattle and horses. Moreover, the Secret Service, the Panhandle stockmen, and Sheriff Pat Garrett had begun to close in on White Oaks.

On November 20, 1880, Billy and several Fort Sumner toughs, including Dave Rudabaugh, appeared in White Oaks with a herd of stolen horses to sell. Two days later Deputy Sheriff William H. Hudgens learned of their presence, recruited a posse of thirteen men, and set out to arrest them. They had departed, however, headed back to Fort Sumner.

About halfway on the road connecting the two towns stood the roadhouse of "Whiskey Jim" Greathouse, which provided a resting place for Billy and other thieves taking stolen stock to White Oaks. The fugitives stopped there. At dawn on November 27 they discovered the house surrounded by the White Oaks posse. Hudgens sent in a note demanding surrender, which provoked laughter.

At length, both sides agreed on talks about surrender. A well-liked White Oaks blacksmith, Jimmy Carlyle, agreed to enter the house if, as Hudgens insisted, Greathouse himself came out as hostage for Carlyle's safe return. As soon as Carlyle reached the interior, Billy took him prisoner. The other men were drinking heavily at the bar, and Billy forced Carlyle to drink, too, so much that he became increasingly drunk. Fearful of his fate, Carlyle pleaded to be released, but Billy refused. At 2:00 p.m. Hudgens sent in a message giving the fugitives five minutes to let Carlyle go or Greathouse would be killed. Probably accidentally, at this juncture one of the posse fired a shot. An alarmed Carlyle smashed through a window and began to run to safety, but a volley dropped him dead. Both sides exchanged fire until the posse gave up and rode back to White Oaks.

Who killed Carlyle? The men inside insisted that the posse itself had fired the fatal bullets. The posse claimed to have seen three men, including the Kid, fire from the window. One of the posse later contended that Billy himself had leaned out the window, taken deliberate aim, and fired the bullet that struck down Carlyle.

Again, like the other killings in which Billy took part, he may or may not have killed Carlyle. The posse itself may have been guilty, or three men inside the Greathouse ranch, or Billy himself.

Less than a week later, Las Vegas editor W. S. Koogler named "Billy the Kid" the captain of an outlaw gang. The killing of the popular Carlyle put "the desperate cuss" at the top of the list of outlaws sought by Sheriff Pat Garrett. Billy tried to redeem himself in a long letter to Governor Wallace, describing all that had happened in terms favorable to himself. The governor simply sent it to Koogler to print in his newspaper. Already, on December 13, the day after Billy wrote his letter to the governor, Wallace had issued a proclamation putting a price on the Kid's head—five hundred dollars for his delivery to the sheriff of Lincoln County.

For the rest of his short life, Billy the Kid devoted himself entirely to trying to evade the clutches of the law.

* * *

The move from Lincoln to Fort Sumner opened a new phase in Billy Bonney's life. For his tastes, Fort Sumner presented an enjoyable place. Usually joined by his pals Charley Bowdre and Tom O'Folliard, he had fun gambling and mixing with other men in the two saloons, dancing and singing at the bailes, courting the so-called queridas, or better still, being courted by them. He felt secure because lawmen rarely appeared.

Far more significant in terms of Billy's future, however, was his turn to outlawry. The killing of Joe Grant was not outlawry but a deliberate act of bravado. Rustling Panhandle beef was outlawry. It stirred up victims and citizens as well and prompted the rise of Pat Garrett as a sheriff determined to get him. It also led to the gun battle at the Greathouse ranch, which bolstered Billy's penchant for gunplay.

Finally, these events, reinforced and embroidered by the Las Vegas newspaper, branded Billy as the number one outlaw in New Mexico. In offering a reward for his capture, Governor Wallace enhanced the image and destroyed all chance that he would extend any form of clemency for the lad with whom he had negotiated in Lincoln, a development that entirely escaped Billy's thinking.

✽ CHAPTER 12 ✽

Stinking Springs

Back in Fort Sumner after the fiasco at the Greathouse ranch, the Kid first learned that he had been styled "Billy the Kid." He also discovered that his pal Charley Bowdre, who had been ranch foreman at the cattle spread of Thomas G. Yerby, had decided to try to square himself with the law. He had moved his wife, Manuela, and her mother into one of the vacant quarters at Fort Sumner and wandered from camp to camp in the cattle country northeast of Fort Sumner.

Billy and the veterans of the fight at the Greathouse ranch drifted from ranches northeast of town into Fort Sumner to visit the Smith and Hargrove saloons. When Bowdre was present, they moved into a vacant room next door to have a place to bunk. Billy's group now usually consisted mainly of Billy Wilson, Tom Pickett, Dave Rudabaugh, and always Tom O'Folliard.

They knew Pat Garrett was hot on their trail. Fort Sumner lay in San Miguel County, where the sheriff of Lincoln County lacked authority. But Garrett also bore a commission as deputy US marshal. Since Billy faced federal as well as territorial charges, Garrett could hunt him anywhere.

Billy and his comrades hid at the ranch of Manuel Brazil northeast of Fort Sumner. Brazil hosted them out of a sense of apprehension combined with a sometime friendship with the Kid. The outlaws pondered leaving the country and taking refuge in Mexico. A heavy snowstorm complicated their efforts to stock up on provisions. Garrett and his posse, which now included six men dispatched by the Panhandle Stockman's Association, rode into Fort Sumner on December 17, 1880, while the snow continued to fall. Garrett conceived an elaborate scheme to lure Billy into Fort Sumner. It worked, for on the night of December 19, the Kid, with O'Folliard, Pickett, Rudabaugh, and Wilson, rode into Fort Sumner, heading for Charley Bowdre's quarters.

Tom O'Folliard rode in the lead, Tom Pickett behind him. At the Bowdre quarters O'Folliard's horse nuzzled up under the portal roof. "Halt!" came the shouted command from the shadow of the portal. Spooked, O'Folliard's horse reared, and Tom drew his pistol. A blast of Winchester fire struck him in the chest. His horse trotted away, O'Folliard slouching in the saddle. Tom Pickett spurred his horse in a mad dash for safety that ended with the collapse of his horse, leaving him to walk back to the Brazil ranch. Billy and the other two, Rudabaugh and Wilson, quickly turned and raced away from the building. Tom O'Folliard's horse walked slowly back to the building.

Garrett's Winchester had hit Tom in the chest. "Don't shoot, Garrett, I'm killed." Possemen helped him off his horse and carried him into the building. They continued their game of poker until Tom finally shuddered and died. Such lack of sympathy and compassion for their fellow man was characteristic of frontiersmen.

At the Brazil ranch, the fugitives delayed until the night of December 22, then struck out through deepening snow to the east, presumably headed for Mexico. Five made up the group: Billy Bonney, Charley Bowdre, Dave Rudabaugh, Billy Wilson, and Tom Pickett.

After a three-mile ride through the snow, they reached a sheepman's abandoned stone hut. Seeking relief from the bitter cold, they tied their horses to the projecting rafters outside and bundled up inside. The hut took its name from nearby Stinking Springs. In the bright moonlit night, they had left a trail in the snow that Garrett and his men easily followed. They arrived at 3:00 a.m. The sheriff positioned his men in arroyos and behind hills to bring the stone bastion under fire from all directions, then settled in to wait for daybreak.

As the day dawned, Charley Bowdre carried a nosebag full of grain outside to feed the horses. He wore a broad-brimmed hat such as the Kid affected. From a distance, he could easily be mistaken for Billy. Winchesters erupted and smashed into Bowdre, who staggered back into the hut.

Billy Wilson yelled that Bowdre had been hit and wanted to surrender. Garrett acquiesced, provided Charley emerged with his hands up. The Kid said, "They have murdered you, Charley, but you can get revenge. Kill some of the sons-of-bitches before you die." He pulled Charley's holstered pistol so it hung from the center of his waist and pushed him out of the door. His hands held up, Bowdre lurched toward the sheriff, then collapsed. Garrett laid him on his blankets and watched him die.

The Kid was not ready to surrender. He grasped the rope that held one of the horses outside and slowly pulled it toward the door. If successful, he and others who attempted the scheme could mount and try to escape. But a bullet from Garrett's rifle dropped the horse in the doorway, blocking any attempt to ride out. He also took careful aim on the ropes that tied the other horses to the roof and one by one cut them with bullets. The horses trotted away.

Stinking Springs marked the end of Billy's free-roaming life. Garrett had ingeniously trapped him, and the Kid could conceive of no way to escape. As he later explained, "I would have ridden out on my bay mare and taken my chances of escaping. But I couldn't ride out over that [dead horse], for she would have jumped back, and I would have got it in the head." The men could have remained in the hut, but they knew Garrett would simply keep them under siege until they ran out of food.

By late afternoon, the smell of roasting meat wafted into the hut. Rudabaugh, who took orders from no one, waved a dirty white rag outside the door and shouted that he wanted to surrender. With

Garrett's consent, Rudabaugh advanced for a talk, then returned to the hut. Shortly, all four emerged with their hands up.

The posse escorted their prisoners, under close guard, to the nearby Brazil ranch, where they had dinner and spent the night. Garrett sent Brazil's wagon back to Stinking Springs to retrieve the body of Charley Bowdre. One of the posse later described the prisoners during the evening, singling out the Kid—"cheerful and chattering, excitement lighting up his face." Even though he had lost his friend Bowdre, he enjoyed his role as burgeoning celebrity.

On December 24, the outlaws were placed in a wagon with Manuel Brazil at the reins and the posse riding closely on all sides. At Fort Sumner, they halted to have dinner and shackle and iron the captives. Garrett also had to deal with "Mother" Maxwell, the widow of Lucien, the original owner of the property. She asked that Billy have a chance to say a last good-bye to her daughter, Paulita—one of his queridas. In the Maxwell house, she implored Garrett to let Billy go into a room alone with Paulita and "talk awhile." He did not go in alone but with two guards and, shackled to his ankle, Dave Rudabaugh. As one of the guards explained the scene, "The lovers embraced, and she gave Billy one of those soul kisses the novelists tell us about, till it being time to hit the trail for Vegas, we had to pull them apart."

In Las Vegas the day after Christmas, the Kid had an opportunity to posture before a crowd in his new role as celebrity. Alerted in advance, citizens poured out to watch the entry of the wagon and its guards. On the hotel veranda, one of the spectators observed that Billy "was in a joyous mood. He wore a hat pushed far back, and jocularly greeted the crowd. Recognizing Dr. Sutfin [the hotel proprietor], he called, 'Hello, doc! Thought I jes drop in and see how you fellers in Vegas air behavin' yerselves.'"

Throughout his days in Las Vegas, Billy played to the crowd. In prison the next day, a reporter was allowed to interview him. Bonney, wrote the newsman, "was light and chipper and was very communicative, laughing, joking and chatting with bystanders." "What's the use of looking on the gloomy side of everything. The laugh's on me this time." Reveling in his notoriety, he said, "There was a big crowd gazing at me wasn't there. Well, perhaps some of them will think me half man now; everyone seemed to think I was some kind of animal."

The reporter went on to describe the Kid, now twenty-one, at this juncture in his life.

> He did look human, indeed, but there was nothing very mannish about him in appearance, for he looked and acted a mere boy. He is about five feet eight or nine inches tall, slightly built and lithe, weighing about 140; a frank open countenance, looking like a school boy, with the traditional silky fuzz on his upper lip; clear blue eyes, with a roughish snap about them; light hair and complexion. He is, in all, quite a handsome looking fellow, the only imperfection being two prominent front teeth, and he has agreeable and winning ways.

No curious throngs greeted the Kid in Santa Fe. Attention and acclaim centered on Sheriff Garrett and his posse. Nor did Billy enjoy comfortable accommodations. Garrett, in his role as deputy US marshal, turned him over to federal officials, who housed him in a frigid cell in the Santa Fe jail.

One block to the north of the jail lay the historic plaza, the end of the Santa Fe Trail, fronted on the north by the ancient Palace of the Governors. That was the residence and office of Governor Lew Wallace.

The governor's promised pardon had turned into a clammy jail cell.

* * *

Stinking Springs signaled the beginning of Billy the Kid's downfall. But for the horse Sheriff Pat Garrett killed to block the stone hut's doorway, Billy would assuredly have tried to escape. His bay mare was widely known as one of the best horses in New Mexico. He would have galloped out of the building, firing his pistol at the posse, and spurred away from his attackers. But too many well-armed marksmen would have aimed their Winchesters at him and likely brought him or the mare to the ground. In the weeks after Sheriff Pat Garrett got on his trail, Billy's alert mind failed to detect the schemes set in motion to trick him and gave his pursuers the advantage. The denouement at Stinking Springs testifies to the skill and persistence of the sheriff of Lincoln County.

Billy's brief reign as a celebrity for curious crowds shows another side of this complex fellow. Instead of being discouraged and downcast after the catastrophe at Stinking Springs, he thoroughly enjoyed being the center of attention and played the role to the utmost. In Santa Fe, however, he had no curious crowds to play to.

At Stinking Springs, Billy lost his longtime comrade Charley Bowdre, a supporter who could be called on for any favor. Did he feel any remorse tinged by guilt over the loss? Judging by his action in shoving the wounded Bowdre out the door to certain death, he seems not to have felt much remorse. Nor did he manifest any regret or sadness over the death of Tom O'Folliard, his worshipful companion for more than a year. Nor McSween. The only person whose death prompted regret if not remorse was Tunstall. One is left to wonder if Billy truly bonded with anyone, whether called friend or not.

❈ CHAPTER 13 ❈
Tried for Murder

Billy the Kid looked forward to almost three months in the Santa
Fe jail until Judge Bristol convened court in Mesilla at the end
of March 1881. Sharing the cell were his comrades from Stinking
Springs, Dave Rudabaugh and Billy Wilson. Rudabaugh awaited ex-
tradition to Las Vegas, and Wilson was slated to entrain for Mesilla
with Billy. Tom Pickett had been detained in Las Vegas; ultimately
his charges were dropped, and he received a pardon.

The Kid's first impulse was to prod Governor Wallace into honoring his promise of two years earlier—a pardon in exchange for
testifying in the trial for the murder of Huston Chapman. If Wallace
had ever truly intended to pardon Billy, the Kid's turn to outlawry
in recent months had consigned it to political irrelevancy. Moreover,
the governor was not in Santa Fe but en route to Washington, DC.

The next stratagem was for all three inmates to try to dig their
way out of the jail. At night they dug slowly at the base of the wall
fronting the street, concealing the dirt and stones in bed ticking,
then in the morning filling the hole with the debris. Throughout
February 1881, they worked at this tedious task. They nearly succeeded, but at the end of the month the sheriff and a deputy US marshal entered the cell and exposed the scheme. The sheriff had grown

suspicious and stationed an informer in the next cell. To prevent more trickery, the sheriff ironed the inmates and kept them under constant guard.

Once more, Billy turned to Governor Wallace, now back from Washington. On March 2, 1881, he penned a letter to the governor, containing a sentence that did his cause no good: "I wish you would come down to the jail to see me. It will be to your interest to come and see me. I have some letters that date back two years and there are parties who are very anxious to get them but I shall not dispose of them until I see you. that is if you will come immediately."

Receiving no response, two days later he wrote again, this time omitting the hint of blackmail.

> I wrote you a little note the day before yesterday, but have received no answer I Expect you have forgotten what you promised me this month two years ago, but I have not, and I think you ought to have come and see me as I requested you to do. I have done everything that I promised you I would, and you have done nothing that you promised me. I think when you think the matter over, you will come down and see me, and I can then explain everything to you.

Almost certainly the governor did not "think the matter over," if he even did more than scan the letter. His thoughts ranged far higher than the "precious specimen" of Lincoln two years earlier. A new president had been elected in November 1880, and Wallace aspired to a posting more congenial than New Mexico. His January journey to Washington may have been to petition the incoming president for an ambassadorial appointment. In May 1881 Wallace got his wish. President James Garfield had read *Ben-Hur* and promptly named Wallace ambassador to the court of the sultan of the Ottoman Empire.

On March 28, 1881, two deputy marshals escorted Billy the Kid and Billy Wilson aboard a railway coach for the journey down the Rio Grande to Mesilla. Two days later Judge Bristol opened the spring term of court in Mesilla. The Kid's trial ranked high on the judge's agenda. Billy still faced both federal and territorial charges. Bristol dismissed the federal charge on a technicality but ordered the Kid turned over to the territory for trial in the murder of Sheriff Brady.

Billy could not afford a defense lawyer, so the judge named a local law partnership as public defender. Former district attorney William R. Rynerson's successor as prosecutor lined up a series of Lincoln's most prominent citizens to testify for the prosecution. No one seems to have backed Billy. In his charge to the jury Judge Bristol came close to demanding a finding of guilty of premeditated murder. And this was the verdict the jury delivered on April 9, assessing a penalty of death by hanging. On April 15, 1881, Judge Bristol imposed this sentence and directed that Billy be turned over to the sheriff of Lincoln County to carry out the sentence.

* * *

After Stinking Springs and his jocular stay in Las Vegas, Billy had almost no way to get out of his predicament. The attempt to dig out of the Santa Fe jail failed. So did his effort to get the attention of Governor Wallace. In his letters, he let the promised pardon exclude all other events of his checkered career. Politically naive, he failed to understand that his turn to outlawry in rustling cattle and engaging in gun battles made any visible effort at clemency by the governor impossible.

* * *

The irony lies in the fact that of all the dozens of participants in the Lincoln County War, Billy Bonney was the only one convicted of any crime.

CHAPTER 14

Escaping the Hangman's Noose

Billy Bonney had to be transported from Mesilla to Lincoln and imprisoned until the date set by Judge Bristol for his execution, May 13, 1881. To ensure that the slippery young man made no attempt to escape, seven men guarded the wagon in which Billy sat handcuffed and shackled by the ankles to the back seat. Three rode horseback, the others seated in the wagon.

At least two of the guards had a long history of hostility toward the Kid. Billy Mathews had headed the posse that killed Tunstall, had shot the Kid in the thigh in the assassination of Sheriff Brady, and had fought for Dolan throughout the Lincoln County War, including the assault on the flaming McSween house.

The other was Bob Olinger, a deputy US marshal and a vicious man who would welcome the least opportunity to shoot the Kid. Olinger held Billy responsible for the death of his close friend Bob Beckwith, a victim of the "big killing" in McSween's backyard. He also called the Kid a cold-blooded murderer. "Pecos Bob" fit the description of one who knew him in the Seven Rivers area:

> Two hundred pounds of bones and muscle, six feet tall, round as a huge tree trunk, with a regular gorilla-like chest that

bulged out so far his chin seemed to be set back in his chest. He had a heavy bull neck, low-browed head, short and wide, topped with shaggy hair, bushy eyebrows, and a hat-rack mustache. His arms were long and muscular, with fists like hams. Despite his build and size he was quick as a cat, and always got the best of the deal in any encounter he figured in. He could take punishment as well as hand it out.

The two hostile deputies, Mathews and Olinger, sat in the wagon seat facing Billy. For five days, the wagon and the guards traveled the road to Lincoln, Olinger and Mathews making every effort to humiliate the Kid. Lincoln's jail, still the barred hole in the ground, "wouldn't hold a cripple," according to Sheriff Pat Garrett. He arranged to confine Billy next to his own office on the second floor of the old Dolan store, now the county courthouse. Garrett assigned two men to keep close watch on the Kid. One was Deputy James W. Bell, the other Bob Olinger, who continued to bully the Kid.

Handcuffed and leg-ironed, Billy conceived of no way to escape, except to take quick advantage of any opportunity. Whereas Olinger constantly taunted the Kid, Deputy Bell treated him kindly. He had good reason to despise Billy because of his close friendship with Jimmy Carlyle, the victim of the shooting at the Greathouse ranch. Commenting on Bell's forbearance, Garrett remarked that "never by word or action did he betray his prejudice, if it existed." Billy, on the other hand, "appeared to have taken a liking to him."

Garrett repeatedly cautioned the guards to keep close watch on their prisoner. "I knew the desperate character of the man, that he was daring and unscrupulous, and that he would sacrifice the lives of a hundred men who stood between him and liberty." Garrett prescribed procedures for the two guards to follow to prevent a bid for liberty.

Late in April Garrett rode to White Oaks to collect taxes. On the evening of the twenty-eighth, Olinger took prisoners from another room across the street for dinner at the Wortley Hotel. Before leaving, he stood in front of Billy and arrogantly loaded a double-barreled shotgun with eighteen buckshot in each barrel. To the Kid, he proclaimed, "The man that gets one of those loads will feel it." Uncowed, Billy responded, "I expect he will, but be careful, Bob, or you might shoot yourself accidentally."

Seizing the advantage of Olinger's absence, the Kid asked Bell to take him down to the privy in the rear of the building. With hands cuffed and legs restrained, Billy had a hard time getting down the stairs to the rear door. Emerging from the privy, he hobbled back to the door and up the stairs, Bell to his rear. Billy reached the top first and turned from Bell's view. His slim hands allowed him to slip off one of the cuffs. As Bell turned back into view, Billy swung the cuff and slashed Bell across the forehead, knocking him to the floor. He then pounced on the deputy and struggled to wrestle his pistol from its holster. When he succeeded, Bell sprang to his feet and sprinted to the stairwell. Billy got there in time to shoot him before he reached the bottom. He staggered out the back door and fell dead.

Godfrey Gauss, the old German who had cooked for the cowboys at the Tunstall ranch, knew Billy. Gauss lived in a shack behind the courthouse. Rushing out, he caught Bell as he fell and died. Gauss then went around to the front of the building. Olinger had emerged from the Wortley with his prisoners. Gauss yelled that the Kid had killed Bell. By then, Olinger had entered the gate at the northeast corner of the building, immediately below the window where Billy had positioned himself with the shotgun Olinger had loaded before leaving.

Recalled the Kid, "I stuck the gun through the window and said, 'Look up, old boy, and see what you get.' Bob looked up, and I let him have both barrels right in the face and breast." He collapsed, torn up by thirty-six heavy buckshot he had loaded into the two barrels of the shotgun.

Billy next hobbled to the back window and told Gauss to throw up a pickax lying on the ground. Gauss did as he was told. The Kid used the tool to break the chain binding his leg shackles and allow him to walk. He had also ordered Gauss to saddle a horse in the corral and bring it around for him.

Leg chain draped over his belt, Billy ventured out on the balcony at the front of the building. People had gathered on the Wortley porch, and a few appeared in the street. None, however, dared challenge him or even display a rifle. Once again a showman, Billy had another chance to play to the crowd, as recalled by one of the men on the Wortley porch:

> It was more than an hour, after he killed Olinger and Bell, before he left. He had at his command eight revolvers and six guns [taken from the arsenal in Garrett's office]. He stood on the upper porch in front of the building and talked with the people who were in Wortley's, but would not let anyone come towards him. He told the people he did not want to kill Bell but, as he ran, he had to. He said he grabbed Bell's revolver and told him to hold up his hands and surrender; that Bell had decided to run and he had to kill him. He declared he was "standing pat" against the world; and, while he did not wish to kill anybody, if anybody interfered with his attempt to escape he would kill him.

Billy slammed the shotgun over the railing and threw the pieces down on Olinger's body. "Here is your gun, God damn you. You won't follow me with it any longer."

Gauss had brought the saddled mare to a hitching rail in front of the building. Billy returned to the back stairs and went down to the back door. Pausing at Bell's body, he said, "I'm sorry I had to kill you, but couldn't help it." Making his way toward the front, he kicked Olinger's shattered corpse and said, "You are not going to round me up again."

On the "borrowed" horse, his chains banging against his legs, Billy trotted west on the road out of Lincoln.

*   *   *

Billy the Kid, Las Vegas editor Koogler's "desperate cuss," had lived up to the reputation his newspaper created. He was now indeed New Mexico's premier outlaw. Governor Wallace even placed another five hundred dollars on the reward for his capture. Billy's exploit in Lincoln produced bold headlines in newspapers in New Mexico and elsewhere in the country. Newspaper commentary conceded that the escape was daring in concept and brilliant in execution but wrathfully condemned him for murdering two deputies. In a single demonizing paragraph, Koogler's paper branded Billy "a terror and disgrace to New Mexico," a "flagrant violator of every law," a "murderer from infancy," "malignant and cruel," "urged by a spirit as hideous as hell," blind to "the drooping forms of widows and the tear-stained eyes of orphans." "With a heart untouched to pity by misfortune, and a character possessing the attributes of the damned, he has reveled in brutal murder and gloried in his shame. He has broken more loving hearts and filled more untimely graves than he has lived years, and that he is again turned loose like some devouring beast on the public is cause for consternation and regret."

Other newspapers indulged in less rhetorical excess, but they all portrayed him as a murdering outlaw ranging the territory as an accomplished criminal inclined to pull the trigger at the slightest excuse. The murder of Olinger and Bell justified public outrage but not the characterization of most newspapers. On the contrary, the "devouring beast" had only one objective: to escape death or capture by the law.

After putting Lincoln behind him, the Kid turned north into the Capitan Mountains. A number of Hispanic friends lived there. One removed the handcuffs and leg irons. Another Hispanic fed him a meal. He ended the day at the home of Yginio Salazar, his companion in the breakout from the burning McSween house.

As Salazar recalled, "I talked with Kid at my house at Las Tablas the next day. The Kid laid off there for three days. He laid out in the hills and came to my house to eat. I told him to leave this place and go to Old Mexico." He had tried once, only to be captured at Stinking Springs. He pondered it again, now that he had shot his way to freedom and had to distance himself from the law.

Possibly with Mexico in mind, Billy rode down the north slope of the Capitan Mountains and turned south to cross the Ruidoso above San Patricio. He then continued south to the Peñasco, where his friend John Meadows had a ranch in partnership with Tom Norris.

That night, May 2, Billy presented himself at the ranch. As recalled by Meadows, the following took place:

> He says, "I've got you covered." I says, "Yes, and what in hell are you going to do with us?" I hadn't discovered who it was. I looked at him, and, by God, I said, "By God, that's the Kid."
>
> We sat down there, and I says, "What the hell are you going to do with us?"
>
> He said, "I'm going to eat supper with you."
>
> I says, "If you can stand these beans, just stand up to it, old top."
>
> He sat down, and him and Tom and me got there and talked until midnight, and I begged him, say I, "You'd better go into Mexico while the going's good. You can make it there now, and you can do well there. You go back to Fort Sumner, and Garrett will get you as sure as you go back. He ain't laying down on his job."
>
> He says, "Garrett will get me if he can, but I've got too many friends there."
>
> I says, "You have got too many of them. One will give you away," and that is just what they done.

Billy Bonney knew the dangers of Fort Sumner, immeasurably heightened by his deadly breakout from Lincoln, but he also remembered the pleasures: the bailes, the bevy of queridas, the fellowship of saloons, the welcoming attitude of the scattered Hispanic sheepmen. He knew he could find safety moving from one of their camps to another. That he spoke Spanish and charmed their women is but one reason the Hispanics liked Billy so well. He was their friend and, unlike most other Anglos, did not condescend to them. He treated them as equals, and they responded with friendship and a readiness to help him whenever he needed it.

But Billy could not keep his presence secret from Sheriff Pat Garrett and other lawmen seeking him.

Why did he choose Fort Sumner instead of Mexico? The explanation doubtless lies in a trait he had exhibited throughout his life: the habit of surrendering long-term goals to the impulse of the moment. Such a moment occurred at the ranch of John Meadows.

The escape from Lincoln, as admitted by some newspapers, was indeed brilliant in conception and bold in execution. He instantly seized an opportunity and imaginatively made the most of it. It cost two men their lives, Bell and Olinger. Almost certainly Billy felt compassion for Bell; he genuinely regretted the necessity of killing him. Olinger, on the other hand, had set himself up for death by bullying and humiliating the Kid. Undoubtedly Billy took great pleasure in blasting two barrels of buckshot into his upturned head and chest.

Despite the rigid restrictions Pat Garrett had placed on the two deputies to ensure that Billy had no chance of escape, they let Billy outwit them. Rather than leave the Kid guarded by only one deputy, Olinger might have had the meals of the other prisoners brought across the street by Sam Wortley. Or Bell might have been more careful in escorting the Kid down to the privy. To let him out of his sight for even a moment proved a fatal error. Even Pat Garrett relaxed his vigilance by leaving Lincoln during a critical period. He could have occupied his office on the second floor of the courthouse for two weeks remaining until the scheduled hanging. Instead, he rode to White Oaks to collect taxes.

Billy himself, as he had done in the burning McSween house, rose to the occasion. What he accomplished was extraordinary. In the Lincoln courthouse, he once more showed his mettle: quick thinking, quick action, unbridled determination to free himself, and the long period of showmanship on the balcony that cowed all who watched and prevented any attempt to stop him. Garrett later characterized the citizens of Lincoln as "terror stricken." "A little sympathy might have actuated some of them, but most of the people were, doubtless, paralyzed with fear when it was whispered that the dreaded desperado, the Kid, was at liberty and had slain his guards."

The feelings of the citizens of Lincoln probably reflected the feelings of the citizens of New Mexico.

✳ CHAPTER 15 ✳

Pete Maxwell's Bedroom

Fort Sumner provided all the pleasures Billy Bonney anticipated—the bailes, the queridas, the saloon society, and Hispanics
who sheltered him and brought him news of the outside world. That
news consisted mainly of newspapers, in which Billy read that he
was the most wanted outlaw in New Mexico and that he was thought
to be somewhere around Fort Sumner. If the newspapers thought he
was there, so did Sheriff Pat Garrett.

Although Garrett was not certain, he centered his attention on
Fort Sumner. He tried to conceive a strategy for confirming Billy's
presence at Fort Sumner and, if so, finding him and taking him prisoner or killing him. The Kid continued the life he had come to Fort
Sumner to enjoy. As the Santa Fe *New Mexican* observed on June
16, "The people regard him with a feeling half of fear and half of
admiration, submit to his depredations, and some of them go so far
as to aid him in avoiding capture." Billy committed no depredations
during these weeks, and those who aided him in avoiding capture
were Hispanics. The mix of fear and admiration was confined to
Anglo ranchers.

Although Billy spent a lot of time on the range with his Hispanic
friends, he occasionally slipped into Fort Sumner in pursuit of his

usual pleasures. Aware that Garrett suspected that he was in the Fort Sumner vicinity and was trying every stratagem to corner him, Billy should have crept into Fort Sumner only with the greatest alertness and caution. One careless mistake could cost him his life.

He made such a mistake on the night of July 14, 1881. He and some of his friends gathered in an orchard adjoining the old Fort Sumner parade ground. They sat talking for a time, unaware that Garrett and two of his deputies were also in the orchard, too distant to recognize anyone or understand the talk.

Soon the group dispersed. One was indeed Billy, clad in dark trousers, a white shirt covered by a vest, and a broad-brimmed hat. He jumped the fence onto the old parade ground and walked to the old quartermaster building. In the rooms lived several people he might have been heading for. One, however, was home to one his queridas, Celsa Gutierrez. Likely that is the room he entered. Inside, Billy took off his hat, vest, and boots, and maybe his trousers. What transpired can only be imagined. But near midnight, the Kid decided he was hungry. He recalled seeing a freshly butchered yearling hanging from a rafter on Pete Maxwell's porch. He could cut a slab from the yearling and bring a steak back for Celsa to prepare for him. Buttoning his trousers, Billy grabbed a butcher knife and his pistol and wandered out in his stocking feet.

A bright moon shone on the parade ground, and the July heat caused Pete Maxwell to leave his bedroom door and window open. A picket fence ran along the front of the porch, separating it from the parade ground. A gate opened on the parade ground. Knife in one hand and pistol in the other, Billy made his way up the pathway between the porch and the fence.

Almost at the entrance to Maxwell's bedroom, Billy suddenly confronted two men. One squatted on the parade ground outside the gate. One sat on the edge of the porch, his legs dangling over the side. Billy quickly pointed his pistol at the man sitting on the porch and jumped to the porch in front of Maxwell's bedroom. "Quien es? Quien es? [Who is it?]," he demanded, assuming the men were Hispanic. The man stood and faced Billy, telling him not to be alarmed;

the two men would not hurt him. The Kid repeated, "Quien es?" as he backed around the door frame into Maxwell's bedroom.

Turning toward Maxwell's bed, Billy asked, "Who are those fellows outside, Pete?" Instead of an answer, in the dark Billy sensed Maxwell rearing up in his bed and heard him almost shout, "That's him!" Adjusting his eyes to the dark, Billy discerned a dark shape next to Maxwell's bed and again asked, "Quien es?"

Those were Billy Bonney's last words. From the crouching figure next to Maxwell's bed a pistol flashed twice in the dark, sending one bullet into the Kid's left breast below the heart. He was dead before he sprawled on the floor.

By even venturing into Fort Sumner that night of July 14, 1881, Billy Bonney failed to exercise enough caution. But that was not the mistake that cost him his life. He had visited the fort more than once in the past few weeks, usually for the same purpose. Unknown to him as he pursued his pleasures, Garrett and his deputies had spent days sneaking around Fort Sumner and vicinity interviewing all the prominent citizens. None would admit to knowing of Billy's whereabouts. On this night the lawmen had all but given up when Garrett suggested one last interview, with Pete Maxwell. Garrett's presence in his bedroom at the same time Billy wanted a beefsteak was a timely coincidence and for the sheriff an accident.

Rather, Billy's fatal error was the momentary pause between sighting the dark shape crouching next to Maxwell's bed and his final "Quien es?" That pause, no longer than a second or two, afforded the moment Garrett needed to draw his weapon and fire. The usually quick and alert Billy would have fired instantly.

* * *

The next morning, July 15, Fort Sumner demonstrated its attitude toward Billy the Kid. As word of his death spread, a throng of residents poured onto the parade ground. They shouted their fury at the lawmen and waved their fists in their air. Deluvina Maxwell ran at Garrett and, sobbing, pounded his chest with her fists. Other women stood in a group talking quietly and sympathizing with one another. The prevailing mood, however, was one of anger, so intense an anger that Garrett and his two deputies, John Poe and Tom Mc-Kinney, barricaded themselves in the Maxwell bedroom with rifles ready to repel an attack.

After a coroner's inquest, the women asked for Billy's body and carried it across the parade ground to the carpenter shop, where a coffin was being assembled. There, as Poe observed, the body "was laid out on a workbench, the women placing lighted candles around it according to their ideas of properly conducting a 'wake' for the dead." "Neatly and properly dressed," added Garrett, Billy was placed in the coffin and carried to the old military cemetery, where citizens now buried their dead. People gathered to pay their respects as the coffin was lowered into a grave next to the graves of Tom O'Folliard and Charley Bowdre.

For two and one-half months after Billy the Kid's breakout from Lincoln, he had reprised the good life of Fort Sumner. He paid for it with his life. Had he taken the sensible advice of Yginio Salazar and John Meadows, he might have lived a long and secure life in Mexico. That would have consigned him, however, to barely a footnote in the history of the American West.

❋ CHAPTER 16 ❋
Legend and Myth

The nation enthusiastically applauded the death of Billy the Kid. Newspapers acclaimed his demise. "His death is hailed with great joy," according to the *New York Sun,* "as he had sworn that he would kill several prominent citizens, and had already slain fifteen or eighteen men." Newspaper rhetoric appeared mild, however, compared with the pulp fiction and penny dreadfuls published within a year. As one example, only a month after the Kid's death, this excerpt characterized the vicious killer:

> "Oh! Billy, Billy," cried the terrified wretch, "for God's sake don't shoot me!"
>
> "Hold your head still, George, so I will not disfigure your face much, and give you but very little pain."
>
> The words were spoken in that cool, determined and blood-thirsty manner, as only the Kid could speak.

The image of the cold-blooded killer who enjoyed killing dominated the pulp market for several years and later gave way to the writings of respectable authors. The only significant publication in the immediate aftermath of the Kid's death was Pat Garrett's own *Authentic Life of Billy the Kid,* which appeared in the *Santa Fe New Mexican* in the spring of 1882, less than a year after Billy's death. Garrett had borne widespread criticism for unfairly killing the Kid in the darkened bedroom and wanted his side of the story told. Actually, most of the book was written by Marshall Ashmun Upson, a wandering newspaperman who had been postmaster at Roswell and knew Billy. Ash Upson concocted a work of fiction masquerading as history. Not until the final chapters, after Garrett came on the scene, does the book ring of authenticity. It achieved modest sales but remained the source to quote for a generation.

Books or articles that appeared for the rest of the nineteenth century and into the twentieth drew almost exclusively on the Garrett-Upson publication. All fit the definition of ephemera and swiftly faded from public view. One exception that attracted notice was Charlie Siringo's *A Texas Cowboy: Or, Fifteen Years on the Hurricane Deck of a Spanish Pony,* published in 1885 and kept in print for forty years. Siringo had met Billy in 1878, but he drew most of his information from Garrett-Upson and added flourishes of his own. The flourishes exploded in 1920 with his book *The History of Billy the Kid.* He packed this book with page after page of fantasy and included many of the myths that endure in popular folklore. Despite Siringo's prevarications, throughout this period and early into the twentieth century, Billy's image remained that of a merciless outlaw.

That image changed radically in 1926 with the publication of Walter Noble Burns's *Saga of Billy the Kid.* Riddled with historical error and contrived episodes, the book nonetheless put Billy back into the public mind. In fact, error proved no detraction. On the contrary, error helped shape a real if fictional character.

Burns portrayed an appealing figure, a likable young fellow, fighting corruption and injustice, fighting for downtrodden Hispanics. Burns interviewed some of the people who had known Billy as an admired friend and used their quotations to embellish his character. The book contained exceptionally readable prose and gave distinction to the newly launched Book-of-the-Month Club.

Thanks to Walter Noble Burns, Billy the Kid took on the character of a legend—a figure out of history whose exploits may or may not have been true but who captured and held the attention of the public. The legend endured.

Coincidentally, *The Saga of Billy the Kid* appeared as silent motion pictures gave way to talking films. The first "talkie" featuring the Kid appeared in 1930. Titled simply *Billy the Kid* and brought to the screen by King Vidor, the picture starred Johnny Mack Brown as Billy and, improbably, Wallace Beery as Pat Garrett. Previewers would not tolerate the death of the Kid, so Vidor altered the ending to present Pat Garrett deliberately failing to kill the Kid and instead watching him and his sweetheart ride into the sunset.

In the shadow of the Vidor production, more than 150 motion pictures centered on the Kid. Many reflected the times. During the Great Depression of the 1930s, people suffering from economic woes crowded the theaters to indulge in a couple of hours of escapism. Several decades later, reflecting the cynicism and antiwar protests of the 1960s and 1970s, Billy as legendary hero gave way to Billy as legendary bad man in productions such as *Dirty Little Billy* (1972).

Most of the pictures, however, were typical shoot-'em-up westerns, although they varied one from the other. In 1938, for example, Roy Rogers, the singing cowboy, starred in *Billy the Kid Returns*. At the same time, Hollywood produced a series of seventeen Kid movies starring first Bob Steele and then Buster Crabb. They were low budget but kept Billy's name before the public. In 1941 Robert Taylor brought Billy to life in Technicolor.

In 1957 Paul Newman played Billy in *The Left-Handed Gun,* adapted from a Gore Vidal script. The title drew on the single authentic photograph of Billy, a daguerreotype with reversed image, showing the Kid's pistol dangling on his left hip. *The Left-Handed Gun* captured the rebelliousness of the younger generation in the years after World War II.

One that swept the nation and mirrored society in the 1970s was Sam Peckinpah's *Pat Garrett and Billy the Kid* (1972). Kris Kristofferson portrayed an idealistic Billy confronted with a corrupt and unjust West, while James Coburn's Pat Garrett ultimately had to kill the young rebel.

Not until 1988 did the screen receive a popular reprise of Kid movies. In *Young Guns* Emilio Estevez as Billy the Kid appealed to American youth, so much so that *Young Guns 2* continued the theme with the same cast in 1990.

Beginning in the 1950s, Billy began to appear on television and ran close competition to the movies. Individually and in series like *Death Valley Days* and, more recently, documentaries on the History and Discovery channels, television continued to keep the name of Billy the Kid alive for the American public.

Motion pictures, many in the tradition of Walter Noble Burns, contributed critically to elevating the legend of Billy the Kid, but other influences embroidered the movies. A stream of novels and even comic books reinforced the movie legacy. In another notable genre, in 1938 Aaron Copeland's ballet *Billy the Kid,* taking its theme from Walter Noble Burns, opened in Chicago and in 1939 debuted to critical acclaim on Broadway.

Another aspect of the legendary Billy was the search for an authenticated photograph to add to the single one that bore the authentic provenance. Many were published because, their owners believed, they looked like Billy and so must be Billy. In the early 1990s, a computer expert, forensic pathologist, and others gathered to measure critical features of the face of the competitors, such as the distance between their eyes, the length of their nose, the shape of their ear, and compare the results with the one known photograph. None achieved a valid comparison. The search continues.

Americans love conspiracy theories. The "Billy Rides Again" syndrome occasionally arises. Pat Garrett shot the wrong man or contrived a fake killing or was outwitted by the Kid. Somehow, he escaped death and lived on into the twentieth century.

John Miller of Rama, New Mexico, was the first. The Mexican women who prepared Billy's body for burial discovered him still breathing, so they substituted another man who had died that night and nursed the real Billy back to health. He changed his name and lived a peaceful life in New Mexico until 1934.

The most prominent claimant, however, has been "Brushy Bill" Roberts of Hico, Texas. Although he died in 1950, and at an age that could not have had him an adult in 1881, citizens of Hico, supported by a vocal following, stubbornly refuse to reject Brushy Bill as the *real* Billy the Kid.

A solid manifestation of the legend is Lincoln as a tourist destination. New Mexico widely advertises Lincoln and associated sites as a place where visitors can recapture the days of Billy the Kid. The Lincoln townscape retains much of its historical integrity, which helps the state's promotion. A brochure describes and depicts on a map the "Billy the Kid National Scenic Highway."

Billy has spawned his own association, the Billy the Kid Outlaw Gang, numbering more than a thousand members. They publish the *Outlaw Gazette* and gather once a year in Lincoln or elsewhere for a picnic and various reenactments designed to portray episodes from the days of Billy the Kid.

As late as 2003, two New Mexico lawmen decided to investigate the death of Billy the Kid. Backed by other so-called experts, they wanted to dig up Billy in Fort Sumner and his mother in Silver City to gain DNA for comparison. Also, a workbench reputed to be the one on which Billy was laid out in preparation for his burial had some streaks surmised to be bloodstains. Those, too, would be compared with Billy's DNA. The lawmen apparently wanted to prove that the fellow buried at Fort Sumner was truly Billy and thus expose Brushy Bill Roberts as a fraud. Furthermore, Pat Garrett may not have told the truth about Billy's escape and death. Enlisting the governor of New Mexico, Bill Richardson, in the project, the proponents dragged it out for years, despite negative court decisions in both Silver City and Fort Sumner. By 2012 the effort seemed to have run its course.

Nor does the legend of Billy the Kid show any signs of expiring.

* * *

Myth buttressed legend and became part of legend. Without sensational stories lacking a shred of truth, the legend would fail to attain so wide a public appeal. Writers repeated them as fact, and they appeared so often that they became part of history.

Many such stories sprang from the imagination of Marshall Ashmun Upson, who incorporated them into Pat Garrett's *Authentic Life*. For decades writers turned to the *Authentic Life* for the authentic story and incorporated Upson's fantasies in books and articles, together with new myths spawned by Charlie Siringo in *A Texas Cowboy* and his 1920 biography of Billy the Kid.

One Upson fantasy that took on its own life was the tradition of a close friendship between the Kid and John H. Tunstall. As Upson wrote, the Kid "frequently came into contact with his employer and entertained for him strong friendship and deep respect, which was fully reciprocated by Tunstall." In fact, Tunstall scarcely knew his young employee and may not even have known his name. For Billy, Tunstall could have been seen as a father figure, but no more than an acquaintance, if that.

Although denied by Upson, a newspaper account of the scene in the burning McSween house on July 19, 1878, gained a secure niche in folklore. Sue McSween sat at her piano playing and singing battle songs until the posse fired volleys that destroyed the piano. This myth, too, appeared in subsequent publications.

At the turn of the century noted writer Emerson Hough wrote of Billy the Kid. To him may be credited the story that gained and held wide popularity. The youth killed twenty-one men, one for each of his twenty-one years. In reality, he alone killed four: Windy Cahill, Joe Grant, James Bell, and Bob Olinger. He shared in the killing of six: Sheriff Brady, Manuel Segovia ("Indian"), Billy Morton, Frank Baker, William McCloskey, and Jimmy Carlyle. In each of the six, he may have fired a fatal shot or he may not have. Although he did not kill a man for each of his twenty-one years, the story is an integral part of the legend.

Another of Emerson Hough's myths credited Billy with watching a party of seven Mexicans ride past. He drew his revolver and calmly shot each from his saddle. Asked why, Billy responded, "Just to see them kick." That myth, too, won a secure place in the legend.

In a myth created by author Arthur Chapman, a contemporary of Emerson Hough's, Billy held cattle baron John Simpson Chisum responsible for promising to pay him for fighting in the Lincoln County War. He surprised a party of Chisum cowboys sitting around a campfire and asked one if he worked for Chisum. When the man answered yes, the Kid shot him, then shot two more. He instructed the rest to tell Chisum his account would be credited with five dollars for every man Billy killed. Other versions of this myth exist, but Chapman wrote the first.

Chapman was also responsible for the myth of Billy's sentencing by Judge Warren Bristol. When standing before the judge at the close of his trial for murder, Bristol intoned that Billy would be "hanged by the neck until you are dead, dead, dead." To which Billy replied, "And you can go to hell, hell, hell."

In *The Saga of Billy the Kid,* Walter Noble Burns made a huge contribution to mythology. He created fictional scenes to add verve to his narrative, and even the fictional scenes he dressed in his overheated prose. They, too, made their way into general acceptance.

* * *

In Billy the Kid, legend and myth demonstrated their power to grasp the public imagination. Billy commands universal fascination in the United States and widespread interest in England. Other characters in the history of the Old West left their legend and myth. None transcends Billy the Kid, even General George Armstrong Custer. Billy the Kid still rides the West as, in historian Paul Hutton's phrase, the "dreamscape desperado."

The mortal Billy the Kid died at the age of twenty-one in the darkened bedroom of Pete Maxwell at old Fort Sumner, the victim of a gunshot fired by Sheriff Pat Garrett. Legend and myth endowed the mortal Billy the Kid with immortality.

Ned Kelly

CHAPTER 17

Father and Son

At the age of twenty-four, the son introduced himself to a man who had been present at his father's burial with these words: "I'm Ned Kelly, son of Red Kelly, and a finer man never stood in two shoes." Red Kelly had been dead for twelve years, yet his son never ceased venerating his father. Ned Kelly repeatedly used this phrase in introducing himself.

Born in December 1854, Edward "Ned" Kelly was the third child and first male in the Kelly family. John "Red" Kelly was the father, Ellen Kelly the mother. Born a Catholic, Ned loosely embraced his religion until near the end of his short life. He was baptized by Father Charles O'Hea, who stood with him on the last day of his life. Ultimately Ellen bore Red eight children.

In the first decade of his life, in the Victorian towns of Beveridge and Avenel, Ned Kelly grew up as a member of an expanding household. He willingly did household chores, briefly attended school, played with others his age, roamed the hills around home, and acquired a sense of the land that proved vital in later years.

But in adulthood, Ned Kelly's name would blaze throughout Australia and elsewhere in the world.

* * *

Red Kelly personified the origins of Australian society. The first generation of white Australians were convicts, transported from England as punishment for crime. Moreover, Red Kelly was Irish, bitterly opposed to the rule of Queen Victoria. In Ireland, John Kelly stole two pigs, an offense punishable by transport. Transported to Australia in 1841, specifically to Van Dieman's Land (now Tasmania, an island off the southern coast of Australia), Kelly served a seven-year sentence before crossing to Melbourne in 1849 and settling twenty-two miles to the north at the small pastoral community of Beveridge, where Ned was born.

English criminals were transported, too, but by midcentury transport was being phased out. Now, both English and Irish immigrated and took up homes in Australia. Whether convict or immigrant, the growing society fought throughout the nineteenth century to exclude other races from Australia. All dedicated themselves to the slogan "White Australia."

As Red Kelly typified, however, Australia evolved from a foundation of convicts. Transport and convict labor are an integral part of Australia's heritage. As a side-effect, convict labor resulted in a great disproportion of males to females and to the origins of a male-dominated culture.

Red Kelly, however, stood for more than criminal transport. As an Irish expatriate, he brought with him memories of long warfare in Ireland between the Irish people and their English overlords. That inheritance found more expression in bitter hostility between Catholic and Protestant. Aside from issues of doctrine, Protestants excoriated the Irish as disloyal rebels who opposed the queen in Ireland and now in Australia. Protestants looked down on the Irish Catholics and their priests as a lower order of society. Protestant sermons condemned the Irish as improvident drunkards and gamblers.

The hostile mix of English and Irish citizens, and Protestant and Catholic doctrine, troubled all Australia throughout the nineteenth century. Protestant lawmakers ensured that Irish did not hold any public or government office until 1901.

Adding to the trouble were two classes of citizens: "Squatters" and "Selectors."

Squatters arrived first, leasing Crown lands largely for the grazing of cattle and sheep. Mainly British, Squatters usually could obtain loans or were already wealthy, which enabled them to obtain and continue their leases. To work their stock, Squatters relied primarily on convict labor. In time, however, a shortage of convict labor and the arrival of more Squatters forced them west. As a remedy, Squatters promoted immigrant labor—Chinese, Pacific Islanders, Indians—and thus angered a population committed to the goal of White Australia. Squatters also took up farming. They regarded themselves as the upper order of society and were generally more prosperous than others.

By the 1860s, the legislative assemblies of each colony, despairing of the unexpectedly modest value of Squatter exports, sought a more lucrative use of public lands and enacted laws that threw open millions of acres for agricultural purposes—laws that resembled the American Homestead Act providing for disposition of public lands. Under these laws, any person, labeled a Selector, could select a block of several hundred acres, paying a deposit on the day of selection and the rest over a period of eight years. Selectors also had to cultivate the land, erect a habitable dwelling, and enclose the selection with a substantial fence. The difficulty in meeting the requirements of the laws condemned most Selectors to a life of squalor, ignorance, and superstition.

Moreover, the Selectors often chose land already occupied by Squatters. Not surprisingly, tension and even hostility existed between the rival worlds of Squatter and Selector.

The two worlds took on special significance in the northeastern part of the colony of Victoria. Ned Kelly would become entangled in these two worlds. As an adolescent growing up in the 1860s, however, he came to know intimately the land that would be Kelly country. Remote from the thriving metropolis of Melbourne to the south, it was a rugged, lightly populated land. Mountain ranges forested with giant eucalyptus trees (called gum by the people)—the Warby,

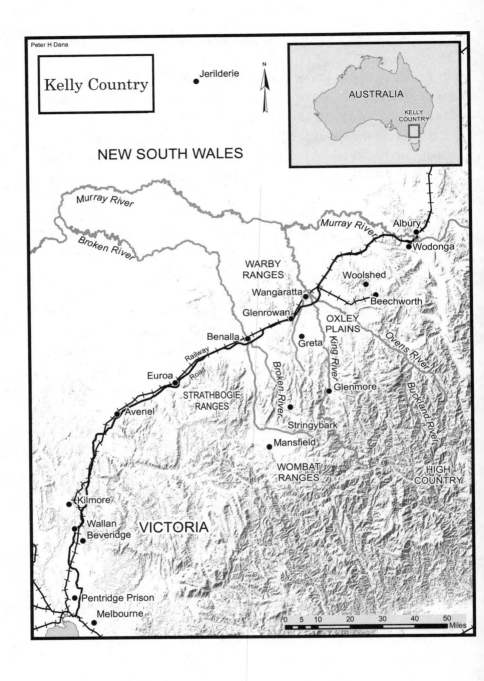

Peter H Dana

Kelly Country

Jerilderie

N

AUSTRALIA

KELLY
COUNTRY

NEW SOUTH WALES

Murray River

Broken River

Murray River

Albury

Wodonga

WARBY
RANGES

Woolshed

Wangaratta

Beechworth

Glenrowan

OXLEY
PLAINS

Benalla

Greta

King River

Ovens River

Railway

Euroa

Road

Glenmore

Buckland River

Avenel

STRATHBOGIE
RANGES

Broken River

Stringybark

Mansfield

WOMBAT
RANGES

HIGH
COUNTRY

Kilmore

Wallan
Beveridge

VICTORIA

Pentridge Prison

Melbourne

0   5   10   20   30   40   50
Miles

the Wombat, and the Strathbogie—gave birth to large rivers that flowed northwest to empty into the Murray River, the boundary between Victoria and New South Wales. The valleys were generally well grassed and well watered, lending themselves to the raising of cattle and sheep. South, toward Melbourne, rolling hills spotted with green thickets and stands of timber grew brush and short grass.

All this landscape, mountain and plain, took on the term "bush," which Australians embraced as part of their heritage. Poets and writers focused on the bush, as in this excerpt from *The Drover's Wife* by Henry Lawson: "There is nothing to see, however, and not a soul to meet. You might walk for twenty miles along this track without being able to fix a point in your mind, unless you are a bushman. This is because of the everlasting, maddening sameness of the stunted trees."

A road and newly completed railroad connected Melbourne with the settlements to the north; it was programmed in a few years to cross the Murray River and continue to Sydney, capital of New South Wales. The road had borne slow wagon traffic for years, which accentuated the remoteness of northeastern Victoria. The railroad brought new life and new commerce to Kelly country, as well as speedy travel to one's destination. Settlements along the road associated with Ned Kelly were Beveridge, Wallan, Kilmore, Avenel, Euroa, Benalla, Glenrowen, Wangaratta, and, at the Murray crossing, Albury. A railway spur ran from the main line through the Woolshed Valley to Beechworth.

*   *   *

In 1841, the same year as Red's transport to Van Dieman's Land, James Quinn and family migrated from Ireland to Melbourne and three years later settled at Wallan, just north of Beveridge. In 1850, at age thirty and one year after his release, Red Kelly married James Quinn's eighteen-year-old daughter Ellen, already five months' pregnant. That first child, a girl, survived only briefly. The couple's daughter Anne (Annie) was born in 1853. Edward (Ned) arrived in December 1854. Another sister, Margaret (Maggie), came in 1857, followed by two younger brothers, James in 1859 and Daniel

(Dan) in 1861, and then two more sisters, Catherine (Kate) in 1863 and Grace in 1865.

Of all his siblings, Ned was closest to Dan, seven years younger. They spent their brief lives as a strong partnership, but Dan would always look and act the junior partner. He lacked Ned's robust physique and projected a quiet disposition. By contrast, Ned looked much older than he was.

In Beveridge, Red Kelly prospered modestly at farming and stock-raising, earning enough to buy a town block and a forty-one-acre property for £651. He had done some gold digging and extracted enough to buy the land. In 1859, he purchased another twenty-one acres for £70. Ned's early education began by day in watching his father erect first a hut and then a cottage in which to live and at night in listening to his tales of the iniquities of the Crown's treatment of the Irish back home. The stories, repeated endlessly, cemented Ned's identity as an Irishman, one who detested the queen's laws, her system of justice, and especially her police.

Beyond his home, Ned received a rudimentary education when a Catholic school opened outside Beveridge in 1862. As pupils, Ned (eight) with his sisters Annie (nine) and Maggie (six) walked to school each morning. Here Ned began learning to read and write. According to a fellow student, he was "a tall and active lad and excelled all others at school games." After only six months, Ned emerged as a semiliterate, energetic, and competitive young fellow.

Interrupting his children's education, Red Kelly abandoned Beveridge. He fell on hard times and had to sell his property at a loss. Hard times were abetted by his increasing addiction to strong drink. As another motive for moving, some of the Quinns, Ellen's family, and his own brother Jim got into trouble with the law. Jim was convicted of cattle stealing, which invited police scrutiny of the Kellys and Quinns. Red also feared that his family would be labeled criminals by the townspeople.

In 1864, therefore, when Ned was almost ten, Red sold his property in Beveridge and moved his brood to Avenel, fifty miles up the road from Melbourne. Red rented a modest farm and tried to build some prosperity with a herd of dairy cows, but grog interfered with this purpose.

Avenel consisted of about thirty shops and houses, a courthouse, a school, three churches, and a police station. Two hotels, or public houses, provided rooms and board. One, the Royal Mail, would figure in Ned Kelly's life. Avenel's economy rested on the grain and wool trade with Melbourne, facilitated by the completion of the railroad.

Ned and his two sisters continued their education at the local school. Ned worked hard, but the teacher was an Englishman, a harsh disciplinarian, and taught from English texts that spurned the Irish Catholicism of the Beveridge school in favor of the Church of England. The Kelly pupils were the only Irish children in the class.

In May 1865, with Ellen pregnant, Red faced charges of cattle stealing. He had stolen a calf from his neighbor and cut the brand from the hide. Strangely, the charge of cattle stealing was dropped, but he was convicted of illegal possession of a cow hide. Confined in the Avenel lockup, he served until October, when he was released two months early for good behavior. During his absence, in August, Ellen gave birth to their eighth child, Grace.

At the age of eleven, Ned had increasingly taken over as the man of the house, caring for his strong-minded mother and his sisters. Red's release did not diminish Ned's role, because his father reverted to old ways with the bottle. Money went for strong drink, and his health began to fail. Two days after Christmas 1866, Red Kelly died. Ned vowed that he would never become addicted to alcohol.

In Avenel, Ned was one of the most prominent boys—strong, active, inquisitive, responsible. He increasingly acquired a knowledge of the bush and honed skills that would serve him well, in honest or dishonest life. He would observe the prominence of cattle theft, or "duffing," the general indifference of many people to the crime, and the harsh reaction of the queen's police. As Ned matured, cattle theft began to hold a certain appeal.

Although still an adolescent, Ned appeared and acted much older. He formed a friendship with an adult who improved his character and knowledge. Esau Shelton managed the Royal Mail Hotel. From Esau Shelton, Ned learned about the Aborigines who occupied Australia before the Europeans arrived. Generally considered a nuisance by whites, they practiced a rich and artistic culture. Shelton took Ned to a nearby camp and introduced him to the local Aborigines. They interacted, unusual for a youth of twelve. Ned absorbed firsthand the elements of their culture and especially their skills. He tried to match their uncanny ability that made them known as "black trackers." They could follow any trail invisible to white people, such as a leaf bent, a rock turned over, a broken weed stem, and other sign only they could notice. In turn the Aborigines, in later years, embedded Ned into their mythology, a tribute no other white person received.

But one incident threw young Ned into bright relief and contributed mightily to his legacy. One morning in 1866, even before Red Kelly's death, Richard Shelton, Esau's seven-year old son, set forth for school. Instead of proceeding to the stone bridge across Hughes Creek, he took a shortcut. Opposite the school a fallen red gum tree spanned the creek, its upper side stripped of bark to provide a precarious footbridge. As young Shelton crossed, his new straw hat blew off and lodged on a tree branch. The boy made his way down to the creek to retrieve his hat but overreached and fell into swirling flood water. Ned, walking on the road along the other side of the creek, quickly dove into the water. He struggled to reach the sinking boy and saved him from drowning. That Ned probably did not know how to swim made the rescue even more valiant.

At twelve years of age, Ned suddenly became the hero of Avenel. Richard's grateful parents at the Royal Mail Hotel presented Ned with a green silk sash, seven feet long and five inches wide, with golden bunting fringing both ends. It endured as Ned's most prized possession, to be worn only on special occasions. It was discovered wrapped around the wounded Ned's waist on the most important day of his life.

The green sash testified not only to Ned Kelly's courage, his instant decision to jump into the water without even knowing how to swim, but more importantly to a fundamental trait of his character. He was a youth of substance and would mature into an adult of substance.

At this young age of twelve, Ned Kelly was remembered as older than he was, five feet four inches tall, stout, broad shouldered, with a smooth face and light brown hair, generally wearing moleskin trousers, a cloth cap, boots, and a jumper (sweater).

* * *

Ned had worshiped his father and continued to worship him in death for the rest of his life. That raises the question of Red Kelly's relationship with his son. Did Red lavish a father's affection on his son? Did he mentor his son in proper behavior, or at least Red's notion of proper behavior? On dealing with the law or the police—a volatile issue in northeastern Victoria? On acquiring the skills he would need as an adult? To be sure, Red was absent at times in court or gaol (Australian for jail), and he was occasionally too drunk to communicate. Still, one looks in vain for some idea of how Red treated Ned, how he inspired such veneration in his son.

For certain, when the family sat around the fire in the evening, Red regaled them with stories—of the interlocking Irish clans and their troubles with the law and the police, of the police force itself, but especially of the motherland, of Ireland, and of the queen's injustice toward the native Irish. Of all these topics Red would have talked, but that was no substitute for a father's close relationship with his son.

Ned's mother, Ellen, a wild and impetuous woman, seems not to have earned devotion comparable to Ned's worship of his father. Only after Red's death did Ned begin to bond more firmly to his mother. The bonds held and grew stronger even as Ellen repeatedly feuded with acquaintances.

Widowed at thirty-three, Ellen Kelly confronted poverty, responsibility for seven children, and enough women in Avenel to feud with. Hot-tempered as ever, she took on her sister-in-law, Anne Kelly. Each charged the other with assault. They stood before a magistrate, who found Ellen guilty and fined her. Three months later Anne's landlord, Thomas Ford, charged Ellen with "abusive and threatening language." She countered that he had assaulted her. Again she stood before a magistrate, together with Ford. Both were found guilty and fined.

Ellen decided she had had enough of Avenel. Her two aunts lived in Greta (pronounced Greeta), fifty-five miles to the northeast. She resolved to put Avenel behind and move her family in with her aunts. Their husbands, Tom and Jack Lloyd, were in Pentridge gaol, on the edge of Melbourne.

Greta lay on Fifteen-Mile Creek, which emptied into the Ovens River. The Wombat Ranges rose to the south, and the Oxley Plains stretched to the northeast, toward Beechworth. Greta was a tiny settlement shadowed by red gum trees and consisting of a few shanties, a dilapidated school, a small police station, and a rundown hotel that catered to the occasional passing wagon. Ellen's two aunts operated the establishment less as a hotel than an unlicensed pub. Ellen moved her family in with them. Thereafter, Greta was the center of Ned Kelly's life.

In Greta young Ned Kelly entered a new phase if his life, the larrikin years.

✳ CHAPTER 18 ✳

The Larrikin Years

Until a home could be found in Greta, Ellen moved the family into a rundown shanty that served as a makeshift hotel, where her aunts lived. Early in 1868, Red's brother James showed up. He had served three years for cattle stealing and on this night was drunk. His antics roused the family, and Ellen drove him out with a stick and a gin bottle broken over his head. He retaliated by setting fire to the building, which burned to the ground. Convicted of arson, Uncle Jimmy began serving fifteen years at hard labor. Neighbors collected money to aid the homeless Kellys. Ellen took the younger children to Wangaratta and moved into a small house, leaving Ned and the older children to stay with the Lloyds in Greta. In Wangaratta, Ellen washed clothing during the day and made dresses at night. Within six months, hard work had earned enough money for Ellen to stake out a selection of land near Greta. It consisted of eighty-eight acres and a hut, which the family occupied. Thus Ellen Kelly graduated into the ranks of the Selectors and, like most, never rose much above poverty.

Meantime, in addition to helping his mother improve the selection, Ned joined the ranks of the local "larrikins," a term that described the younger generation that had been born in Australia. In song and verse, "The Wild Colonial Boy" symbolized the youthful larrikins who came of age in the 1870s. Larrikins regarded as heroes the "bushrangers" whose era was now drawing to a close, men who, folklore had it, robbed the rich and gave to the poor. Australia and its constituent colonies owed fealty to Queen Victoria, her laws, her colonial rulers and institutions, and her police and courts. Larrikins detested the royal presence and displayed their contempt through antisocial behavior—indulging in horse, cattle, and sheep theft, drinking grog to excess, affecting special dress that dramatized their "flashness"—so unruly and troublesome that they drew police harassment and passed time in police custody, the courts, and the gaols. Larrikins were indeed "Wild Colonial Boys."

> Come along my hearties,
>   We'll roam the mountains high,
> Together we will plunder,
>   Together we will ride.
> We'll scar o'er the valleys,
>   And gallop o'er the plains,
> And scorn to live in safety
>   Bowed down by iron chains.

For the larrikins, the Victoria Police Force symbolized the "iron chains." And for the police, the larrikins symbolized the behavior of the Wild Colonial Boy. As a consequence, the police constantly harassed the larrikins and their families, intimidated them, and arrested them on the slightest charge, sometimes fabricated.

In addition, Ned had collected a herd of horses and a flock of sheep—whether or not honestly is not apparent. He mastered horsemanship and grew immensely fond of a horse's back between his legs. He also learned the art of sheepshearing. As a lad of fourteen, he had acquired skills usually associated with adulthood—horse breaker, log splitter, fencer, stonemason, and carpenter.

Instead of putting these skills to productive work, however, Ned passed the time riding with the fledgling Greta Mob of larrikins. He adopted their flash attire, sporting a red sash, a hat cocked forward with the chinstrap under the nose, tight-fitting bell-bottomed trousers, and boots with disproportionately small heels. As a larrikin Ned drew close attention from the police, who constantly harassed the entire Kelly family and their kin.

In fact, the Victoria police suffered from incompetent leadership and unqualified troopers. The city police, in Melbourne, were as inept as the bush force. The chief commissioner, Frederick Standish, had served in the army but had no background in the police. He lived at the swank Melbourne Club and enjoyed the pleasures of the club as well as the seamier side of life in the capital. As Victoria's top policeman, he lacked judgment, experience, and any sense of how to command a police force.

Even worse than the urban police of Melbourne, the field police were neither trained nor able to understand the bush and the people who lived in it. They were also sufficiently dishonest to contrive excuses for arrest and perjure themselves on the witness stand. A worthless policeman would play a critical role in the life of Ned Kelly.

* * *

In 1869, at age fourteen, Ned Kelly met a man destined to set his life on a new course. Under the name Johnstone, the man had escaped from Pentridge gaol near Melbourne. Now he called himself Harry Power, the last of the bushrangers. Harry was an Irishman with a clumsy appearance that belied his skills as a holdup professional who could ride at furious speeds through the rough, forested countryside. He spoke with a deep, intimidating voice and carried a double-barreled shotgun to back up his commands.

Bushrangers enjoyed a long tradition in Australia, and the roster of names that evolved over the 1850s and 1860s bore some of the most prominent names in the country's history. Many were escaped Irish convicts. Their specialty was "bailing up" (Australian for "hands up") travelers, preferably English Protestants, and relieving them of their valuables. All but Harry Power had been killed or captured by police.

After his escape in February 1869, Harry Power headed for Glen-more, far up the King Valley. Glenmore was the domain of Grandpa James Quinn, a Selector who had taken up twenty thousand acres in this remote valley in an attempt to prevent his errant sons from straying to the wrong side of the law. Harry had probably learned of Glenmore in Pentridge from Tom and Jack Lloyd, cousin and uncle of Ned Kelly. Either at Greta or at Glenmore, Harry met the fourteen-year-old. By May 1869, Power had taken on an apprentice bushranger named Ned Kelly.

Like his fellow larrikins, Ned longed for excitement and adven-ture. Even at this early age, he must have admired the long se-quence of bushrangers known to all the people. Bushranging offered an uncertain income, but so did cattle and sheep "duffing," both of which drew police scrutiny. Knowing the history of the Kelly and Quinn clans' collisions with the police and the Victorian system of justice, Ned seems to have had no doubts about abandoning an hon-est, hardworking life for one beyond the law.

The first adventure of Harry Power and his young apprentice almost ended their career. They rode up into the Wombat Ranges toward Mansfield. Harry had some grand exploit in mind but did not confide in Ned. Their horses, however, had become jaded riding into the mountains. Harry decided that they would steal two horses from the station (Australian for "ranch") of Dr. J. P. Rowe. As they crept down a rocky slope above Rowe's corral, an attendant spotted them and called out to Rowe. The doctor and his son armed themselves and gave chase on foot. Mounting their horses and riding furiously through the forest and brush, Harry and Ned eluded their pursuers —a feat of horsemanship that impressed the old bushranger. Rowe could not identify the lad who rode with Power; the name of the ap-prentice remained a mystery. Afterward, Ned returned to Greta to help improve his mother's selection. He worked at axing ironwood trees and splitting them for firewood. With a surplus, he sold enough wood to help the family.

In October 1869, at his mother's home, Ned got into trouble with the police. A member of the large Chinese community, Ah Fook, stopped at the Kelly home for a drink of water. Annie Gunn, Ned's older sister, gave him a cup of creek water. Offended, he treated Annie roughly. Ned rushed to the scene to defend his sister. Three versions of what happened next lead to one conclusion: the two men got into a sparring match with a long bamboo cane that Ah Fook carried. Ned chased the man off the property. Ah Fook went at once to the police at Benalla and claimed that he had been attacked and robbed. Sergeant James Whelan and Constable David McInerny accompanied Ah Fook to Greta. Spying their approach on horseback, Ned raced out the back door and ran toward the boundary fence. He failed to reach it before Whelan grabbed him. Ned was taken to the Benalla police station and held until he stood before a police magistrate. Confronted with the contradictory stories Sergeant Whelan drew from witnesses, the magistrate dismissed the charges and Ned went free. An angry and embarrassed Whelan would not forget Ned Kelly.

In March 1870, Ned again teamed up with Harry Power. The family needed money because Ellen had become pregnant by an Englishman, Bill Frost, who had promised to marry her but had then skipped out. In their first escapade, the two bushrangers bailed up Robert McBean, a Squatter prosperous and influential enough to make the bushrangers' holdup a big mistake. They relieved McBean of his prized watch and mare and left him afoot. Later the same day, on the edge of the Strathbogie Ranges, they bailed up another traveler and took his saddle and bridle. By bushrangers' standards, however, the day's haul had been not been impressive. Yet McBean took great offense at the theft of his watch.

Into April 1870, police scrambled to find the bushrangers as Harry and Ned robbed more travelers. Ned continued to escape identification, though speculation occasionally named him as Power's accomplice. By the end of April, a leak by police, based on McBean's word, appeared in the newspapers naming Ned Kelly as the youth about whom all were curious. Filthy, exhausted, and resentful of his treatment by Harry, Ned parted with him and returned to Greta. There he found his mother with a new baby, the vanished Bill Frost the father. The morning after Ned's arrival, four policemen burst into the shanty and arrested him.

Confined in Beechworth gaol, three times Ned Kelly faced the court, first on the charge of robbing McBean, then twice on successive robberies. The police, however, hoped to use Ned to capture Harry Power. In court, therefore, no one would positively identify Ned as the culprit. On the third charge, robbery, the victim identified him.

Ned was remanded to Kyneton and then to Melbourne. While there, he even received a visit from Commissioner Standish. Although the public suspected Ned of betraying Harry Power, the betrayer was Uncle Jack Lloyd, who coveted the reward for Power. The police succeeded in trapping Harry in his lookout high above Glenmore. Harry returned to Pentridge gaol.

Back at Kyneton, Ned faced the court on the third charge, robbery. The victim failed to appear, and Ned was discharged.

Ned Kelly's bushranging days had ended. He was fifteen and had experienced enough police and judicial attention to keep him repeatedly on the wrong side of the law—and repeatedly in the eyes of the police.

Shortly after his release from Kyneton, Ned met a man who was to play a major role in his life: Isaiah "Wild" Wright. He was a tough farmer from Mansfield who loved to fight and provoked many a contest just for the fun of it. Wright came one day to the Kellys for business with Alex Gunn. He rode a handsome horse he had "borrowed" from the Mansfield postmaster. When he prepared to leave the next morning, his horse had drifted away. Ned loaned him his own horse, and in exchange Wright said to use his strayed mount when he found it. Ned found it and rode to Wangaratta for a holiday.

On his return to Greta, he was stopped by Senior Constable Edward Hall, a huge man with a spotty record as a policeman recently placed in charge of the new Greta police station. On the pretext of signing papers relating to his release from gaol, Ned dismounted, only to be informed by Hall that he was under arrest for horse stealing. Hall of course had no knowledge of the horse's origins, but he jumped at Ned and threw him to the ground. Ned struggled, broke free, and ran to catch the escaping horse. Hall drew his revolver and shouted, "Stand!" Ned turned to face the constable, who pointed his pistol straight at Ned's face and pulled the trigger. Three times the gun misfired before Ned sprang on his opponent. In the fight, Ned tried to wrestle the pistol from the constable's hand but instead was struck repeatedly on his skull, his scalp laid open so deeply as later to require nine stitches. Several burly onlookers responded to Hall's call for help, and together they subdued a bloody Ned and dragged him into the police station. The next morning, two policemen hauled a bound Ned in a wagon to the Wangaratta lockup.

Not for the first time, Constable Hall perjured himself on the witness stand at Beechworth. He had no way of knowing that Ned's horse was not stolen but was a stray Ned had acquired from Wild Wright. When no evidence could be produced to back Hall's accusation, the charge was amended to read "receiving" a stolen horse. On this flimsy verdict, the judge sentenced the hapless youth of sixteen to three years at hard labor. Such was the "justice" that the Kelly clan endured from the Victoria police and courts. Even if the horse had been stolen, three years in prison was an arbitrarily harsh punishment for a teenager.

Ned Kelly began his imprisonment in Beechworth gaol in October 1871. In February 1873 he was transferred to Pentridge gaol and, in common with all entering prisoners, placed in solitary confinement for the first month. On February 4, 1874, Ned walked out of Pentridge, an embittered young man of nineteen sporting the beginnings of a beard fringing his chin and jaw.

Early in August that same year, Ned wandered into a pub in Beechworth. Wild Wright came in, too, the first time the two had met since the affair over Wright's borrowed horse that landed Ned in gaol. They got into an argument that swiftly escalated to the point of violence. The publican intervened and suggested they settle their argument outside, in a sportsmanlike way—boxing.

Wild Wright was a widely known fighter and outclassed the younger Ned, who nonetheless had his own abilities, shaped by his days axing trees and breaking stone. A photograph reveals Ned in underwear covered by a pair of shorts. They boxed with their fists, without gloves, which was the custom. They fought with determination, round after round, hour after hour, with neither man yielding. After twenty rounds, Wild Wright gave up. He later admitted that Ned had given him the "hiding of my life."

The contest yielded no enmity. In fact, Wild Wright became a devoted friend and supporter of Ned Kelly for his remaining four years. Ned's fame spread as the boxing champion of the Northeast.

*   *   *

In 1871, during Ned's term in gaol, Ellen Kelly had sued Bill Frost for child maintenance and won, but the baby died before Bill had to ante up. In 1874, Ellen married George King, a man of shady antecedents who had just been released from gaol after serving a sentence for horse theft. He agreed to be listed as the father of Bill Frost's child. Observing how compatible the marriage appeared, Ned quickly bonded with his stepfather, and together they continued George's business—stealing horses. This partnership lasted until early 1878, when George, suddenly and without explanation, disappeared from the life of the Kellys, leaving Ellen three months' pregnant.

The defection of George King coincided with entry into Ned's life of another player, a crucial one who would end one era and open another in the life of Ned Kelly. In April 1878, Constable Alexander Fitzpatrick took over the police station in Greta.

*   *   *

Ned Kelly's larrikin phase lasted nine years, from his apprenticeship to Harry Power until the appearance in Greta of Constable Fitzpatrick in April 1878—from Ned's age of fifteen to twenty-four. Three of those years isolated him in Pentridge gaol.

The larrikin years defined a young man with many fine qualities. By age twenty-four, he was tall (five feet ten) and strong, handsome, almost beardless, and with a well-rounded personality that appealed to people. He loved his mother and sought to protect his large interlocking brood of family, many of whom repeatedly stood before the courts or served time in gaol. He was kind, courteous, and solicitous of women. At the same time, he quickly resented insult and did not back away from physical combat, especially with errant police officers such as Constable Hall.

While pursuing his career as a horse thief—he adored horses—he roamed his rugged domain, forming in his mind a detailed map of mountains and valleys, rivers and tributaries. He easily navigated the rough mountain ranges. In his brief life as a bushranger, he gained a sense of the bush that enhanced his skill at using the environment to his advantage.

From Red Kelly, Ned had acquired a deep knowledge and love of his Irish heritage. Red had familiarized his son with the inequities the English had visited on Ireland and the tyranny of the mother country's ruling class in his father's beleaguered homeland. In Australia the police and all the apparatus of the queen's rule symbolized the oppression she had visited on Ireland.

Ned Kelly dreamed of somehow ridding Victoria of that oppression.

❋ CHAPTER 19 ❋

Stringybark

Constable Alexander Fitzpatrick, age twenty-one, took over the Greta police station on April 15, 1878. Fitzpatrick's brief record as a policeman had been one of unreliability, dishonesty, and excessive indulgence in grog. Indeed, on his ride from Benalla to Greta he had paused at a pub to fortify himself for the arrest of Dan Kelly, Ned's brother, for whom a warrant was outstanding.

Ned Kelly knew the new policeman. They became acquainted in Benalla in August 1877. Ned judged Fitzpatrick an agreeable fellow. The constable seems to have reciprocated. However, the sergeant in charge of the Benalla police, James Whelan, urged Fitzpatrick to use the friendship to push Ned to commit some minor transgression that would allow the police to strike a blow at his flashness and prestige. On September 20, 1877, Fitzpatrick did just that.

Never known for drunkenness, Ned wandered out of a Benalla pub to be arrested by Fitzpatrick for drunk and disorderly conduct. Almost certainly Fitzpatrick or a compatriot had drugged Ned's drink. Placed in the Benalla lockup, Ned awoke the next morning certain that he had been drugged.

Noting his foul mood, Sergeant Whelan ordered three policemen to help escort Ned to the nearby police court: Fitzpatrick, Constable William Lonigan, and Constable Day. En route, Fitzpatrick suggested that Ned be handcuffed. Ned was not resisting. Why cuff him? And this from a "friend" whom Ned doubtless now credited with drugging his drink. Ned burst free and ran into a boot maker's shop. A wild melee followed, with the police, helped by the boot maker, struggling to place manacles on Ned. Lonigan "blackballed" Ned, squeezing his testicles so hard and for so long that it produced intense and lasting pain. Even so, he continued the conflict until a justice of the peace entered and reprimanded the police for brutality. Ned then submitted tamely, crossed the street, confessed to a variety of charges, paid his fines, and went free. Sergeant Whelan's plan had backfired; Ned's prestige rose and his flashness remained undiminished.

Ned would never forgive Lonigan for blackballing him, and a personal enmity endured between the two.

Such was the background of Ned's relationship with Constable Fitzpatrick when he rode toward Greta on April 15, 1878. Fitzpatrick carried no warrant for Dan Kelly; he had simply read in the *Police Gazette* that one existed. On this pretext, however, he stopped at the Kelly home. A stronger pretext was his months-long attraction to daughter Kate, a pretty fourteen-year-old.

In the Kelly home, Fitzpatrick found Dan Kelly eating supper. The policeman sat at the table waiting for Dan to finish. Ellen Kelly berated Fitzpatrick and, since he carried no warrant, ordered him to leave. As Kate walked by, however, he drew her to his knee. Dan leaped up and threw the constable to the floor. Rising, he drew his revolver just as Ned walked in. Fitzpatrick swung the revolver to point at Ned. Dan struck Fitzpatrick a blow that caused the revolver to fire at the ceiling. Ned fired back, but his bullet scarcely grazed the constable's wrist. Ellen hit the constable over the head with a fire shovel and ordered him out of the house. He rode to Benalla to tell his story.

Based on Fitzpatrick's highly distorted account of what had happened, warrants were issued for the arrest of Ned and Dan Kelly, Ellen Kelly, and two other men who had been present but not taken part in the ruckus. They were Bill Skillion and Brickey Williamson. The charge: attempted murder of a police officer.

To escape arrest, Ned and Dan rode to their hideout on Bullock Creek in the Wombat Ranges. It was a sturdy log hut where they had unsuccessfully looked for gold in earlier times. Now they planned to build a still and manufacture whiskey. At this time Dan was of lesser stature than Ned. His head bore no resemblance to his brother's. A thick cap of hair rested on a crown smaller than Ned's and a rounded face with a thin mustache.

Two close friends from Greta, both former convicts, joined them at Bullock Creek. They were Joe Byrne and Steve Hart.

Joe Byrne, two years older than Ned, had ridden with him in George King's horse-stealing enterprise. Tall and muscular like Ned, Joe cut an impressive figure. He seemed a quiet lad, but he was a member of the Greta Mob of larrikins.

Steve Hart, Ned's age, also had a fondness for horses belonging to other people. He rode them exceptionally well, performing impressive feats of horsemanship and riding at times as a jockey. Tall, slim, beardless, and handsome, Steve had a "sullen temper, easily ruffled," according to one who knew him. Like the other three, Steve was a member of the Greta Mob of larrikins.

While Ned and Dan hid from the police, Ellen, Skillion, and Williamson were arrested and on May 17, 1878, stood before a police magistrate in Benalla. After the Crown presented its case, the magistrate ruled that the three would stand trial at Beechworth on October 9, five months hence. Bail presented an impossible obstacle for Ellen, and she and her baby faced the prospect of spending those five months in the frigid Beechworth gaol. Finally, two Greta farmers scraped together fifty pounds for bail that allowed Ellen to live at home until the trial.

With her sons safe from the police, Ellen stood trial on October 9, 1878, in Beechworth, together with Skillion and Williamson. They had the misfortune to be tried in the court of Judge Sir Redmond Barry, known for the severity of his sentences and his contempt for the Kellys. The charge read "aiding and abetting the shooting of a police constable." She had hit a constable over the head with a fire shovel, defined grandiosely as "aiding and abetting."

All three defendants were convicted, and Judge Barry demonstrated more than his usual harshness in the sentencing. Ellen Kelly, with a baby in her arms, would spend three years in gaol at hard labor. The verdict led to her immediate incarceration in an unheated cell of the Beechworth gaol.

High in the Wombats, Ned and Dan were surprised and outraged at the verdict, another example of the Crown's injustice. The brothers resolved to find a way to liberate their mother. They knew of a compassionate police magistrate at Benalla, Alfred Wyatt, who had expressed his opinion that their mother's sentence was excessive. Through an intermediary, they approached Wyatt and proposed surrendering themselves in exchange for their mother's release—a huge sacrifice in view of Judge Barry's statement in sentencing Ellen that if Ned stood in the dock with her, his sentence would be twenty-one years' hard labor.

Wyatt replied that the best he could do was to make every effort to accomplish such an outcome, but he could not make that a promise. Ned had made a remarkable demonstration of his love for his mother, one that would condemn him to breaking bluestone and hammering it into building blocks for the best years of his life. Wyatt's counterproposal to try but not promise led the Kellys to withdraw the offer.

Ellen served part of her term in the Beechworth gaol, the rest in the Melbourne gaol. Ned and Dan denounced their mother's cruel sentence repeatedly in coming months, holding it up as another example of the official harassment of the Kelly family.

Rarely did Ned and Dan venture from their hideout on Bullock Creek in the Wombat Ranges. It was a sturdy log hut. With police searching for Ned and Dan to stand trial for attempting to murder a police officer, the brothers, Joe Byrne, and Steve Hart fortified the hut so that it was almost impregnable to attack. All they lacked was firearms. Two ancient percussion-cap rifles and one pistol made up their armament. If police found the fortress, they would not face a deadly fire.

Word came from Greta that a four-man police search party had set forth for the Wombat Ranges, striking southeast. Shortly afterward, they learned that a second party had left Mansfield, moving northwest. Clearly, the police had determined that the wanted men had to be found and either killed or captured. With two parties of police converging on their haunts, the four men had to find more weapons and ammunition if they were to defend themselves.

The men thoroughly scouted the area of their hideout, looking for horse tracks that would betray the presence of police. On October 25, 1878, Ned and Dan discovered tracks, but especially four horses with a packhorse headed toward a clearing that had been created by gold diggers in a stand of tall stringybark trees and scattered white gums. Stringybark Creek flowed nearby. That night they discovered that a party of four policemen in plain clothes had camped in the clearing, scarcely a mile from their hut. The troopers had raised a tent and built a fire. With other police converging, Ned knew that they soon would be discovered unless they took some action.

They did. At dusk on October 26, the four outfitted themselves as larrikins, with hat tilted forward and chinstrap buckled under the nose. Ned donned a red sash as a symbol of leadership. Quietly they crept through spear grass that edged the camp on the south. They spotted only two men in the camp. Spreading into a skirmish line, with Ned on the right, they rose and walked into the clearing, Ned aiming his antique carbine. "Bail up! Throw up your hands!" Ned commanded. One of the officers raised his hands, but the other scampered behind a fallen log and rose to aim his pistol. Ned fired and hit the man in the forehead. He struggled to his feet, stumbled forward, and pitched into the grass, dead. The other officer remained submissive as Ned walked over to look down on the fallen officer but failed to recognize him as none other than Constable William Lonigan, the trooper who had "blackballed" him in the fight at Benalla.

The other policeman was Constable Thomas McIntyre. After securing his revolver, Ned allowed him to put down his hands. He also gathered all the guns and ammunition in the tent. McIntyre admitted that two other officers had ridden out on patrol looking for Ned and his men. They were Sergeant Michael Kennedy and Constable Michael Scanlan. As the four larrikins sat enjoying a meal of ham, biscuits, and tea that McIntyre had prepared, they heard the approach of Kennedy and Scanlon. Ned ordered McIntyre to sit on a log and not give an alarm. The four then took cover to wait.

Kennedy was the first to appear. McIntyre rushed forward, shouting for him to surrender, but Kennedy failed to take the warning seriously. As Scanlan rode into view, all four men ran forward, yelling, "Bail up, bail up!" Kennedy pulled his pistol from its holster and swung to the offside of his horse to fire at the aggressors. A bullet grazed Dan Kelly's arm. All four kept shouting, "Bail up, bail up," signaling that they did not want to kill the officers but wished to take them prisoners.

At the same time, Scanlan's horse took fright and reared. Scanlan turned his carbine, still strapped to his shoulder across his back, and fired an unaimed shot. Joe Byrne fired back. The bullet struck the officer, who slid off his horse to the ground and rested on his knees, trying to unsling his carbine. In this position he exposed himself to Joe, who fired a round that lodged in Scanlan's side and killed him.

Kennedy had begun to run through the forest, trying to escape. Ned followed. Kennedy ran from tree to tree, pausing to fire back at Ned. One bullet grazed Ned's rib, and he promptly fired back. Kennedy kept running but finally stepped from behind a tree, dropped his pistol, and began to raise his hands in surrender. In the fading light of dusk, Ned failed to see the dropped pistol and believed the rising arms to be preparation to fire. Ned fired at once and struck Kennedy, who fell, mortally wounded and in agonizing pain. Ned and his comrades gathered around the fallen officer and stood over him. He had been shot three times, and after a brief and touching conversation, in sympathy Ned placed his revolver at the sergeant's chest and ended his misery.

As the drama unfolded, Constable McIntyre mounted Kennedy's horse and made a wild attempt to escape. Terrified, he constantly anticipated a bullet in his back. Tree branches shredded his clothing and finally unhorsed him. His exhausted mount could carry him no farther. He unsaddled and sent the horse away. On foot, the bedraggled officer crawled into a wombat hole and spent the night. The next day he hobbled into Mansfield, where he entered the police station and related the entire sad story.

Back at the clearing, the four men robbed the corpses, cleared out the tent and set it afire, and departed on the police horses. Back at their own hut, they burned it also.

During the affair at Stringybark, Constable McIntyre intently studied each of the attackers. He judged Ned older than twenty-three and estimated his height at six feet. The policeman observed a "sallow complexion, dark-brown hair, full beard and mustache of a dirty, dark red colour, mustache cut square across the mouth, hazel eyes with a greenish tint, wore dark tweed clothes, red silk sash, dark low hat." As for the beard and mustache, photographs reveal Ned with various styles of facial hair. McIntyre also noted that "a string from the hat under the nose was indulged in by all four bushrangers, and the hat was worn tipped well over the eyes"—the defining flashness of the Greta Mob, which was now the Kelly Gang.

Heavy rain prevented the destruction of their hut, but they rode north, heading for New South Wales. Tom Lloyd, a close friend of the Kellys who had served as lookout at Stringybark, accompanied them as far as his home in Greta, where they were fed. Tom stayed behind as the four continued to the north. Rain still fell in sheets, and flooding rivers blocked the path. They turned west to the Warby Ranges, hoping to find Aaron Sherritt in his home in the Woolshed Valley. He was Joe Byrne's closest friend—or "mate." Mateship was a venerable Australian tradition. In the bush, two lonely men developed an abiding trust in each other, men who stood together in work and against any threat. Such was the relationship between Joe Byrne and Aaron Sherritt. Aaron led the gang high on the rocky cliff behind his home and ushered them into a large cave. Here they could dry out and sleep. Aaron walked guard. No pursuers could find them here because the rain had washed out their tracks.

The four men knew that they now were considered outlaws because on October 28, as soon as the word of Stringybark hit the telegraph wires, Premier Graham Berry announced a reward of eight hundred pounds for Ned and Dan and two persons unknown (Joe and Steve), two hundred pounds for each. Aaron Sherritt informed them at the cave that the reward had been increased to two thousand pounds, five hundred for each.

The gang abandoned Aaron Sherritt's cave and again made their way through the floodwaters to the Murray River and New South Wales. They reached the raging torrent of the Murray on October 30 and stood up to their necks in water as police searched the area.

By November 1 they had given up on the Murray and retreated southward, again through floods. Back in Melbourne on this day the Legislative Assembly (lower house) of Victoria's Parliament enacted the Felons Apprehension Act. Modeled after a similar law passed earlier in New South Wales to bring down the celebrated bushranger Ben Hall, it branded named criminals as outlaws. Men outlawed could be captured, shot, or killed by any citizen who recognized them. The Legislative Council (upper house) promptly adopted the same bill.

The Felons Apprehension Act granted Ned and Dan Kelly and two persons unknown until November 12 to surrender at the Mansfield Courthouse. If they failed to do so, the government would declare them outlaws. Although the Mansfield Courthouse remained open all day on November 12, the fugitives did not appear. Three days later the government issued a Declaration of Outlawry by the Chief Justice and immediately thereafter a Proclamation of Outlawry.

For the Legislative Assembly to outlaw anyone without trial, even though the law was almost never invoked, stood in vivid contrast to the American system of justice. In the United States, no one could be legally outlawed without having been found guilty in a trial by jury. The US Congress or state legislatures could not constitutionally outlaw a person. Thus the difference between the Kelly Gang's outlawry and that of Billy the Kid.

Under the terms of the Legislative Assembly's action, as outlaws the Kellys could be arrested or killed by any citizen. Fortunately for Dan and Ned, northeastern Victoria was home to hundreds of Irish Kelly sympathizers. The Kellys' reputation as killers, moreover, was forbidding enough to discourage hostile Squatters from such an attempt. The risk was not great.

* * *

Whatever Ned Kelly's previous encounters with the law, sooner or later he had always emerged a free man. That was no longer possible. The gang now had to live outside the law.

More than Ned or Dan, Joe Byrne or Steve Hart, one man bears prime responsibility for the chain of events that led to Stringybark and the Proclamation of Outlawry: Constable Alexander Fitzpatrick. By his advances on young Kate Kelly and his encounter with Dan, Ned, and Ellen, followed by his distorted story of what had actually occurred at the Kelly home, Fitzpatrick caused Ned and Dan to be men wanted for murder. But more important, the issue of the warrants caused Ellen Kelly to be sent to gaol with three years' hard labor. The imprisonment of their mother anguished Ned and Dan. She did not deserve such harsh punishment. Constable Fitzpatrick bears the blame for this outrage. Fitzpatrick's story resulted in the warrants that sent police swarming in search of Ned and Dan, which led to Stringybark and the Proclamation of Outlawry.

Ned planned Stringybark well. It went awry because the troopers failed to heed his commands. That forced him to shoot. Ned later summarized his own feelings that day. "Had they been my own brothers I could not help shooting them, or else lie down and let them shoot me which they would have done had their bullets been directed as they intended them."

More than once, Ned took all the blame for the police killings on himself and expressed his regret that the police had failed to do as he ordered. His motive was not murder but simply to obtain guns and ammunition for defense against the police patrols searching the

Wombats for him. Ned was not a killer; the three policemen were his first killings.

For the rest of their lives, Ned and Dan were outlaws. Anyone could shoot and kill them. They successfully behaved as outlaws. Not, however, as ordinary outlaws. Ned made it clear that they were not the usual bushrangers. They robbed no one, later sent payment for what they had received, and were unfailingly kind and courteous to any people they met, especially women. They intended to be a type of outlaw such as Victoria had never witnessed. And for the last two years of their outlawry, Ned and Dan practiced these precepts.

They committed more criminal acts, but they carried them out as gentlemen, adopted a unique style of their own, and displayed a courtesy, compassion, and generosity constantly noted by friendly newspapers.

Stringybark marked a watershed event in Ned Kelly's life. It would never be the same as during the larrikin years. And neither would he. Stringybark transformed Ned Kelly. He grew more serious and mature. The frivolous larrikin behavior vanished, submerged by the demands of outlaw life. He had not lost his sense of humor, however, as his elaborately staged criminal exploits demonstrated.

During the last two years of his life, Ned Kelly laid the foundation for his emergence as a memorable element of the Australian heritage.

❋ CHAPTER 20 ❋

Euroa

Two weeks before the Proclamation of Outlawry, the Stringybark killings signaled a massive police pursuit. Superintendent John Sadleir had charge of the Northeast Police District, but Superintendent Charles Nicolson was assigned to command the pursuit. During the next few weeks, 79 policemen were dispatched to the Northeast. Added to those already assigned to the district, more than 150 policemen took up the chase. Extra rifles, pistols, and double-barreled shotguns further armed the troopers.

Both Nicolson and Sadleir were experienced and competent policemen. They looked the part and even resembled each other. Both had high foreheads, piercing eyes, and well-tended beards and mustaches. Sadleir's beard was gray, Nicolson's dark.

As Ned Kelly and the other three outlaws and their led horses struggled through floodwaters to the Murray River and New South Wales on October 30, Nicolson concluded that this was the most likely course the gang would follow. Police confronted the raging Murray but failed to find the fugitives, who retreated without being discovered. They preferred to return to Greta, but that route would be cut off. That left the Warby Ranges. Wangaratta and the railroad blocked this path. At great risk, unaware that twenty-two additional

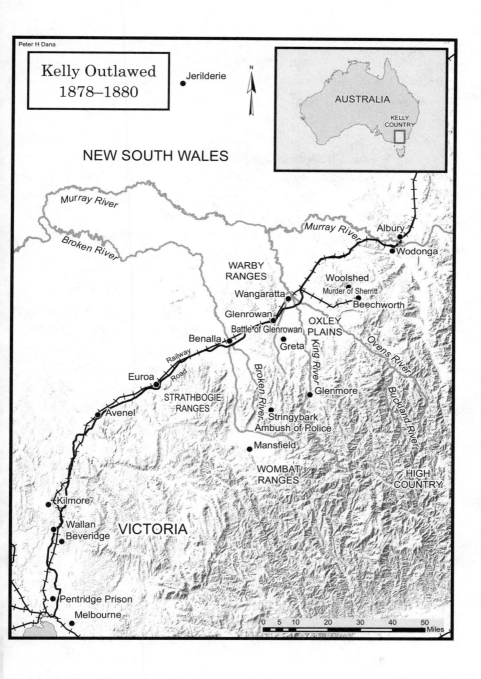

Kelly Outlawed
1878–1880

Jerilderie

N

AUSTRALIA

KELLY
COUNTRY

NEW SOUTH WALES

Murray River

Broken River

Murray River

Albury

Wodonga

WARBY
RANGES

Woolshed

Wangaratta

Murder of Sherritt

Beechworth

Glenrowan

OXLEY
PLAINS

Battle of Glenrowan

Benalla

Greta

King River

Ovens River

Railway

Euroa

Road

Glenmore

Buckland River

Avenel

STRATHBOGIE
RANGES

Broken River

Stringybark
Ambush of Police

Mansfield

HIGH
COUNTRY

WOMBAT
RANGES

Kilmore

Wallan

VICTORIA

Beveridge

Pentridge Prison

Melbourne

0   5   10   20   30   40   50
Miles

policemen stood guard at Wangaratta, the gang and their horses worked their way through the waters of the Ovens River under the railway bridge and emerged to ride through the streets and out of town on the west. Leaving Wangaratta behind, they quickly climbed into the Warby Ranges.

The task of searching the gang out of the Warbys fell first to Inspector Alexander Brooke Smith, who had arrived in Wangaratta with a contingent of twenty-two police charged with pursuing the gang. Brooke Smith was corpulent, lazy, muddle-minded, and a veteran of thirty undistinguished years in the Victoria Police Force, rising to the rank of inspector by seniority. Ned Kelly wrote about him that "he knows as much about police as Captain Standish does about the mustering of mosquitos and boiling them down for their fat." Brooke Smith was hardly the officer to lead any pursuit.

Superintendents Sadleir and Nicolson were, but Smith was a favorite of Commissioner Standish. All three officers led scouts around the base of the Warbys. In one instance, a party under Sadleir or Nicolson—neither admitted to leadership—swooped down on Joe Byrne's house at Sebastopol, in the Woolshed Valley, to find the family peacefully pursuing their daily lives. This embarrassing fiasco came to be known as the Great Sebastopol Raid, a reference to the city that figured in the Crimean War.

Meantime, Brooke Smith led his men around and then into the Warby Ranges. One of his men, Senior Constable Charles Johnston, discovered tracks and, in an orange grove, fresh orange peels, evidence of the nearby presence of the Kellys. In fact, Johnston discovered where the gang had crossed a fence and left a trail down the mountainside. To Johnston's disgust, however, instead of following the trail, Smith judged his men "nervous and excited" and returned to Wangaratta, intent on resuming the search the next morning.

Smith planned to get under way at 4:00 a.m. but decided to sleep longer. Not until 7:00 had he climbed out of bed and joined his men. He ordered them to return to the orange grove and he would follow. He followed slowly and failed to appear until early afternoon, and then not to command but only to accompany the men looking for more tracks. After camping overnight, they picked up a warm trail leading down the Warbys. Again Smith halted the pursuit and ordered a return to Wangaratta.

And so it went, as the police leadership demonstrated its inability to catch the Kellys, even when Brooke Smith had the best opportunity that would fall to the police. From the chief commissioner in Melbourne, pleasure-loving Captain Frederick Standish, to the officers in the field, Nicolson, Sadleir, and others, the Victoria police had demonstrated themselves unable to run down the Kelly Gang. In fact, did they truly want to face the guns of the Kellys? In several instances the police were deliberately diverted from a known target or aimed for a destination they knew was far from the Kellys or ordered to call off a promising operation altogether. Police still swarmed over northeast Victoria, but under leadership hampered by the ignorance of Captain Standish in Melbourne.

* * *

As Ned and his comrades made their way north through the floodwaters, then turned back to the adroit maneuver under the railroad bridge at Wangaratta and into the Warbys, they needed money to carry out their designs. That led to Ned's decision to rob a bank.

While Ned and his comrades plotted which bank to rob and by what strategy, on November 14 a member of the Legislative Assembly in Melbourne, Donald Cameron, took to the floor to quiz Premier Graham Berry about what was being called "The Kelly Outbreak." What were its origins? Why were the police unable to capture the Kelly Gang? Cameron's purpose was simply to embarrass the premier, who promised to investigate if provided evidence.

To Ned Kelly, who read the newspapers, the call for evidence represented an invitation to supply such evidence—his own story. Ned and the more literate Joe Byrne sat down to draft a recital of Ned's story. The recounting came to more than three thousand words of rambling, chaotic prose but nonetheless did tell Ned's story. It even included a description of Stringybark. Mostly, however, it proclaimed his innocence of crime and heaped scorn on the police. Constable Fitzpatrick headed the list of scorned police. If Fitzpatrick were not brought to justice, he would be "the cause of greater slaughter to the rising generation than St. Patrick was to the snakes and toads of Ireland." As for himself, "his conscience is as clear as the snow in Peru." He ended with "a sweet goodbye from Edward Kelly, a forced outlaw." The missive, later copied on suitable paper, was eventually dispatched to Melbourne. It came to be known as the Cameron letter.

Pocketing their draft letter, Ned and Joe plotted a bank robbery. They needed money to support their lifestyle and help their friends, but chiefly a place to arrange an elaborate drama that would advertise the gang's new identity throughout the colony. Several towns with banks were considered but rejected as not fitting their plan. They finally settled on Euroa, which offered not only a bank but a stage for their theatrical production, which involved a cast of more than a score of townspeople.

Euroa was a small settlement of three hundred people forty miles north of Melbourne. Fertile fields surrounded the town, the economy resting on agriculture. In addition to neat dwellings, Euroa had a railroad station, two hotels, a police station, and, most critically, a bank.

Four miles north of Euroa and 150 yards east of the railroad stood a substantial brick homestead called Faithfull's Creek, set in a stand of willows and tall gum trees. The homestead embraced eleven thousand acres that supported five thousand sheep. Behind the homestead, a small slab storage shed with one door and one window stood near the stables. Ned selected the cramped storage shed as a place to hold hostages taken during the bank robbery. Ned bailed up the attendants working in the stable and took prisoners of others who wandered in, confining them in the hot and stuffy shed. Among the newcomers were a few who were not truly prisoners but allies of Ned. That evening, "hawker" (traveling salesman) George Gloster arrived. When Ned informed Gloster who he was and trained a pistol on him, Gloster ran to his wagon to get his pistol. After a rowdy scene, a bystander persuaded Gloster to calm down. The drama concealed from the others Gloster's identity as a Kelly ally.

By nightfall fourteen prisoners settled down in the shed. Ned entertained them not with a speech but with what he called "yarning"

—relating story after story, about his family, about the police and their harassment, and about Stringybark.

Why did Ned feel the need for prisoners, or hostages? Euroa had only one policeman. Alerted, the officer could have summoned help, although not in time to interfere with the holdup plan. Probably two motives lay behind this aspect of Ned's strategy: showmanship and an element of his dramatic demonstration to the authorities that he was not a typical bushranger but a powerful new presence in the Northeast.

At dawn Ned walked to the homestead, where Dan, Joe, and Steve had spent the night. Joe sat at a desk writing a neat copy of the Cameron letter and the rest of the morning making another copy for Superintendent Sadleir. Begging stamps from the homestead cook, they posted the Cameron letter later in the day.

After lunch, with Dan guarding the prisoners, Ned, Steve, and Joe took a hatchet to the railway line running between the town and the homestead and cut and twisted the telegraph wires. In his wagon, Gloster had brought a change of clothing for the gang. They shed their bushranger outfits, even burned them, and decked themselves out as civilized men. They wanted to present a civilized appearance while robbing the bank.

In late afternoon of December 10, 1878, with Joe Byrne remaining in the storage shed to guard the prisoners, Ned, Dan, and Steve rode spring wagons, including Gloster's, into Euroa. Ned knocked at the front door of the bank. A clerk cracked it to say the bank was closed. Ned shoved the door open and sent the clerk sprawling. As Steve came in the back door, Ned pushed open the office door of the bank manager, Robert Scott. Both Ned and Steve pointed two pistols at him and demanded the keys to the safe. He resisted until his wife entered and, charmed by Ned, produced the keys. Ned already had £300 or £400 in cash from the manager's office. In the safe he discovered more in gold and securities that brought the total to £2,260.

As was Ned's custom, he spoke courteously and gallantly to Mrs. Scott, her maid, and her mother and won them to his side. The three women and twelve men taken prisoners, fifteen in all, were herded to the shed, where the other twenty-three remained in Dan

Kelly's custody. After a dinner prepared by the homestead's cook, Ned indulged in further showmanship—trick riding on his mare. His feats of horsemanship—he had developed many—greatly amused the prisoners. At 8:30 p.m. Ned informed the prisoners they were free to go, but only after affording the gang three hours' start. The gang galloped off in a cloud of dust with their bag of loot from the bank.

*   *   *

Ned Kelly had achieved his purpose. He had staged a performance that gripped Victoria. And all to critical acclaim. Newspapers quoted the remarks of his prisoners, all complimentary. He spoke kindly, and he wore the clothes of a typical citizen, even with a handkerchief tucked in his breast pocket. The story played out against the background, also reported by the newspapers, of fumbling police efforts to find him.

As the gang made their exit, bank manager Scott asked Ned where they were going. Ned's reply rang truthfully. "Oh, the country belongs to us. We can go where we like." It did and they could. Continued police incompetence left them in command of a country where they could go where they liked.

Ned's brash reply revealed a new cockiness in his demeanor. Even the Cameron letter contained brazen rhetoric. Since the Proclamation of Outlawry, Ned had also made himself into a showman. Neither trait had been characteristic of Ned, not even during his larrikin years. Cocky showmanship, however, would define Ned whenever he had an audience.

The bank loot had not approached the ten thousand pounds Ned had hoped for. It was still sufficient, however, for people who had been poor and cashless to begin spending money. All, not surprisingly, had long been supporters of Ned Kelly. Robin Hood he was not, but distributing money among people who needed it illustrated another Kelly trait: generosity.

The Euroa robbery also dramatized what Ned had been emphasizing ever since Stringybark and the Proclamation of Outlawry: the members of the Kelly Gang were no ordinary bushrangers; they were outlaws committed to grand deeds of outlawry.

G. RICHARDS,   PHOTO.   BALLARAT.

"Ned Kelly the Bushranger," drawn from a photograph by George Rogers sometime in 1870s. The hat and the small heels on his boots signified larrikin "flashness." (Courtesy State Library of Victoria.)

(above) *Ellen Kelly, Ned's mother, photographed in 1890, when she would have been fifty-eight years old. The horse could possibly be Ned's horse Music, which bore him to Glenrowan ten years earlier. (Courtesy State Library of Victoria.)*

(right) *Aaron Sheritt, Joe Byrne's "mate," acted as police informer for a time and finally alienated the Kelly Gang. His murder by Joe Byrne on June 24, 1880, was supposed to trigger the confrontation of the Kellys with the police at Glenrowan. The chinstrap under the nose was another sign of larrikin flashness. (Courtesy State Library of Victoria.)*

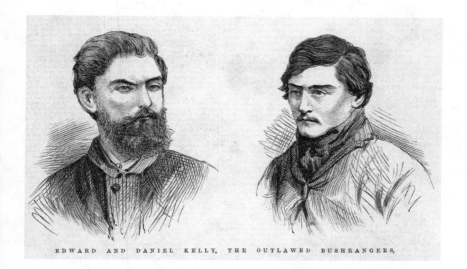

EDWARD AND DANIEL KELLY, THE OUTLAWED BUSHRANGERS,

W. E. BARNES,   PHOTO.

(above) *Ned and Dan Kelly, a wood engraving made for a Melbourne newspaper on November 28, 1878, shortly after the two were outlawed for the Stringybark killings. (Courtesy State Library of Victoria.)*

(left) *Steve Hart, one of the four members of the Kelly Gang, photographed by Wangaratta photographer William E. Barnes in 1878. Steve died in the burning hotel during the Glenowan fight. (Courtesy State Library of Victoria.)*

MURDEROUS ATTACK ON VICTORIAN POLICE BY KELLY AND HIS GANG.

THE MURDER OF SHERRITT.
(FROM A SKETCH TAKEN IMMEDIATELY AFTER THE DEPARTURE OF THE KELLY GANG.)

BIRD'S EYE VIEW OF GLENROWAN.

1.—Jones's Hotel.   2.—Out House.   3.—Railway Station.   4.—Stationmaster's House.   5.—M'Donald's Hotel.   6.—Platelayers' Tents.
7.—Positions Taken by the Police.   8.—Trench : Lieutenant O'Connor and Black Trackers' Post.   9.—Spot Where Mr. Hare was Shot.   10.—Paddock
where Horses were Shot.   11.—Tree where Ned Kelly was Captured.   12.—Road to Bracken's Station.   13.—Half a Mile from Here the Rails were Taken up.

(facing page, top) *Stringybark. Wood engraving in the* Illustrated
Australian News, *November 28, 1878. The engraving depicts the gang's
attack on Sergeant Kennedy and Constable Scanlan. The figure hailing
Scanlan to surrender is Constable McIntyre. Lying in the foreground is
Constable Lonigan, shot by Ned. The four remaining figures are the
Kelly Gang. (Courtesy State Library of Victoria.)*

(facing page, bottom) *Joe Byrne kills Aaron Sherritt at the door of his hut,
the event that was to bring police speeding north by train to search for
the Kellys. The murder set off the battle at Glenrowan. The engraving
was published in the* Illustrated Australian News *on July 3, 1880,
immediately after Glenrowan. (Courtesy State Library of Victoria.)*

(above) *This view of Glenrowan was published in the* Illustrated
Australian News *on July 17, 1880. The numbers of the most important
sites are (1) Jones Hotel, (3 and 4) railway station and stationmaster's
house, (5) McDonald's Hotel, (7) positions taken by the police, (8) trench
where the black trackers took position, (9) site of Superintendent Hare's
wounding, (11) tree where Ned Kelly was captured, (12) road to station of
Constable Bracken and school of Thomas Curnow, (13) half a mile
farther on the railway where the rails were taken up. (Courtesy
State Library of Victoria.)*

NED KELLY AT BAY.
FROM A SKETCH DRAWN ON THE SPOT BY MR. T. CARRINGTON.

Ned Kelly in armor exchanging fire with the police at Glenrowan. This
wood engraving appeared in the Australasian Sketcher, *July 3, 1880.*
(Courtesy State Library of Victoria.)

A STRANGE APPARITION—NED KELLY'S FIGHT AND CAPTURE.

W.E.BARNES.   PHOTO.

(above) *Ned Kelly in armor confronts line of police. Wood engraving published in the* Illustrated Australian News, *July 17, 1880. (Courtesy State Library of Victoria.)*

(left) *Sergeant Steele, whose shotgun blasted Ned Kelly's legs and caused his collapse under the weight of one hundred pounds of armor. (Courtesy State Library of Victoria.)*

THE CAPTURE OF NED KELLY.

W.E. BARNES,   PHOTO.

(above) *Ned Kelly captured at Glenrowan. Sergeant Steele and another man struggle with the gravely wounded Ned, who managed to fire one shot with his pistol before surrendering. Wood engraving published in the* Illustrated Australian News, *July 3, 1880. (Courtesy State Library of Victoria.)*

(left) *Constable Bracken, who saved Ned Kelly from being shot and killed by Sergeant Steele after Kelly collapsed, photographed by Wangaratta photographer William E. Barnes in 1880. (Courtesy State Library of Victoria.)*

KELLY IN THE DOCK. — A SKETCH FROM LIFE.

Ned Kelly's committal hearing in Beechworth, August 6, 1880, wood engraving printed in the Illustrated Australian News, *August 28, 1880. Ned's useless right hand rests on the dock, his other clasps his lapel. After extensive testimony, the presiding magistrate decreed that Ned would be tried for the murder of two policemen. (Courtesy State Library of Victoria.)*

THE KELLY TRIAL—THE SCENE IN COURT

(above) *Ned Kelly's trial, wood engraving in the* Illustrated Australian News, *November 6, 1880. Judge Sir Redmond Barry presides. Ned stands in the dock facing the judge. (Courtesy State Library of Victoria.)*

(facing page, top) *Ned requested a picture for his family, which was taken against a wall of the Old Melbourne Gaol the day before his execution on November 11, 1880. His useless left hand is hooked over his belt, holding up the chain extending to his leg-irons. (Courtesy University of Melbourne.)*

(facing page, bottom) *Ned had a more formal portrait taken the same day, November 10, 1880—his last picture. (Courtesy State Library of Victoria.)*

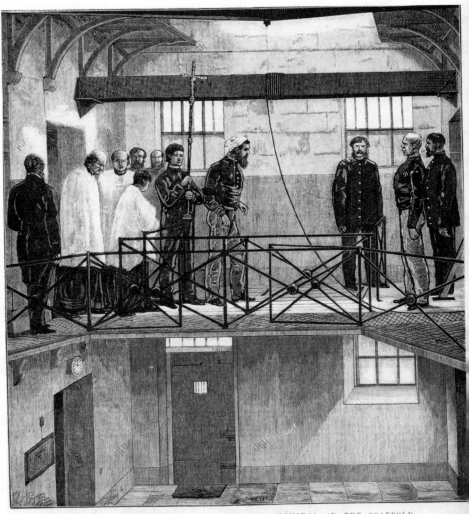

LAST SCENE OF THE KELLY DRAMA: THE CRIMINAL ON THE SCAFFOLD.

The gallows, November 11, 1880, 10:00 a.m. Wood engraving published in the Australasian Sketcher. *Ned faces the rope, the hood already in place on his head. The executioner faces forward. Priests stand behind Ned. Facing Ned is presumably the gaol superintendent, John Castieau. (Courtesy State Library of Victoria.)*

❊ CHAPTER 21 ❊
Jerilderie

News of Euroa ignited predictable outrage in Melbourne. The reward jumped to £1,000 for Ned, totaling £2,500 for the entire gang. Chief Commissioner Frederick Standish dispatched 58 additional policemen to northeast Victoria to guard against another robbery, raising the total to 217. More rifles, pistols, and shotguns increased police armament. Regular army soldiers stood sentry at the banks.

Standish also intercepted the Cameron letter, which arrived at the assemblyman's desk on December 17, 1878. Standish had read the copy provided to Superintendent Sadleir and at once induced Premier Graham Berry to prevent Cameron from reading it in Parliament. The newspapers were shown copies but not allowed to print the letter. Nevertheless, the press conveyed enough for the public to understand its contents and intent.

Superintendent Nicholson had been in charge of the Kelly pursuit. But Commissioner Standish's favorite, Francis Hare, now relieved Nicholson. The usually decisive Hare tried to decide where the gang was and how to go about finding them.

Commissioner Standish had his own idea, which both Sadleir and Hare considered a serious mistake, as it turned out to be. The Kelly Gang relied on friends and sympathizers throughout the area

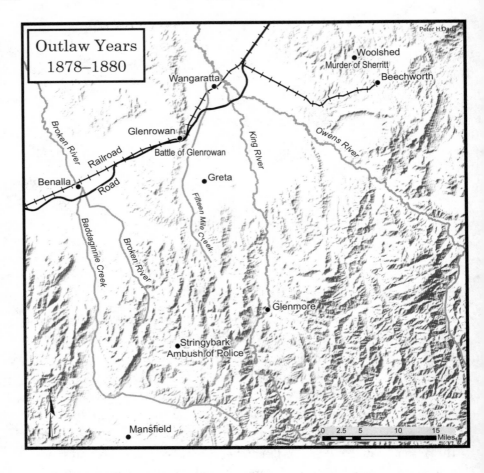

Outlaw Years
1878–1880

Peter H Dana

Woolshed
Murder of Sherritt

Beechworth

Wangaratta

Glenrowan

Battle of Glenrowan

Broken River

Railroad

King River

Owens River

Benalla

Road

Greta

Baddaginnie Creek

Broken River

Fifteen Mile Creek

Glenmore

Stringybark
Ambush of Police

Mansfield

0   2.5   5   10   15
                            Miles

to keep them informed of police movements. The Felons Apprehension Act provided that known Kelly sympathizers could be arrested and made to stand trial for the offense. Standish gathered officers from all stations in the district and asked for the names of men who should be arrested. On January 2, 1879, warrants were obtained for more than twenty men, all of whom had to be arrested on the same day to prevent their scattering. Police fanned out and arrested all those named in the warrants. By train and wagon, the prisoners were taken to Beechworth gaol to stand trial for their presumed sentiments.

In a special court convened in the gaol, twenty-one men stood before a police magistrate. No evidence could be presented to prove that anyone was a Kelly supporter, so all were remanded to their cells for seven days to await another hearing. For three and a half months this scene was repeated, with the sympathizers remanded each time for seven days. These sordid proceedings, widely reported in the press, alienated the public and earned more hostility for the police and more support for the Kellys. Those arrested represented only a fraction of the Kelly sympathizers scattered across northeast Victoria, a total augmented by the arbitrary police persecution of the twenty-one.

* * *

The gang conceived another dramatic performance: to rob a bank in New South Wales, where banks were not guarded by soldiers. Such a robbery would obtain money to help pay for the defense of the re-manded sympathizers and once again stage a drama that would spread their names and deeds throughout Australia. Their target was the small town of Jerilderie, about forty miles north of the Murray River.

Late on the night of February 7, 1879, the gang reached the front of the Jerilderie police station, Ned on horseback and the others converging along the porch. When two police officers came out, half dressed, Ned bailed them up. One was Senior Constable George Devine, the other Probationary Constable Henry Richards. Devine's wife emerged from the home, attached to the police station. She begged the gang not to harm her husband. Ned assured her that the constable was in no danger so long as he behaved. Ned and his comrades ushered the two policemen into the station, gathered all the arms and ammunition, dressed themselves in police uniforms, and placed the two men in the lockup. Devine implored Ned not to harm his wife. Ned answered in terms he had used before: "No female could say otherwise than that he and his mates had treated women with the greatest respect and courtesy, more than could be said about many of the Victoria Police." "Mrs. Devine and her children would have every respect shown them."

That he did as he promised led Mrs. Devine later to declare Ned "the kindest man I ever met."

The gang took turns sleeping in the Devine parlor. The next day, accompanied by the hostage policemen, they scouted the town's main street. Adjoining the Royal Mail Hotel was a small building, the Bank of New South Wales. The robbery would take place the next day, patterned after the Euroa heist.

Ned had another purpose in Jerilderie. He had explained himself in the Cameron letter. That had failed. He would try again. This time he had a stack of paper, fifty-six pages crammed with 7,500 words. To ensure that it would not be ignored like the Cameron letter, he intended for the local newspaper to print it in its entirety. Based on the Cameron letter, the Jerilderie letter was twice as long and twice as detailed.

The Jerilderie letter also contained a significant new element, a hint of the dream that had been flowering in Ned's mind for months. Doubtless with the imprisonment of his mother in mind, he railed against the injustice of the queen's laws and police in Australia. But he went a step further, adverting to the suffering of the Irish who had been transported to Australia and "bravely died in servile chains but true to the shamrock and a credit to Paddy's Land." As a remedy, Ned referred to the green that no Irishman dared wear but pledged to "reinstate it and rise old Erins Ilse once more from the pressure of tyrannism of the English yoke which has kept it in poverty and starvation and caused them to wear the enemy coat." Ned also used the phrase from the Cameron letter citing the snakes and toads of Ireland; but he again hinted at his future plans. If the government would not grant the Irish liberty, he would "open the eyes of not only the Victorian Police . . . but the whole British army." He also referred to the Union Jack as a target. "I do not wish to give the order full force without giving timely warning but I am a widow's son outlawed and my orders must be obeyed."

What he intended to order is not specified, only implied in the soaring rhetoric about liberating the Irish from the "English yoke." How he thought that could be accomplished is left unsaid.

The next day, February 10, with Ned in a police uniform, the gang invaded the Royal Mail Hotel and took everyone there, and all who entered later, as prisoners.

While Dan and Steve guarded the hostages, Ned and Joe entered the back door of the bank next door. They bailed up the accountant, Edward Living (Liveing) and gathered the cash in the safe, £691. But the inner safe required two keys. Living had one, but the manager, who was absent, had the other. The junior clerk, who had been waiting outside for the manager to return, then entered the front door and also was bailed up. Fortuitously for Ned and Joe, at this time John Tarleton, the manager, entered the back door and drew water for a bath. Bailed up, he had to climb out of the tub and get dressed. He then did as he was told and opened the inner safe, which yielded £1,450. Like Euroa, not an impressive haul.

Ned had more important matters on his mind than money. He wanted the Jerilderie letter printed. The newspaperman, Samuel Gill, sensing a story in the making, had been nosing around town. When he learned of the Kelly holdup, he hurried out of town and out of reach. Living escorted Ned to the newspaper office. Ned asked Gill's wife where her husband was. She said she did not know. Living then offered to take the document and give it to Gill. Ned instructed him to make sure Gill printed it. The accountant agreed.

Gill did not print the letter and may not even have seen it. Living turned it over to the police. This so-called Jerilderie letter had no more effect than the Cameron letter. It did not become public until after Ned's death, when a copy was introduced as evidence in the proceedings of a royal commission convened to investigate the Kelly outbreak and especially police conduct.

The robbery had ended. All that remained was to deal with the thirty hostages in the hotel. Ned made a long speech to the hostages, dwelling mainly on the iniquities of the police. He again told the story of Stringybark. At the end, he enacted another drama; he summoned Constable Richards to the front of the crowd. "Now," he announced, "I'm going to shoot Constable Richards before I leave."

Richards had been one of a contingent of police that opened fire on a boat of four men crossing the Murray River. Although the four men in the boat were Victoria police, Ned pretended they were the gang.

"You were one of those who fired."

"Yes, I fired across the river at them."

"You did your best to bring us down."

"Yes, I did my best."

"You did not know me, and yet you tried to kill a man you never saw before, or who never did you any harm?"

"I was doing my duty. You were outlawed at the time."

"You would have taken my life if you could, so you now cannot blame me for shooting you."

"Yes, I can," responded the courageous constable. "We were both armed then and had an equal chance in a fight. If you shoot me now, you shoot an unarmed man who has not chance of his life. Give me a loaded revolver and I'll fight you now, and if you shoot me, it will be a fair fight."

Ned let a few seconds pass for the effect on his audience. Then he exclaimed: "You can go now, for I'm damned if I don't like your pluck, but if we ever meet again, I'll shoot you."

The constable did not turn away. Fixing Ned with his eyes, he replied, "That's all right, so long as the two of us are armed; it will be you and me for it."

The exchange not only restored Constable Richards's dignity after a day of humiliation. It also assured the people of Jerilderie that they had a policeman they could respect, one who had stood up to the feared Ned Kelly.

Ned Kelly had probably staged this drama deliberately to accomplish just this purpose. Few were aware that Ned disliked shooting anyone, that the only men he had shot and killed were the three policemen at Stringybark Creek. And he blamed them for forcing him to shoot.

With the two policemen in the lockup, the gang rode out of Jerilderie with their paltry loot but with Ned's vain hope that his letter would reach the public.

* * *

The affair at Jerilderie added few insights into Ned Kelly's personality. The robbery, the hostages, the handling of the police, the small sum of the loot, and even the failed Jerilderie letter simply reflected Euroa. The hostages, too, provided the same service in Jerilderie as they did in Euroa: they praised Ned Kelly to the newspapers.

Two insights did surface: Ned's respectful dealing with Constable Devine's wife and his revealing episode with Constable Richards, when he threatened to shoot him. In the first, he repeated what he had always said about women. In light of Ned's dislike of policemen, his treatment of Constable Richards appears strange. For one thing, however, this was not Victoria. For another, he had enough compassion to understand and remedy the officer's feelings of disgrace for the day's events.

Jerilderie prompted the government of New South Wales to reach out to the government of Victoria and boost the reward for the Ned Kelly Gang. The total now stood at eight thousand pounds, two thousand for each of the outlaws. Beyond that, the audacity of the raid failed to provoke as much outrage in either colony as Euroa, which was an unprecedented criminal drama.

As the Kellys roamed the wilderness for the rest of 1879, the police followed one lead after another, only to have it vanish. The stature of the gang grew, as sympathizers celebrated their achievements and applauded their engagement of lawyers to stop the endless chain of remands that the police inflicted on sympathizers. The gang became the subject of song and ballad, sung or recited in households all over northeastern Victoria.

> Sure Paddy dear and did you hear the news that's going
>   round
> On the head of bold Ned Kelly they have placed two thou-
>   sand pounds
> For his brother Dan, Joe Byrne, Steve Hart, a similar sum
>   they'll give.
> But if they doubled that amount, the Kelly gang would live.

Doubtless the gang rejoiced at such tributes, as well as the futility of the scores of police trying to find them. One kind of police Ned did fear: "black trackers." He learned of Aborigines in his youthful days in Avenel. He marveled at their uncanny ability to follow tracks that no one else could see. Queensland offered a contingent of black trackers to Commissioner Standish to track the Kellys. Standish wanted no part of them, reflecting widespread racism. Before he could react, however, in March 1879, Sub-Inspector Stanhope O'Connor of the Queensland Police showed up in Benalla, followed few days later by six Aboriginal Mounted Police.

Ned and his comrades took to a winter hut high in the mountains, hoping to elude the black trackers. They need not have worried. The mountainous Victorian climate, contrasting with the humid Queensland climate, eroded their health. Besides, Captain Standish still detested the black trackers and made sure they were misused. A discouraged O'Connor saw his men sidelined, although not relieved of duty for almost a year. The gravest threat Ned had faced subsided.

In their mountain hideout, the gang plotted their next adventure.

✻ CHAPTER 22 ✻
A Republic?

After Jerilderie, Ned Kelly and his companions passed the autumn of 1879 in the mountains, first to avoid the black trackers imported from Queensland and second to conceive another adventure like Euroa and Jerilderie. Critical to one of the plans they were pondering was Aaron Sherritt, mate of Joe Byrne.

A resident of the Woolshed Valley, Aaron was the same age as Ned but bonded with Joe Byrne. Aaron was tall with dark brown hair, unkempt, only slightly educated, and a Protestant in a uniformly Catholic neighborhood. The two probably met at the Catholic school.

With the gang's full knowledge, Aaron became a double agent. He knew their plans and passed misleading versions on to the police; and he kept them informed of the police plans.

At the time of the Great Sebastopol Raid in November 1878, Aaron had exacted a promise from Commissioner Standish to spare Joe Byrne's life in exchange for playing the role of police informer—a promise Standish had no intention of keeping. In the Benalla police station, before Jerilderie, Aaron sat with Superintendent Francis Hare to play his role. British to the core but not too bright, Hare was to turn up repeatedly in Ned Kelly's life.

Aaron's first act as an informer was to tell Hare that the gang intended to rob a bank in New South Wales. He revealed that the crossing of the Murray River would take place on the road to Goulburn. That led the police to concentrate at a point on the Murray where the gang would have to cross if headed for Goulburn. The crossing proved to be 160 miles downstream from the actual crossing point, and the bank was at Jerilderie.

After Jerilderie, the credulous superintendent continued to place his trust in Aaron, who now concocted another stratagem to mislead the police. Joe Byrne's home, where his mother lived, lay in the Woolshed Valley, below the plateau where Beechworth stood. On the north, the plateau rose abruptly in a steep cliff with a cave overlooking the valley. Aaron persuaded Superintendent Hare that he and a party of police hide themselves during the day in the cave and spread out around the Byrne house at night. When Joe Byrne visited his mother, the police could grab him. What Aaron did not tell Hare was that he had positioned the police so they could not see the path by which Joe approached his mother's house. Hare allowed this pointless charade to continue for a month.

Meanwhile, however, Aaron's careless mistakes compromised his role as double agent. He never informed Mrs. Byrne of the police surveillance, and she grew increasingly suspicious. He also allowed himself to be seen riding with police patrols. He was engaged to marry Joe Byrne's sister Kate, but that went awry in a complicated imbroglio that landed in court. Kate Byrne stood in the witness box and, staring at Aaron, declared, "We had a falling out about his giving the police assistance. I thought that Aaron was giving assistance to the police in the pursuit of the bushrangers." For unknowing sympathizers, Kate's testimony branded Aaron a traitor to the gang.

Superintendent Hare, an exhausted wreck, gave up and was replaced on July 3, 1879, by Superintendent Charles Nicolson. Both Nicolson and his superior, Superintendent John Sadleir, were a greater threat to the Kelly Gang than Hare.

As the cave farce played out in the autumn of 1879, another took its place, one that Commissioner Standish should have perceived would strengthen the Kelly Gang. Selectors and applicants for selections made up the target of the new plan, which was conceived by Standish and reluctantly carried out by Superintendent Sadleir. As Sadleir recognized, Selectors were the very people the remand policy had alienated. Now they were hit by one much more painful and ill-advised.

Unlike the Squatters, most of the Selectors were Kelly sympathizers. Many already occupied selections. Many more, including Aaron Sherritt, applied for selections of their own. When Selectors sought title to their selections, and when men applied for their own selections, the Lands Department refused to grant them. Asked why, officials could answer only that the police had recommended it.

The Selectors had been struck two hard blows—deprived of their land and deprived of their drought-ridden crops. The Squatters enjoyed the spectacle, which almost escalated into violence between the two classes. Ned wanted to help the impoverished sympathizers and considered robbing another bank to provide the cash. But he gave that up when he recognized how closely guarded they all were.

Aaron continued to play the informant role with Superintendent Nicolson, although that officer lacked respect for Aaron and distrusted him. Nicolson wanted to rid himself of Aaron, but Commissioner Standish refused to permit it. Another cave party resulted, with police hiding in the cave by day and spreading out in front of the Byrne home at night.

In December 1879, Aaron Sherritt married Ellen Barry and moved in with his wife's family in the Woolshed Valley. Marriage did nothing to dim the growing suspicion of Aaron as a scoundrel, a betrayer of Joe Byrne. So widespread was the belief—and the talk—among sympathizers that even Joe began to doubt Aaron's loyalty.

Meanwhile, the embattled Selectors grew even more outraged. They talked openly of a revolt in northeast Victoria. This had long been Ned Kelly's dream: liberation from the queen's laws and police. That the idea now spilled into public stoked Ned's dream of liberation.

In the late summer of 1880, Ned and his fellows busied themselves fashioning suits of armor. Ned may have thought of using armor in robbing banks. More likely, he anticipated using it in an armed revolt against the queen's rule. Joe Byrne thought the idea impracticable and opposed it, but Ned insisted. Using steel mold-boards from idled plows, the gang pounded them into desired shapes over fallen gum-tree logs. Sympathizers donated many of the mold-boards, although in March 1880 the gang had stolen a few. The com-pleted suit consisted of a helmet, a backplate and a breastplate, side plates, shoulder guards, and an apron. The full suit weighed almost a hundred pounds. Friendly blacksmiths constructed such suits for Dan, Joe, and Steve.

Superintendent Nicolson perceived that something unusual was taking place. Rumors of stolen moldboards, of vigorous activity among the embattled Selectors, and of multiple sightings of the Kelly Gang stirred him to heightened investigation. Then in May 1880 he re-ceived word that he would be replaced by Commissioner Standish's favorite, Superintendent Hare, who had surrendered the position to Nicolson a year earlier. The transfer took place on June 2, 1880. An embittered Nicolson withdrew to Melbourne.

The cave scheme continued in progress. Aaron, however, now spent the night at his wife's house in the Woolshed Valley while the four policemen kept watch on the Byrne house.

Meanwhile, Ned worked on plans for an uprising of sympathizers designed to establish a Republic of Northeastern Victoria. He and the better-educated Joe Byrne even drew up a proclamation and had it printed, although how widely it was distributed, if at all, remains unknown. Full of the wild rhetoric of the Jerilderie letter, the proc-lamation concluded with the demand written in the Jerilderie letter: "I do not wish to give the order full force without giving timely warning but I am a widow's son outlawed and my orders must be obeyed." Again, one is left to wonder what form the order was to take.

Joe Byrne had already concluded that Aaron Sherritt was a trai-tor to the gang, and he resolved to kill him. Ned decided that Aar-on's death would be the event that launched his ambitious plan. He reasoned that as soon as Melbourne learned that Ned Kelly had emerged from hiding, a train full of troopers would speed north to take up the chase. The police contingent and their horses, together with some black trackers, had been held in Benalla for this purpose.

Ned settled on the tiny community of Glenrowan as the place where the uprising would begin. Just east of the Glenrowan station, the railroad curved northward around the base of the Warby Ranges. Here they would pull up the rails, leaving the special police train to plunge into a deep gully. Ned and the others, meanwhile, would have bailed up the town residents and held them captive in McDonnell's Railway Tavern. When the train crashed, they would shoot any of the surviving troopers and send Chinese signal rockets into the sky to alert the small army of sympathizers held in reserve south of the station. Then all would wage guerrilla war against the authorities until the republic became a reality.

The scheme contained many flaws, many what-ifs, and it was doomed from the beginning. Ned floated alternative plans, but these may have been merely diversions or a sign of genuine uncertainty. Glenrowan would determine the future of northeastern Victoria—and Ned Kelly.

* * *

Postscript: Is the concept of a Republic of Northeastern Victoria a genuine part of the life of Ned Kelly, an element of the legend of Ned Kelly, a fanciful story concocted to explain the drama of Glenrowan, a tale to be ridiculed, rejected, or ignored altogether? Only one of Ned Kelly's major biographers has taken the idea of a republic seriously and explained it in convincing detail. Ian Jones is universally conceded the definitive biographer of Ned Kelly. His interpretation and documentation of the republic in *Ned Kelly: A Short Life* is detailed and persuasive. Ned's other biographers either ignore the issue, refer to Jones without explicitly embracing his narrative, or concoct a new theory, such as the idea that the train would be halted at Glenrowan and the police taken hostage and held for the release of Ned's mother, an approach that would avoid any loss of life. The narrative here is based almost entirely on Ian Jones's reconstruction.

One book that challenges Jones and all other pro-Kelly writers appeared in 2012: Ian Macfarland's *The Kelly Gang Unmasked*.

Though Macfarland makes many persuasive arguments, this author has also found it deeply flawed. Ian Jones remains the reigning authority.

Although with occasional resort to Macfarland, the narrative that follows is based almost entirely on Jones's reconstruction.

❋ CHAPTER 23 ❋
Glenrowan

By June 1880, deep into winter, Ned Kelly was totally dedicated to his project to engineer an uprising that would lead to an independent republic in northeast Victoria. He had perfected some of the arrangements, such as choosing the village of Glenrowan as the focus of the uprising, sending out a summons for sympathizers to assemble at Glenrowan, and launching the revolt as soon as the gang had wrecked the expected train loaded with police and shot down the survivors.

The first requirement, however, was to set the trigger that would bring the police train to Glenrowan. Backed by Dan Kelly, Joe Byrne would kill his former mate Aaron Sherritt at his home in the Woolshed Valley. That would bring forth the four policemen inside the Sherritt house as part of the scheme for keeping watch on the Byrne home. They would raise the alarm that the Kellys had emerged from hiding and bring the police train north from Benalla toward Beechworth, near the murder scene, where the police would begin a search. Meantime, Ned and Steve Hart would reach Glenrowan to tear up the tracks half a mile east of the railway station and organize the sympathizers.

The murder occurred on Saturday night June 24, 1880. Joe had loaded his double-barreled shotgun with two heavy slugs. He stood to one side of the door in the dark as Aaron stood in the open door. Joe then moved to confront Aaron, raised his shotgun, and fired one barrel into Aaron's face, the slug punching a large hole in his throat. Before he could fall, Joe fired the second ball into Aaron's chest. With two massive wounds pouring forth blood, Aaron fell backward to the floor.

The first setback in the plan now occurred. Fearing that the gang was still in the vicinity, the four policemen hesitated to leave the Sherritt hut—hesitated in fact for twelve hours, until daylight Sunday. During that time, the telegraph operator at Beechworth could not know to alert the police at Benalla that the Kelly Gang had come out of hiding and bring the train full of troopers and their horses north to Glenrowan.

Meantime, Ned and Steve had reached Glenrowan. Their first task was to twist the rails east of the railway station. The railway divided the small town. To the south stood McDonnell's Railway Tavern, the assembly point for the small army of sympathizers and the place where Ned and Steve tethered their horses, two riding horses and two packhorses. The heavy armor had been hauled behind in a buggy. To the north of the railway lay the small, shabby Glenrowan Inn of Ann Jones, in the shadow of the Warby Ranges.

Ned and Steve had brought tools to lift the rails but discovered that they were not heavy enough. Ned went to four tents housing railway workers and ordered them to get the rails loose. They had no tools. Exasperated, Ned roused the stationmaster, John Stanistreet, and ordered him to get the workmen to do his bidding. Stanistreet replied that he would need two platelayers (tracklayers) who lived farther south along the rails. While Ned went to get the platelayers, Steve ordered the workmen to break open the toolhouse and bring tool chests to the site. The platelayers came with Ned and succeeded in loosening the rails, although they stalled the brief task so that it took an hour and a half. They threw the rails into the thirty-foot gully running beside the curving railway line. The platelayers did not finish until well past 1:00 a.m. on Sunday.

Joe and Dan arrived to report that Aaron Sherritt had been killed and the police train should soon be on the way from Benalla. At the Glenrowan Inn north of the railway, Ned had roused Ann Jones from her sickbed and forced her and her young daughter to accompany him. Angry at first, she turned hospitable during the adventure and invited Ned to bring the people he had taken prisoner from the railway crossing to the hotel and have breakfast. Ned decided to change his base from McDonnell's to Ann's Glenrowan Inn. Leaving the women and children behind at the stationmaster's house under guard of Steve Hart, the gang and their prisoners trooped up to Ann's hotel. Fire blazed in the fireplace, and Ann Jones prepared a breakfast of ham and eggs. Sympathizers began to arrive, swelling the number of people in the hotel.

Among the prisoners was the local schoolteacher, Thomas Curnow, who had been apprehended by Ned late Sunday morning at the railway crossing. Curnow had been driving a buggy seating his wife, sister, and baby, accompanied on horseback by his brother-in-law, Dave Mortimer. Ned informed the teacher that he and Mortimer were now prisoners. His wife and sister remained with the other women and children at the home of John Stanistreet, while Curnow and Mortimer walked up to the Glenrowan Inn and entered the ranks of the prisoners.

At the inn's bar, Joe Byrne had downed enough drinks to tell Curnow why they had come to Glenrowan and describe how they planned to wreck a special train loaded with police headed for Beechworth to pick up the outlaws' trail. Alarmed, Curnow behaved like a sympathizer while trying in his mind to form a plan to avert the atrocity.

Although eighteen hours had elapsed since Aaron Sherritt had been killed and there was still no police train, what should have been cause for great worry did not inhibit a raucous scene in Ann Jones's inn. With Dave Mortimer pumping a concertina, most of the prisoners danced, men with men since the women remained at the Stanistreet residence. The fun grew livelier as men lined up at the bar. Curnow played up to Ned while still trying to decide how to stop the Kellys.

By nightfall Sunday, twenty-four hours had passed since the murder. The train should have arrived hours earlier.

Curnow begged Ned to let him get his family and go home. "I assured him," Curnow recalled, "that he had no case for fearing me, as I was with him heart and soul." Ned sympathized with the teacher and his family and regarded him as harmless. Often ready to extend unmerited trust, he consented. Moreover, riding with the teacher's carriage would afford him the opportunity to take custody of the local policeman, Constable Hugh Bracken, who lived beside the road to Curnow's. Ned and Joe donned their armor and mounted, slinging their helmets over the necks of their horses.

Earlier, visiting his family at the Stanistreets', Curnow had noticed that his sister wore a bright red scarf. His plan began to form around the scarf. The armor-clad gang accompanied Curnow on the road as far as the home of Constable Bracken. After making him a prisoner, Ned turned to Curnow and said, "Go quietly to bed, and don't dream too loud." As Curnow's buggy rattled down the road, Ned and Dan, with Constable Bracken, turned back to the Jones inn.

After reaching home, Curnow hastily climbed the railway embankment behind the school and began to walk toward Benalla. He had scarcely begun the hike when he heard a locomotive laboring up the slope from Benalla. As the engine's headlamp came into view, Curnow lit a candle and held the red scarf in front of it. The engine slid past Curnow and, hauling only a single coach, came to a stop. The man in the coach shouted, "What's wrong?" "It's the Kellys," replied Curnow. The locomotive was a pilot preceding the train loaded with police. After Curnow told the engineer about the twisted rails and the planned execution of the police, he sounded short blasts of the whistle to warn the following train.

When Ned and Joe returned to the inn with Constable Bracken, they found the party still under way—dancing, drinking, and now singing. Ann Jones told her frail thirteen-year-old son to sing. He resisted, but finally, as the rest of the crowd grew silent, he sang "The Wild Colonial Boy," traditionally set to the strains of "The

Wearing of the Green." It was an appropriate metaphor for what the Kelly Gang hoped to achieve at Glenrowan.

As Ned talked with Constable Bracken, the women and children were brought from the Stanistreets' house, and the dancing and partying resumed. Ned tried to call the quadrilles but got confused. Dave Mortimer had been kept a prisoner when Curnow had been released. He then took over the dance from Ned. Ned cavorted happily around the room with Ann Jones and other women, even though he should have been deeply worried about the long delay of a response to Aaron Sherritt's murder. The dancing slowed as the children tired and were put to bed. After some verbal byplay between Ned and several men, especially Constable Bracken, Ned told the prisoners they could leave. First, however, Ned climbed on a chair to give what Anne Jones called a "lecture," although he spoke only a few innocuous words before he stepped down.

At this point, about 2:00 a.m. Monday, before any prisoners had left, Joe Byrne rushed in the back door and said, "The train's coming." Ned stopped all activity while he and the other three of the gang went to another room and donned their armor. When outfitted, they put on long smocks and rode their horses down to the railway. There they spotted the train, halted and with interior lights being extinguished. They rode back to the inn and instructed Ann Jones to put out all the lights. A second time they rode down to check on the train. This time, they made out the headlamp of the train slowly approaching, suggesting that the police had been warned. Meantime, Constable Bracken, who had slipped the front door key into his trouser cuff, went about the throng telling everyone to lie flat on the floor. As the train slid to a stop, Bracken unlocked the front door and ran to the train. "Over there," he shouted, "the Kellys—not five minutes ago—stuck us all up—the four of them—quick, quick."

Superintendent Hare had charge of the police. Heeding Bracken's "quick, quick," Hare yelled, "Let go the horses! Come on boys! They are at Jones's!" Confusion reigned. Not all heard Hare, while others tried to saddle their mounts and still others struggled to control frightened horses. Without pausing to organize an attack, Hare sprinted up toward the inn, followed by only a few men.

A bright moon above the Warbys cast the inn in shadow and illuminated the police. Ned stood in the dark at the end of the edge of the veranda, his three companions standing spread out on the veranda. As Hare raised his shotgun, Ned took aim with his rifle and fired. The bullet struck Hare's left wrist. "Good gracious," exclaimed Hare, "I am hit the very first shot."

From the veranda Dan, Joe, and Steve opened fire at policemen taking cover in a ditch and among a grove of trees. The police returned fire. "Fire away you bloody dogs," Ned shouted from behind his helmet, "you can't hurt us." He ventured down into the moonlight to fire again, but with his rifle raised, a bullet plowed through his bent left arm, inflicting four wounds. At the same time, another bullet hit his toe and exited at the heel. Despite the disabling wounds and profuse bleeding, he succeeded in making his way back to the inn.

The shattered wrist drove Superintendent Hare back to the railway platform, leaving no one in command. Although he returned to the battle line once, he remained only a few minutes. With the telegraph line buzzing with word of the Glenrowan fight, at shortly after 5:00 a.m. a special train from Benalla arrived bearing reinforcements but, perhaps more important, a better leader than Hare—Superintendent John Sadleir.

Throughout the night, the half-circle of thirty-four policemen in the front and to the left side of the inn aimed volleys that shredded the front of the inn and swept over and into the civilians. One of the first bullets struck Jack Jones, Anne Jones's young son. After the affair ended, Jack died in a hospital in Wangaratta. Two other men received mortal wounds. Someone shouted to the police to stop firing, women and children were inside. During a lull in the firing, the women and children made their escape, although one family encountered police fire and ran back to the inn.

Down at the railway crossing, Jack Lloyd, the member of the Lloyd clan closest to Ned, had been assigned the task of firing the rockets that would alert the sympathizers. He hesitated and then finally decided to fire two. Ned saw them and, although grievously wounded, resolved to ride down and, rather than risk the lives of his sympathizers, tell them to disperse. He would then return to rescue the other three members of the gang. Ned succeeded in this task and labored back to the inn. He entered to find Joe Byrne drinking at the bar. At that moment a police bullet smashed into Joe's groin and killed him.

Ned thought that Dan and Steve had escaped the inn and decided to challenge the police alone. Outside, up the slope near the paddock containing the horses, he met Tom Lloyd, who wanted to know where the others were. Ned then understood that Dan and Steve were still inside the hotel, but before he decided on his next move, he fainted from loss of blood. While Tom prepared Ned's pistols, he recovered enough to drag his hundred pounds of armor back down to the inn to save Dan and Steve.

As Ned made his labored way toward the inn, dawn brightened behind him, causing mist to rise from the ground. He looked to the police like some otherworldly monster. They fired at him, but the bullets simply bounced off the armor. Those that struck the helmet, however, produced bruises and two black eyes, as well as causing Ned to recoil. Ned fired back, although because of weakness from loss of blood and vision restricted by the eye slit in the helmet, his bullets went astray. Also, his wounded hand made it difficult to reload the only cartridge revolver he had and impossible to reload the cap-and-ball weapons. "Good shots, boys," he bellowed. "Fire away you buggers. You cannot hurt me."

At the same time, Dan and Steve took positions at the hotel and fired at the police. Bullets continued to bounce off Ned's armor as he made his way to a fallen gum tree he thought might offer a firing station. When almost there, his legs attracted the attention of nearby Sergeant Arthur Steele, who finally understood what the police confronted. He aimed his shotgun and sent a load of buckshot into Ned's right knee, then a second load into his hip behind the steel apron. "I'm done, I'm done," Ned gasped as he crashed to the ground at the gum tree.

He was not quite done. He had a revolver in his hand. Two officers grabbed his arms, but Ned thrust the hand with the pistol behind him and fired, grazing the side of Sergeant Steele's face. This was his last burst of strength, destroyed at last by twenty-eight wounds. A gathering group kept Ned pinned to the ground, his arms immobilized. Steele pulled off the helmet. "By God," exclaimed a policeman, "it's Ned." Steele, an old enemy, aimed his pistol at Ned's head, determined to kill him. But Constable Bracken, Ned's prisoner the night before, straddled the fallen Ned and, with shotgun ready, vowed "to shoot any bloody man that dares touch him."

None did, but an infuriated Dan Kelly rushed out of the inn firing at the group. Police fired back, but their bullets bounced off the armor. Finally one hit a leg, and Dan limped back into the inn. At the same time, Dr. John Nicholson attended Ned, as others removed his armor so the doctor could examine his body. Wrapped around his waist, Dr. Nicholson discovered the gold-fringed green sash Ned had been awarded as a youth in Avenel for saving young Dick Shelton from drowning.

That Ned had chosen this symbol of his youthful triumph for this day of reckoning, whether victory or defeat, demonstrates the significance he attached to the dream of an independent republic; the sash was green, the color of Ireland. More important, the sash may reveal a strong sense of who Ned believed he was or who he wished he had been. He had treasured this sash for many years, so it clearly meant something of continuing value to him, something more than a keepsake, something that went to the heart of his persona.

Nicholson believed that Ned had lost so much blood that he was certain to die. Nevertheless, Steele and Bracken helped Ned stagger down to the railway station. There he was laid out on a stretcher in the stationmaster's office. Superintendent Sadleir treated Ned with unusual kindness, helped make him comfortable, and saw to his other wants, mainly brandy and bread. Standing nearby was Chief Commissioner Standish, who had hurried up from Melbourne. He left matters to Sadleir.

At midmorning Monday, the police quit firing, and the remaining prisoners were told they could come out of the inn. They did, about thirty. That left Dan and Steve in the hotel, together with two wounded men. The police now had to decide how to get them out.

Monday lingered on quietly, with the inn cordoned by police but no one firing. Sadleir considered several options for getting Dan and Steve, including a cannon brought from Melbourne. Finally, in mid-afternoon, Constable Charles Johnston proposed setting fire to the inn. Sadleir approved and assigned the task to Johnston, who hurried off to find straw and kerosene to ignite the flammable building. Piling the straw against the west wall, he poured the kerosene on and struck a match. The straw smoldered, but the flame died. Once again Johnston lit the straw. This time it sprang to life and ignited the inside of the wall, where combustible wall and ceiling hangings quickly caught fire.

As crowds of curious people gathered in Glenrowan, the police tried to keep them restrained. Three other arrivals were significant: Ned's three sisters Kate, Grace, and Maggie Skilling. Catholic priest Matthew Gibney tried to persuade the sisters to get Dan and Steve to surrender. Only Kate agreed, but the police would not let her approach the burning inn.

In addition to Dan and Steve, two young boys lay in the inn. Father Gibney sprang through the flames and reached them. He found both dead. He could not reach Dan and Steve because the blazing ceiling hanging fell on them. He quickly retreated as the building burst into full flame. Almost immediately it collapsed. The burning corpses of Dan and Steve could be seen in the rubble. Police used a long pole to lift and pull them out. The corpses were carried down to the railway station, where Ned still lay in Stanistreet's office.

To avoid trouble, Sadleir released the bodies of Dan and Steve to Ned's sisters, who took them back to Greta for a wake. Ned and the body of Joe Byrne were loaded into a railway coach and speeded south to Benalla and then, for Ned, on to Melbourne. Here he was quickly spirited into the Melbourne gaol, safely out of Kelly country.

Although Ned's little army of sympathizers hung menacingly around Glenrowan, they accomplished no more than to worry the police. The design for a republic in northeast Victoria had collapsed in the flames of Ann Jones's inn. Even had Ned succeeded in wrecking the train and shooting the survivors, the design would still have collapsed. His contingent of sympathizers could hardly have contended with the forces of the government.

The immediate cause of the outcome at Glenrowan lay in two factors: first, in the failure of the four policemen in Aaron Sherritt's hut to emerge and raise the alarm, as Ned expected; and second, in the courage, ingenuity, and betrayal of Thomas Curnow in stopping the police train when it finally did arrive.

Even before the Glenrowan saga began as the police train slid to a stop before reaching the broken rails, Ned Kelly knew he had failed in his ambitious enterprise. He told his sympathizers that he had failed and to disperse and go home. In what amounted to a suicidal determination, the badly outnumbered gang resolved to fight to the end, which they did. The alternative was to give up. The gang had been outlawed by act of the Legislative Assembly for two years. Twice, in the Cameron and Jerilderie letters, Ned had tried to explain his thinking and his behavior. Both had failed. He regarded himself as unjustly treated by continued police harassment, and he deeply resented the imprisonment of his mother based on such trivial evidence as striking Constable Fitzpatrick on the head with a fire shovel. He knew that the authorities, backed by the large segment of the population that did not sympathize with him, would resort to any means, legal or not, to see him hanged. He preferred to go down fighting rather than endure that humiliation.

Under the terms of the Felons Apprehension Act, Ned could have been hanged at once, without further proceedings. Instead, the authorities strung his punishment out for almost six months to wring all the publicity possible from the drama. Humiliation or not, what they accomplished, combined with the spectacle of Glenrowan, laid the groundwork for the evolution of Ned Kelly into an Australian legend.

CHAPTER 24

Path to the Gallows

As Ned Kelly lay grievously wounded at the railway station in Glenrowan, he had already been launched on his way to being an Australian icon. Folklore, balladry, and widespread hero worship among the sympathizers of northeast Victoria had begun to lay the path. But Ned had also to travel the path to the gallows, a painful journey that would add to his stature as an icon.

* * *

Ned Kelly did not remain long in Glenrowan. The night of June 28, 1880, with Ann Jones's inn still smoldering, he was rushed aboard a train and taken to the Benalla lockup for the night. Commissioner Frederick Standish was there. He telegraphed Chief Secretary Robert Ramsay from Benalla seeking permission to transport Ned to Melbourne and lodge him in the Melbourne gaol. The normal destination would have been Beechworth, but Standish wanted to hasten Ned out of Kelly country as soon as possible. The cadre of sympathizers had not entirely disbanded yet. Even more than Standish, Chief Secretary Ramsay desired Ned Kelly to be under central government control. Ramsay entertained strong religious feelings that placed the Kellys far beyond redemption. He quickly authorized Standish to spirit Ned Kelly out of Benalla and thus the normal legal system.

When the morning train arrived in Benalla on June 29, an extra coach was attached. Ned was carried out to be loaded on the coach, escorted by six troopers, Superintendent Francis Hare, and Dr. Charles Ryan. A crowd had already gathered, anxious for a glimpse of the famous Ned Kelly. Emerging from the crowd, Kate Lloyd, Ned's sixteen-year-old cousin, bent over him with a handkerchief dabbing at tears and exchanged a few words with him. Kate had long been believed to be the only woman Ned truly loved, although evidence of a romantic relationship rests on rumor. On board the train as it steamed toward Melbourne, Dr. Ryan worked on the painful wounds in Ned's arm and leg. Ned endured the pain but never complained, said Ryan, but he was also "suffering from a severe mental shock, and moreover wants to die."

Word of Ned's approach had reached the public in Melbourne, and a crowd had gathered at the Spencer Street Station. But Ned had been taken off the train at the North Melbourne Station and hastened to the Melbourne gaol, a giant bluestone castle with massive gates. Here he was taken to the gaol hospital and placed under care of Dr. John Shields. A priest visited Ned and then went to the cell confining his mother, Ellen, and told her of Ned's apprehension and Dan's death. The next day, the gaol's governor, John Castieau, brought Ellen to see Ned, their first visit since she had been gaoled almost two years earlier. Neither displayed much emotion, probably because about a dozen people stood watching them. After twenty minutes Ellen was returned to the prison laundry, where she worked.

Ned was fortunate to be delivered into the custody of John Castieau, the gaol governor. He was a kind, thoughtful, and humane man with long experience as a gaol administrator. On several occasions he visited Ned in his cell. Not so admirable was the resident policeman, Sergeant Arthur Steele. He had played a major role in the pursuit of the Kellys and committed some indiscretions that later got him censured. At Glenrowan, for example, Steele had tried to kill the fallen Ned only to be stopped by Constable Bracken.

For Chief Secretary Ramsay and his subordinates, Ned's seizure alive opened a host of difficulties. Under the Felons Apprehension Act, he could be hanged at once, which everyone expected. But the act had expired with the adjournment of Parliament. Since few were aware of the complexities of the situation, Ramsay resolved to proceed with an ordinary criminal trial. Crown Solicitor Henry Gurner and Crown Prosecutor Charles Smyth were the two officials who would conduct the prosecution.

As further evidence of Secretary Ramsay's attitude, he forbade any visits from family or others without his written permission. His reasoning was that someone might slip Ned an instrument to help him escape, give him some poison to take his own life, or, most notably, to delay as long as possible the formation of a defense team.

Even so, late in July, Maggie Skilling, Ned's sister (separated from William Skilling and living with Tom Lloyd), engaged William Zincke, a Beechworth lawyer who had previous dealings with the Kellys. He traveled at once to Melbourne and talked with Ned, who was content to leave the preparation of his defense to Maggie.

Under the expert care of Dr. Shields, Ned's health steadily improved. His left arm remained useless, his hand clenched in a fist, while his right leg forced him to use crutches. Nevertheless, his spirits had revived, and he was pleased that a defense was taking shape.

Ned was due to appear at City Court on August 2 for a committal hearing on whether he should be placed on trial. But on July 31 a secret proceeding took place in the gaol's kitchen. Chief Secretary Ramsay, Henry Gurner, and Charles Smyth appeared before a police magistrate and, with Ned present, conducted the hearing in secret. Ned's attorney, William Zincke, had been informed of the meeting but had deliberately absented himself and had gone to Beechworth. He had recognized the case as a loser and planned to withdraw. The magistrate decreed that Ned be taken to Beechworth to face the committal hearing on August 6.

The next morning, Sunday, August 1, escorted by gaol governor Castieau and Sergeant Arthur Steele, Ned was helped into a hansom cab and driven through the gaol gates. A wagonette followed bearing three policemen, two of whom Ned knew well: Constables McIntyre (lone survivor of Stringybark) and Bracken (of Glenrowan notoriety). As soon as he recognized them, Ned said, "I suppose you fellows are going to hang me. There is McIntyre and I know he is going to do it."

At Newmarket Station, three miles north of Spencer Street Station, a light locomotive pulling a single car waited. A guards van (a small coach with a single brake operated by a "guard") stood in front and one in rear. Sergeant Steele helped Ned board the forward van and sat with him next to a window. Six troopers now stood guard. The train sped northward with Ned in a jocular mood. He pointed out his birthplace at Beveridge and took delight in the appearance of the Strathbogie Ranges. Passing Euroa, his disposition began to darken, and it grew darker still as the train labored up the steep grade into Glenrowan. Opposite the ruins of Anne Jones's inn, Ned pointed and declared, "A good man fell there." Sergeant Steele unwisely answered, "You weren't such good shots as you thought you were." Ned exploded and, despite his injuries, ripped off his jacket and flung it into Steele's face. The other troopers quickly wrestled Ned back into his seat.

At Beechworth late Sunday afternoon, the special train deposited Ned on the platform to be taken charge of by the gaol governor, Henry Williams. Escorted to the gaol, he was confined in an unheated cell to await the committal hearing. Williams had been troubled by Ned's lack of legal representation. William Zincke was no longer his attorney. When Maggie and Tom learned that Zincke had not been present at the kitchen hearing, they fired Zincke. At Beechworth Ned would be represented instead by David Gaunson, an accomplished and well-known Melbourne lawyer. Maggie and Tom had engaged him immediately after discharging Zincke.

Gaunson's motives are unclear. He was not a barrister and so could not plead Ned's case in the higher court that would try him for murder. The Beechworth committal hearing was routine and its outcome certain. Gaunson thought he could find a barrister in Melbourne who would not demand a high fee. In any event, Gaunson was deep into politics and may have believed an association with Ned Kelly would further his ambitions.

Gaunson hastened to Beechworth for the committal hearing. He was permitted to enter Ned's cell and interview him. Ned's response is a good indication of his state of mind as he approached the hearing:

All I want is a full and fair trial, and a chance to make my side heard. Until now, the police have had all the say, and have had it all their own way. If I get a full and fair trial, I don't care how it goes; but I know this—the public will see that I was hunted and hounded on from step to step; they will see that I am not the monster I have been made out. What I have done has been under strong provocation.

He had been trying to make his side known ever since the Cameron and Jerilderie letters, but they had achieved no effect. At Euroa, Jerilderie, and even Glenrowan, he had impressed people not as a monster but as a likable and courteous young man. He had indeed been hounded by the police and given provocation to perpetrate the Stringybark crime. The imprisonment of his mother was incitement enough. Now he professed not to care what his fate was. He knew the law enforcement establishment would succeed in leading him to the gallows. But first, he wanted to have his say.

* * *

The Beechworth hearing opened on the morning of August 6 in a packed courthouse. Magistrate William Foster sat on the bench, which was also occupied by Police Commissioner Standish. Since most of the witnesses would be subordinate policemen, this was a gross impropriety, objected to by Gaunson but unreported by the newspapers. Ned limped to his seat in the prisoner's dock.

As portrayed by the press, Ned made a handsome figure standing in the dock. Both hair and the beard covering his collar were neatly combed. His left hand clenched his coat collar, and his useless right hand rested on the dock's railing. He looked nothing like a bushranger or a larrikin but like a substantial citizen and businessman. He had appeared similarly on other occasions, notably Euroa and even Glenrowan. During the first hour of the hearing, lawyer Gaunson argued forcefully for a delay to give him time to prepare the defense. He knew little of the major events that had brought Ned to the dock. Exasperated, Foster finally granted a delay—he added an hour to the lunch break. Testimony of the principal Crown witness, Thomas McIntyre, lasted six hours, into the next day. As the sole survivor of Stringybark, only he knew what had happened, at least what he thought or wanted people to believe had happened. But much that he said did not coincide with the evidence. Gaunson had no basis for cross-examination to break down his falsehoods but nevertheless gave McIntyre a vigorous and painful cross-examination.

With a Sunday break, the proceedings dragged on through witness after witness (most of them policemen who could not help observing Victoria's top officer sitting beside the magistrate). To no one's surprise, on August 11, Magistrate Foster decreed that Ned Kelly would be placed on trial for the murder of Constables Lonigan and Scanlan (McIntyre had fled before Sergeant Kennedy was killed). The trial would take place in Beechworth early in October. Although expected, the prospect of a trial whose outcome was also expected threw Ned into a state of depression. He feared the effect it would have on his family, a feeling reinforced by the presence in the courtroom of two of his sisters. The next morning Ned was aboard a train taking him back to Melbourne gaol.

On September 18, Henry Gurner and Charles Smyth, the Crown prosecutors, appeared before the chief judge of the Victoria Supreme Court, Sir Redmond Barry, and requested a change of venue for Kelly's trial from Beechworth to Melbourne. In Beechworth, they argued, jurors might be intimidated or threatened. The change of venue was granted. Judge Barry announced that he himself would preside over the trial.

The chief judge could not be expected to preside in a nonpartisan manner. His decisions were severe, even vindictive. He had sentenced Ellen Kelly to gaol for attempting to murder a policeman when all she had done was hit him on the head with a fire shovel.

The judge had already made known his conviction that Ned Kelly deserved to die on the gallows. He openly demonstrated his belief that a different moral code applied to the likes of Ned Kelly and to his own class. He lived at the Melbourne Club and was widely known for his sexual and gambling proclivities. Ned faced a trial in which the Crown solicitor and prosecutor, Gurner and Smyth, as well as the presiding judge, would enjoy every advantage. The chief judge, moreover, was the ultimate authority; no avenue of appeal existed.

The trial opened on October 18. In the crowded courtroom Maggie Skilling, Ned's sister, had found a seat. Ned was led to the dock and asked how he pled, guilty or not guilty. He hesitantly glanced at the defense table, but no one sat there. On the third request, he mumbled, "Not guilty." In entering a plea, Ned had firmly locked himself into the judicial system. The prosecution no longer had to worry about the Felons Apprehension Act complicating their case.

Belatedly a man rushed to the defense table and explained his absence. His name was Henry Bindon, a Victorian who had been in London furthering his law credentials throughout the Kelly saga. Thus he knew nothing of the case and asked for a delay until November to prepare the defense.

Gaunson had been unable to find a Melbourne barrister willing to undertake the case for a price Maggie could afford. Although Bindon would serve as barrister, Gaunson remained an activist adviser throughout. He wanted Judge Barry replaced. Under the Supreme Court's rules, a move to November would shift the case to another judge. A hurried consultation among the prosecutors led the judge to commend them for their fairness to the defendant and to set the trial to open on October 28, ten days later. Unless concluded in one day, however, it would intrude on the holiday set for the running of the Melbourne Cup, but Judge Barry would continue to preside, Henry Bindon representing Ned.

With a jury of ordinary citizens seated, the judge resplendent in shoulder-length white wig and fur-trimmed red robe, and with Maggie Skilling and Kate and Tom Lloyd in the courtroom, the trial opened as scheduled on October 28. It lasted only two days. The

Crown paraded forth the same witnesses who testified at Beech-worth. Henry Bindon called no witnesses for the defense and conducted blundering cross-examinations of the Crown's witnesses. On the second day the testimony ended, and Judge Barry delivered the summing up. His rambling discourse violated some legal requirements and misled the jury in the Crown's favor. The jury retired and required only half an hour to reach the expected verdict: guilty of the murder of Constable Thomas Lonigan.

Following judicial precedent, the clerk of the court asked Ned if he had anything to say. "Well, it is rather late for me to speak now," he began. But he proceeded to state that on the evidence presented, the jury could have reached no other verdict. He lamented that he had not cross-examined the witnesses, but declared, "It is not that I fear death. I fear it as little as to drink a cup of tea." He blamed no one, he said, but only he knew the true story. He had not spoken because it might have looked like "flashness," "So I let it go as it was."

Now came the time for Judge Barry to pronounce the sentence. A few remarks would have conformed to custom and precedent. But Barry could not resist beginning with an extraordinary nonjudicial dialogue with the prisoner, one that drew the distinction between his class and Ned's. At one point, Barry intoned, "I do not think that anything I can say would aggravate the pain you must be suffering." "No," responded Ned. "I declare before you, God and man that my mind is as easy and clear as it possibly can be." "It is blasphemous for you to say so. You appear to revel in the idea of having put men to death." And so it went until Judge Barry moved to the next phase, the sentence.

"I have now to pronounce your sentence. You will be taken from here to the place from which you came, and thence on a day appointed by the Executive Council to a place of execution, and there you will be hanged by the neck until you are dead. May the Lord have mercy on your soul."

But Ned had the last word: "I will go a little further than that and say I will see you there, where I go." His rejoinder was prophetic. On November 23, 1880, barely two weeks after Ned's execution, Sir Redmond Barry died.

On November 3, the same day the Executive Council met, Ned dictated a letter to the governor of the Executive Council. The letter repeated all the arguments of the Cameron and Jerilderie letters but failed to reach the governor before the council convened. It would have made no difference. Judge Redmond Barry attended and blocked any attempt to interfere with the trial and sentence. The council set the day of execution as November 11, 1880.

Meanwhile, Ned's sisters and David Gaunson, who had not lost interest in Ned, organized petitions, street rallies, and public meetings seeking a reprieve from the hangman's noose for Ned. Night after night, with torches blazing, thousands of people marched in the streets of Melbourne to protest the execution of Ned Kelly. Typically, the press described them as "the laboring class," "idle and seedy." The mass protests were accompanied by a drive to get petitions for clemency signed. On November 5, four thousand people packed the Hippodrome while two to three thousand more gathered in the streets outside. They kept Melbourne astir but, despite a meeting with the governor himself, had no chance of gaining clemency for Ned. The execution would proceed despite all the protests. Notwithstanding the governor's ruling, the petition drive continued until the day set for Ned's execution. Gaunson, Maggie, and Kate presented 32,424 signed petitions to the governor's secretary. Gaunson declared that with more time, he could have obtained 60,000. That such vehement protests and street rallies existed at all, however, testifies to the growing iconic status of Ned Kelly.

In the gaol, as the day approached, gaol governor John Castieau took careful preparations to make certain nothing went wrong. He had been friendly with Ned, often visiting with him in his cell. Other personnel also disliked changing roles so suddenly from gaolers to executioners. Castieau tested every component of the process: the beam from which the rope hung, the strength of the rope, the exact specifications of the noose, the mechanism that opened the trapdoor, and the trapdoor itself. He ensured that the hangman, prisoner Elijah Upjohn, a big, strapping man, knew exactly the procedure.

As the end approached, Catholic priests ministered to Ned. He received them warmly and gave evidence that he had embraced his childhood religion once again. At night he could be heard humming and singing hymns from his past. Each night he sang his favorite, "Sweet Bye and Bye."

On the day before the 10:00 a.m. execution, Ned was allowed family visits. Castieau brought Ned's mother, Ellen, for a final farewell. She may have concluded with "I mind you'll die like a Kelly, son," or some such remark that has come down in folklore. Others came to say good-bye: family members Kate and Tom Lloyd, Jim, Kate, and Grace Kelly. Gaol governor Castieau brought his young son to meet the famed bushranger. Ned put his hand through the bars, laid it on the boy's head, and said, "Son, I hope you grow up to be as fine a man as your father." Two priests ended the parade, speaking at length with Ned. He had already made known that he believed in an afterlife, especially in his response to his sentencing by Judge Redmond Barry. One of the priests, Dean Charles O'Hea, lifelong minister to the family, would administer last rites in the cell immediately before the procession to the execution platform began.

Ned wanted a final picture for his family. The gaol photographer stood Ned against the gaol wall, with his hair and long beard combed, his useless right hand clutching his belt, his left holding up the cord tied to his leg-irons. It was a more realistic if less romantic portrait than the newspaper illustration made at Beechworth.

The night of November 10, Ned slept restlessly until 2:00 a.m., then soundly until 5:00. He awoke, rolled out of bed on his knees, and prayed for twenty minutes, then climbed back into bed. He arose at 8:00 and sang until a blacksmith came to remove his leg-irons.

At 9:00 he was escorted from the Condemned Cell through the gaol gardens to a cell that opened to the gallows platform. Inside, with door closed, Ned knelt and Dean O'Hea administered the last rites. Castieau knocked on the door and opened it. "The last hour has come," he announced. As the executioner, Elijah Upjohn, bound Ned's arms behind his back with a leather strap, Ned told him that was not necessary; moreover, it hurt his injured arm. With Upjohn in the lead, the procession formed. A novice priest held aloft a cross.

Ned walked next, flanked by gaol warders. Then came Dean O'Hea and another priest murmuring prayers. They walked out onto the gallows platform. Below, a crowd of witnesses gathered, including members of the press.

Ned stepped onto the trapdoor beneath the gallows. Upjohn had already positioned a white hood atop Ned's head. He now pulled it down over his face. Ned murmured something, but the hood muffled the sound and no one understood him. Even so, several remarks have made their way into the legend. "Such is life" is one of the most quoted; another is, "Ah, I suppose it has come to this." The noose was fitted around his neck, and a doctor checked the position. Upjohn pulled the lever springing the trapdoor, and Ned dropped eight feet. He died quickly, at the age of twenty-five.

The path to the gallows had ended beneath the gallows. During the entire drama, Ned displayed no apprehension. As he had remarked at his trial, he cared for his life as much as a cup of tea.

* * *

After cut down from the rope thirty minutes later, Ned Kelly's remains took another path, much grimmer than a cup of tea. His body was placed in a cart and pushed across the gaol courtyard to the deadhouse. The hood was removed to reveal a peaceful expression. The manager of Melbourne's waxworks shaved his hair and beard and made a mold for a death mask, which went on display at the waxworks the next day. Then a team of doctors and medical students took over. They sawed off Ned's head and extracted the brain, examined it carefully, and placed it in a jar of preservatives—its whereabouts unknown today. The head, stripped of flesh, vanished, as author Ian Jones states, presumably to serve as a paperweight for some government official. A newspaper described the next proceeding:

> The students particularly went in heavily taking part of the body and generally examining every organ. It was a ghastly sight—indeed, hardly ever paralleled. I am told that portions of the corpse are now in nearly every "curiosity" cabinet in

Melbourne medical men's places. The skull was taken possession of by one gentleman, and it is probable that hereafter he
may enlighten us on the peculiarities of the great criminal's
brain.

What remained was placed in a rough coffin and buried in the
Melbourne gaolyard, unmarked. When that mass grave closed in
1929, the bodies were reinterred in the Pentridge gaol mass graves.
When Pentridge was closed and partly demolished in 2009, the bodies were exhumed. One of the skeletons had no head. It was chosen
for scientific examination. In 2011, DNA tests run against a Kelly
descendant positively identified the headless skeleton as the remains of Ned Kelly. They were returned to the family and, in 2013,
buried in the Greta cemetery.

Although after 130 years Ned Kelly's grave site is a certainty, what
matters more than the resting place of his mortal remains is the
immortality he has demonstrated through all those years as Australia's premier legendary icon.

❊ CHAPTER 25 ❊
Australian Icon

Many modern Australians believe that Ned Kelly is the nation's only true hero. Others lament that he is a criminal blot on their history. But even the detractors cannot ignore him. That he is the focus of so much attention—almost worldwide—in all forms of media, as a tourist attraction, as a magnet of continuing controversy, as a creature of legend and myth, and as a topic the public cannot disregard qualifies him as a genuine Australian icon.

Most such icons carry a burden of legend and myth. Ned Kelly has been no exception. That he is widely perceived as Australia's only bona fide hero owes much to the legend that has evolved over the decades since 1880 and before. Even before his death, books, pamphlets, and articles in newspapers and magazines began rolling off the press. They celebrated Ned Kelly both for his exploits and his person; some portrayed him as the hero who robbed the rich and gave to the poor, while others condemned him as criminal bushranger rampaging around Victoria preying on banks and travelers.

None of this literature rose to the memorable. One, however, deserves mention. Peter Carey's *True History of the Kelly Gang* (2000) was a fictional retelling of Ned's life by Ned himself. It won the prestigious Booker Prize, which alone gives it high rank in Kellyana.

Other modern books featuring Ned Kelly are identified in the bibliographical essay.

Despite the mediocre early literature, legend stands behind reality. A real Ned Kelly did real things. The legend—a story, whether or not true, believed to be true—shapes modern beliefs more than the reality that only the few know.

That Ned Kelly is deeply embedded in Australian memory may be linked to the nation's convict origins. Aside from the Aboriginal peoples, the first Australians were convicts transported to Australia from England as punishment for crime. Convicts conceived many founding oral traditions, which expanded with each generation. Although he was a generation removed from the convict heritage, Ned Kelly and his exploits took their place in the growing body of oral tradition. "Game as Ned Kelly"—bold as Ned Kelly—is an Australian colloquialism used in everyday speech. They are integral to Ned Kelly folklore, understood by Australians but rarely by outsiders.

Transportation from England for crime no longer existed by 1850. Traditions of equality in economic, political, and social affairs took root and elevated many convicts to positions of prominence where the past could be conveniently forgotten. Mate and mateship evolved from the accompanying idea that people judge one another without reference to birth, class, or reputation. Thus Ned Kelly could be idolized without the onus of the convict past.

Ironically, the society developing in Australia stood in marked contrast to the rigid class society of Victorian England. Transport to Australia supposedly punished perpetrators of English crime. In Australia they found a land that was evolving a society of egalitarianism. Convicts did escape, to play their own role in the new society. To maintain subsistence, they took to outlawry in the bush and added their own word to the Australian vocabulary: "bushranger." Ned Kelly himself was for a time an apprentice bushranger. He stole cattle and sheep as acts of defiance against colonial oppression.

Ned's story took root with the first motion picture in 1906, *The Story of the Kelly Gang*. It was the first movie in the world to run sixty minutes. It was remade several years later. A noted film historian commented: "Notoriously, Henry Southwell cast Godfrey Cass as Ned Kelly in his first two Kelly films. Godfrey Cass was a beefy man, in his 50s at the time, and he did not grow a long bushy beard for the part. Nevertheless, I have to say, he brought more charisma to the role than anyone before 1970—even if it was a villainous, melodramatic charisma."

The same director, Henry Southwell, labored for fifteen years to turn out three more Kelly dramas: *The Kelly Gang* (1920), characterized as of "indifferent quality," *When the Kellys Were Out* (1923), and *When the Kellys Rode* (1934). Southwell encountered political sensitivities, with any pro-Kelly material liable to be banned.

Others followed, notably the controversial *Glenrowan* in 1951. As another Australian film critic described it:

The Glenrowan Affair features the bushranging exploits
of Ned Kelly and his "wild colonial boys" on their journey
of treachery, violence, murder and terror. Told from the
perspective of an aging Dan Kelly in present day Benalla,
[Rupert] Kathner presents the narrative as a factual retelling despite his obvious embellishment of the Kelly myth. The
production of the film generated more controversy than the
film itself due to creative fallouts between Kathner and the
film's original director, Harry Southwell . . . and the casting
of local football hero, Bob Chitty as Ned Kelly. . . . The Carlton strongman was cast as Ned Kelly in this movie by Rupert
Kathner, which was narrated by popular actor Charles "Bud"
Tingwell. The project was ambitious, but critics were not kind.

The two most notable modern movies, both titled simply *Ned Kelly,* were the 1970 production starring Mick Jagger and the 2003 drama starring Heath Ledger. Critics were not kind to Heath Ledger either.

Ballads were popular and, besides being widely sung, crowded the airwaves after the advent of radio in the 1920s. Balladry was a prominent feature of Mick Jagger's 1970 motion picture. One au-

thority labeled the ballads "anthems of defiance." A sample suggests
their content:

> Ned Kelly fought the rich men in country and in town,
> Ned Kelly fought the troopers until they ran him down;
> He thought that he had fooled them, for he was hard to find,
> But he rode into Glenrowan with the troopers close behind.
>
> "Come out of that, Ned Kelly," the head zarucker [police
>   trooper] calls,
> "Come out and leave your shelter, or we'll shoot it full of
>   holes."
> "If you'd take me," says Kelly, "that's not the speech to use";
> I've lived to spite your order, I'll die the way I choose!"
>
> "Come out of that, Ned Kelly, you done a lawless thing;
> You robbed and fought the squatters, Ned Kelly, you must
>   swing."
> "If those who rob," says Kelly, "are all condemned to die,
> You had better hang the squatters, for they've stolen more
>   than I."
>
> "You'd best come out, Ned Kelly, you done the government
>   wrong,
> For you held up the coaches that bring the gold along."
> "Go tell your boss," says Kelly, "who lets the rich go free,
> That your bloody rich man's government will never govern me."
>
> They burned the roof above him, they fired the wall about,
> And head to foot in armour, Ned Kelly stumbled out;
> Although his guns were empty he made them turn and flee,
> But one came in behind him and shot him in the knee.
>
> And so they took Ned Kelly and hanged him in the jail,
> For he fought singlehanded although in iron mail.
> And no man singlehanded can hope to break the bars;
> It's a thousand like Ned Kelly who will hoist the flag of stars.

Art has assumed a prominent role, none more so than Sydney Nolan's series of twenty-five paintings dating from 1946–47 and now displayed in the National Gallery of Australia in Canberra. The Nolan paintings are unique if not iconic—featuring Nolan's own surrealistic style. Most of the episodes of Ned's life are represented, in all of them with Ned's head symbolized by a black rectangular box with eye slits, designed to suggest his moldboard helmet. The Nolan paintings are admired throughout Australia as representing the heritage of Ned Kelly as well as the nation.

As the British Empire waned after World War II and British institutions in Australia lost their power, Australians sought a uniquely Australian national identity. Before the 1960s, the colonial governments opposed the legend of Ned Kelly in all its manifestations. Kelly movies that were judged to portray the police unfavorably were banned. The Victoria Police Force had evolved by midcentury into a highly competent organization, hardly representative of the police of Ned Kelly's time. Those troopers deserved to be shown unfavorably, yet the government suppressed what should have been a matter of free speech.

In the 1960s, however, the government changed its attitude. A powerful nationalistic movement began in that decade, as the government and the people groped for Australian meaning to fill the void left by the decline of British influence. Ned Kelly became part of the new national identity, cultivated by all levels of government, cultural and historical institutions, and commercial enterprises. His image has grown year after year since the 1960s.

Tourists, foreign and domestic, cannot avoid Ned Kelly. Every town or site with even remote connections showcases the Ned Kelly story. Glenrowan exploits the final shootout between the police and the Kelly Gang. A tourist center tells the story, and cutout fiberglass figures represent the police and the gang. A statue of Ned clad in armor dominates the town. It has been stolen and replaced so often that a fence surrounds it. Glenrowan enjoyed its moment in the sun in July 1970, with the world premiere of the film featuring Mick

Jagger. Visitors were greeted with a long canvas sign proclaiming WELCOME TO THE REPUBLIC OF VICTORIA—FIRST PRESIDENT NED KELLY.

Stringybark is not as easy to get to as Glenrowan, but a plaque and a "Kelly tree" mark the site.

For all the government's promotion of Ned Kelly, it has badly neglected historic preservation. Ned's boyhood home in Beveridge has been allowed to fall into ruin. One finds hardly anything left of the rude buildings in Greta that housed Ned and his family. The Euroa bank is gone.

The exception is Beechworth, which is especially notable for its surviving buildings associated with Ned Kelly and its visual integrity as a historic town.

Melbourne displays many Ned Kelly venues, especially the Old Melbourne Gaol, with Ned's cell and the platform trapdoor where he was hanged. A suit of armor stands next to the plaque explaining the hanging.

The widely publicized Ned Kelly Trail describes a dozen of the most important places in Ned Kelly's life. Guides to the trail are widely available in printed form and on the Internet.

Especially symbolic of Ned is his suit of armor, replicas of which appear in many museums and many sizes for sale. Parts of the original suit were taken by police at Glenrowan as souvenirs. The State Library of Victoria succeeded in locating all the parts and reassembled them. The suit is now on display in the library, along with other Kellyana, including the Jerilderie letter. The library is located in Melbourne.

Another significant symbol is the long green sash with gold trim awarded to Ned for saving the young Shelton boy from drowning in Avenel. He wore it around his waist in the final battle in Glenrowan. The sash may be viewed today in a museum in Benalla.

For the truly engaged, one can purchase an honorary membership in the Ned Kelly Fan Club.

Like many famous people, the Ned Kelly story has its own conspiracy theory. Ned of course is dead, but Dan Kelly and Steve Hart were burned beyond recognition in the fire that leveled Anne Jones's inn. That opened the possibility that somehow they had escaped. The story most quoted is that both wound up in South Africa and fought in the First Boer War.

Genuine and fake artifacts represent the Ned Kelly story in reasonable fashion, but other commercial offerings border on the absurd. Examples: "Ned Kelly Outlaw Whiskey," "Old Ned" aftershave lotion, "Glenrowan Beer Shampoo," which was shampoo sold in a beer bottle. The marketing of Ned Kelly constantly expands.

* * *

In these multiple ways, the legend of Ned Kelly undoubtedly will live forever. Whether heroic or not, Ned Kelly remains a shining Australian icon.

CONCLUSION

This book originated in the desire to seek the comparison of Billy the Kid and Ned Kelly that suggested itself during my visit to the Old Melbourne Gaol in 1999. The substance for such a comparison is contained in the previous biographical treatments of the two men. The comparisons and differences derive from those biographies. A few brief observations of Billy and Ned establish a basis for a more detailed examination.

Billy the Kid was a skilled horseman and gunman. After the escape from the burning McSween house in Lincoln, he also displayed qualities of leadership. Ned Kelly was a skilled horseman, too, but not a gunman. His leadership of the Kelly Gang was outstanding, more so than Billy's of his followers.

Billy was fun-loving, Ned less so. Ned, however, could extract humor from some of his escapades.

Billy made little effort to be polite and solicitous of other people, except Hispanics. Ned was unfailingly polite and caring, especially to women.

Billy was never noted for generosity; he was self-centered. One of Ned's central traits was generosity. Much of the proceeds from his bank robberies went to impoverished Irish sympathizers.

Billy acted on impulse. He had one long-term goal: to set up a ranch with a friend. But that slipped into obscurity and was never pursued. Ned, on the other hand, thought constantly of the future and set goals that he worked toward. The most ambitious, of course, was to establish a republic in northeast Victoria.

Ned's attempt to create a republic ended with defeat at Glenrowan. If his sympathizers had not been halted by Ned, they might have risen in guerrilla warfare. Billy's involvement in the Lincoln County War was just that—a soldier in war. He probably did not understand that the conflict was war, any more than Ned understood what war would involve had not Glenrowan intervened.

Billy's one known serious romance was with Sallie Chisum, daughter of the reigning cowman on the Pecos River. When she vanished from the scene, Billy truly loved none of his paramours, although they eagerly sought his affection. His sexual relationships undoubtedly scattered some descendants in the Fort Sumner area, and a sexual rendezvous led to his death. Ned Kelly is believed to have loved only one woman, his cousin Kate Lloyd. His courtesy and kindness to all women won him admiration but not romantic liaisons.

Billy's legacy was legend loaded with myth, which inspired decades of literature, movies, and other forms of media. Ned's legacy was legend but not as many myths as Billy spawned. Ned was a man of quality. He expertly maneuvered through his outlaw years. He tried repeatedly to explain to the public what had driven him to outlawry. Unrealistically, he plotted an uprising of sympathizers that would lead to a republic in northeast Victoria. His twin aims in this enterprise were to uplift the downtrodden Irish and to rid Kelly country of the English queen's hated police and apparatus of justice. He went to his death with dignity.

Billy the Kid was a teenager who never matured. He acted as he pleased at the moment, not thinking of the consequences or the future—such as his return to Fort Sumner and the sheriff's pistol instead of fleeing to Mexico and freedom after escaping from Lincoln. He is widely regarded as a well-known if not important figure out of western American history, but by almost no one as a hero. He was simply a young fellow who knew how to ride a horse and shoot rifle and pistol. He was brave enough to engage in shootouts with the law, and clever enough to engineer a daring escape from confinement before hanging. Unlike Ned Kelly, he died because he paused a split-second before firing at the sheriff hidden in a darkened bedroom. The sheriff fired first.

Both Billy and Ned had several traits in common. They possessed charisma. Billy was always the happy, smiling, joking youth, charming everyone he associated with. Ned also was charismatic—kind, generous, and concerned for his fellow citizens, especially women. Both demonstrated novelty that caught people's eye. Billy twice escaped by climbing up a chimney—first by fleeing Sheriff Whitehill's jail, again when trapped in a cabin surrounded by soldiers. Ned attracted universal attention by "telling his side of the story" and by fashioning suits of armor for the final reckoning.

Both Billy and Ned have been colorfully and imaginatively painted by an American painter. Thom Ross of Santa Fe, New Mexico, has rendered scores of likenesses of both men, including items inserted for their symbolism. Ross, moreover, paints on multiple media, including plywood, an exceedingly difficult base for painting. The Australian Sydney Nolan painted only Ned. Thom Ross painted them both.

* * *

Both Billy and Ned revealed much about themselves and their environment during the three stages of their lives: their youth, their early manhood, and their outlaw years. Such an examination helps answer the question of why these two men appeared at the same time half a world apart. Environment, culture, and the times contribute much to the answer. More meaningful comparisons emerge from these details.

Henry McCarty (one day to be known as Billy the Kid) experienced a vastly different youth than Ned Kelly. Henry and his brother followed their widowed mother, Catherine, from New York west and finally, in 1873, wound up in Silver City, New Mexico, a mining town where Henry's new stepfather hoped to find wealth.

Henry was now Henry Antrim, taking his stepfather's name. He dearly loved his mother, who, declining with tuberculosis, often took to bed. But she exerted an influence on him even after the family settled in Silver City. At first, she was healthy enough to provide bed and board, bake cakes for sale, and take in laundry. She also attended dances. A friend remembered Catherine as "a jolly Irish lady, full of life, fun, and mischief." That Henry was so popular and well-behaved as a youth before she took to her bed suggests that Catherine McCarty Antrim was a good mother. Henry seems not to have had much feeling for William H. H. Antrim, nor did Antrim for Henry. With his mother dying and his stepfather looking for riches, Henry did as he pleased. His friends remembered him as a slender, good-looking young fellow, always ready for fun and for pranks. He liked to sing and read. He starred in a minstrel show. But he was on his own, with no family life. His mother died in September 1874, when he was fifteen. His stepfather disappeared for long periods and when present ignored Henry. Despite lacking any family life, he remained a popular youth in Silver City—until he got in trouble that landed him in the Silver City jail. His escape and flight to Arizona opened a new phase in the life of Henry Antrim.

Henry Antrim's brief Silver City years reveal a youth with potential to grow into a mature, productive adult. A concerned mother and father would have helped ensure such an outcome. But lacking true parents, he failed to receive the guidance that would have facilitated the process. Instead, after his Arizona adventure, he took up with men who showed him a new life that overcame the potential of the Silver City years.

Ned Kelly's youthful years bore little resemblance to Henry Antrim's. Ned was a member of an ever-expanding family—he had eight siblings by the time of his father's death. Henry McCarty had only a brother, and they seem not to have been close. With the death of his father, John "Red" Kelly, in 1866, Ned became the head of the household and played that role faithfully and efficiently. After Henry's mother died, he became essentially a loner. In Arizona, after his escape from the Silver City jail, Henry indulged in horse stealing, his first genuine crimes. Killing Windy Cahill was judged a crime but was committed in self-defense. Ned, on the other hand, early became expert at cattle and sheep "duffing," as Australians labeled livestock theft. As Ned acquired a sense of the bush, Henry came to know only the areas of his roaming in southwestern New Mexico and eastern Arizona. In later years Henry would know a much larger area intimately: all southeastern New Mexico.

In Ned's early years he developed lasting personality traits. He firmly bonded with family and clans, as well as his closest friends. He matured more quickly than normal by assuming adult responsibilities. He was protective of his sisters and helped his mother, Ellen, improve her selection. His loyalty to his mother led him to offer to surrender to the law in exchange for her release from prison—in effect giving up the rest of his adult life. He set one prominent goal: to free his Irish compatriots from the queen's rule.

Ned briefly attended two schools long enough to become literate. In school he liked the competition of outdoor sports and engaged in them intensively. Henry also attended school long enough to become even more literate than Ned, but he did not participate in sports. The physical commitment to sports helped Ned grow tall and muscular, leading people to believe he was older than he was. Henry was active enough on horseback, especially in his brief ranch work in Arizona, to keep him physically fit.

At age twelve, Ned rescued young Richard Shelton from drowning, an act that made him the town hero. At the same age, Henry Antrim, newly arrived in Silver City, confronted no such emergency. Had he been in Ned's place, witnessing an emergency requiring quick and heroic action, he was not likely to have taken a chance, or even thought of it. That Ned took quick and heroic action revealed him as a youth of more intellectual power, courage, awareness of the value of human life, and personal substance than Henry.

In Silver City, Henry was exposed to virtually no family life. His dying mother exerted enough influence to inspire love in her son, but she could muster the strength to do little more; and besides, she died little more than a year after the family arrived in Silver

City. Henry's stepfather exerted no influence over his stepson, who in escaping to Arizona separated himself permanently from parental oversight and affection. Ned by contrast had not only a father and mother whom he loved but a large family and interlocking clans scattered around Kelly country. Neither father nor mother extended any supervision but left him to make his own way. With many family members and friends, that was easy and had a strong effect on who he was and would become.

Both Henry and Ned emerged from Irish backgrounds. The McCartys were Irish immigrants who landed in New York. Their life there is unknown, but a widowed Catherine McCarty headed west and, with a new husband, settled in Silver City. Therefore, Henry Antrim's heritage was Irish, although he did not cherish it nor probably even know of it.

Ned's Irish heritage was a dominant influence in his life. He was proud of it, boasted of it, and fought for it. His father was transported from Ireland for an English crime. In Ned's youth, his father passed on his love of Ireland and its people and his hatred of Queen Victoria's oppression of the Irish, both in Ireland and in Australia. Early in his life Ned's Irish patrimony became a major element of his personal identity.

Religion meant nothing to Henry Antrim. He doubtless gave no thought to it and its ramifications. In his circle of acquaintances, religion played hardly any role. In Australia, however, Protestant and Catholic feuded incessantly. To be Irish in Australia meant to be Catholic. Ned Kelly was a lifelong Catholic, but until near his death religion seems to have meant little to him. The Irish Catholic identity of many of his friends, however, involved him in the quarrels with Protestants.

Ned's involvement with the law and the police began with his brief role as an apprentice bushranger. Thereafter, he was constantly in trouble with the police, who targeted him as a troublemaker who had to be constantly watched and dragged into the police station for the slightest offense. Henry Antrim lived in a milieu where law enforcement was rudimentary if it even existed. Henry's experience with Sheriff Harvey

Whitehill brought him into connection with the only lawman in Silver City. In later years Henry would encounter more lawmen, but nothing approaching the number that harassed Ned Kelly.

For both Henry and Ned, the place where they lived their early years exerted an influence. Henry lived in the mountain world of Silver City. He was a popular lad, and after his adventures in Arizona, where he killed his first victim, he could have remained in Silver City. He might have become a miner or further developed his outlaw proclivities that had taken root during his time in Arizona. But Henry did not remain in Silver City, and the wild land east of the Rio Grande became his country. In Silver City, full of miners and entrepreneurs and cramped by mountains, he would not have had the freedom to behave in a fashion that produced Billy the Kid. He probably would not have been known beyond Silver City's mountains.

Ned Kelly's youthful homeland was the bush of northeast Victoria. The bush put few limits on Ned. Forested mountain ranges, substantial rivers, and rolling plains gave Ned space to roam, pursue pleasures, and commit deeds of outlawry. In contrast to urban areas, the bush was lightly populated. Except for the railroad, development had yet to encroach. Towns along the railroad afforded Ned opportunities to mix with people when he wanted but also places where he had to confront the police and the courts.

Like Billy and Silver City, this place could have produced a different man than Ned became. Had his father not moved out of the vicinity of Melbourne, Ned may have mixed with youth his own age in the city. Gangs were prevalent, and vice was rampant. Would he have succumbed to that life or grown into the man he did farther north in Kelly country? Melbourne's lure would have been substantial, but his obligations to family were strong. Reinforcing family, he may have resisted out a sense of revulsion or to be true to values already taking root as he moved north.

The youthful years of Henry Antrim and Ned Kelly, roughly fifteen and younger, reveal two active, physically fit, literate youngsters destined for a life of occasional outlawry. Both in New Mexico and in Australia, outlawry depended on what authority happened to be defining outlawry. What constituted a broken law turned on the lawman's knowledge of the law or even personal bias. Thus Ned incurred the enmity of the police, often for spurious reasons. Henry, as he morphed into Billy, encountered lawmen pursuing a personal or factional vendetta or acting out of simple ignorance. But the boys' youth set them on a collision course with the law. Few youths in either setting, New Mexico or Victoria, entered early manhood with the influences and experiences that Henry and Ned carried with them from their young years. This background equipped both to lead even more adventurous lives as they approached maturity.

For Ned Kelly and Henry Antrim, early manhood occurred at different ages. Ned was only fourteen when he embarked on this period of his life. Henry Antrim, soon to be known as Billy Bonney, was eighteen at a comparable time in his life. At fourteen, Ned was an accomplished horse breaker, log splitter, fence builder, stonemason, and carpenter. At this age he chose a life of intermittent crime. Billy was eighteen when he blundered into a group of outlaws. He was a good horseman and expert with rifle and pistol; guns obsessed him all his life. Beyond that, he lacked the many abilities that Ned, four years younger, had achieved.

By chance, at Silver City, Billy fell in with a gang of outlaws called "The Boys." Billy traveled with The Boys as far as the Pecos River in eastern New Mexico. He obtained a good feel for the country in which he operated the rest of his life, but he also discovered that the blatant outlaw life of The Boys was not for him. Even so, southeast New Mexico, Lincoln County, was now Billy the Kid country.

Lincoln County consisted of a mountain world and a plains world. Billy functioned in both. Lincoln, the center of his life, nestled among the mountains. Fort Sumner, beside the Pecos River in the plains below, was a frequent resort. Both were important in shaping his life. Lincoln gave him the freedom to use his skill with rifle and pistol in a culture of violence. Fort Sumner was a refuge from the law and a place to indulge his love of pleasure. This land, so wild and lightly populated, allowed him to go where he wanted and do what he wanted, always on horseback. The country strengthened his inbred free spirit and his self-centeredness.

The population of Lincoln County consisted mainly of Anglos and Hispanics. Hispanics, commonly called "Mexicans," lived in villages and the valleys draining east into the Pecos, some for generations. With primitive but time-honored methods, they tilled the soil and, in the canyons and on the mesas, herded sheep and goats. With sheep and goats, Hispanics also dwelled in small villages on the Pecos River.

Billy related warmly to the Hispanics and they to him. They afforded him friendship, pleasure, and if necessary refuge from the law. His special friends were at Fort Sumner and San Patricio. Hispanics formed a sort of surrogate family, welcoming and hiding Billy when he was in trouble, providing the pleasures he longed for, communicating in their language, and harboring none of the bias of other Anglos, especially Texans.

Anglos, many Civil War veterans, began arriving in Lincoln County after the war. They too farmed and raised cattle. Many acquired Hispanic wives or, in the absence of clergy and to avoid the license fee, "partners."

The army at Fort Stanton was a small but influential part of the population. The officers and men were largely a closed society, rarely socializing with other Anglos. They did, however, play a conspicuous part in the Lincoln County War, as well as in pursuing outlaws and lending their jails to civilian lawmen. The commanding officer of Fort Stanton targeted Billy as an especially bad outlaw and used his authority to aid lawmen in trying to capture him.

The cowboy gunmen on the Tunstall ranch became Billy's comrades in the Lincoln County War. Richard Brewer employed him on the Tunstall ranch and demonstrated how ranches were run as well as how to take orders from authority. More direct was lawyer Alexander McSween. Under McSween's oversight, Billy rode with the Regulators until the end of the Lincoln County War. Like Brewer, McSween represented authority, and Billy respected it until, in the burning McSween house, the lawyer lost whatever courage he possessed and followed the Kid's bidding. All the Regulators gave Billy comradeship and the opportunity to display his skills with rifle and pistol. Finally, in the last days of the Regulators, the remaining few acknowledged him as their leader.

Territorial governor Lew Wallace, headquartered in Santa Fe, came to Lincoln and sought out Billy. Wallace wanted Billy to testify to a murder he had seen committed; he persuaded Billy to testify in exchange for freedom. Billy obliged, but the governor failed to keep his part of the bargain. Billy turned to outlawry, making it impossible for Wallace to keep his promise. From his jail cell, Billy revived the correspondence, even hinting at blackmail. The relationship with the governor stamped Billy as a young man who was so self-centered and politically naive that he did not understand how his actions made an enemy of Governor Wallace.

In 1869, Ned Kelly, at fourteen, had served as an apprentice to Harry Power, a famous bushranger, and learned the techniques of robbing travelers. He served in this role twice, while the police tried to identify who rode with Power. At the same time, he became a larrikin, the young men whose dress and insolent behavior infuriated the police. Billy would not have thought of taking on a new identity such as that offered by the larrikins. At the Tunstall ranch, he did the job for which he was paid, his only diversion a preoccupation with rifle and pistol. Like Ned, however, he was well liked by his associates.

At fifteen, Ned got into trouble in a controversy over a stolen horse. A policeman perjured himself, and Ned was sentenced to three years' hard labor. From 1871 to 1874, ages sixteen to nineteen, Ned sat in jail. Not until near the end of his life did Billy see the inside of a jail.

Billy's role in the Lincoln County War was as a gunman for Tunstall and, after his murder, lawyer Alexander McSween. The drawback was that the county sheriff, William Brady, was an ally of the opposition. To remove this obstacle, Billy participated with five others in the assassination of Sheriff Brady. In jumping over the wall and approaching the sheriff's body, Billy demonstrated courage and boldness as well as recklessness. The consequence was a bullet in his thigh. The year was 1878, Billy's age eighteen.

Influences playing on Billy the Kid and Ned Kelly had much to do with the times in which they lived. For Billy and Ned, the times were the late nineteenth century, roughly 1875–85. In the United States, industrialization had begun to eliminate the western frontier, but the American Southwest of Billy's time still retained its essential frontier characteristics: lightly populated mountains and plains, still untrammeled by the influx of people. Billy could roam freely, unhampered by the trappings of industrial civilization. The freedom afforded by the times and the place therefore reinforced Billy's sense of independence and self-regard. They opened the way for his form of behavior, which would not have been possible even two decades later. The times also endowed him with the power to project himself as legend and myth into the distant future.

The culture of Lincoln County was dominated by violence. Billy the Kid's guns fit well into the Anglo culture, including Texans. A six-shooter hung from almost every man's belt, a Winchester in a boot strapped to his saddle. These weapons were not there for show but for use, and they were used somewhere nearly every day. The Lincoln County War was only one manifestation of the prevalence of violence. Other, lesser fights occurred, with gunfire the medium for settling disputes. An example is the so-called Horrell War of 1872–73, pitting Texans against Hispanics.

Texans moving north up the Pecos with cattle brought their own brand of violence, fueled by resentment over the outcome of the Civil War and the iniquities of federal Reconstruction in Texas. They disliked Hispanics and Indians alike, and detested black soldiers.

The culture also relied on whiskey. Nearly every man drank every day, so nearly every man was more or less intoxicated most of the time. Whiskey led to fights and fighters resorted to six-shooters. Everyone was quick to resent a perceived insult and to settle scores with their firearms. "I'll die before I'll run" was the motto Texans brought with them from Texas.

Few murderers paid the ultimate price. Lawmen and courts took a lenient view of mayhem that ended in death. Even so, hangings were frequent enough to qualify as public events. Citizens of Lincoln anticipated the hanging of Billy the Kid, only to be disappointed by his spectacular escape.

Six-shooter and Winchester symbolized the paramount culture of Lincoln County and also much of the western frontier. Billy the Kid shared that culture but not as fully as most Anglos. He rarely if ever drank, so he was always sober. This proved advantageous when facing off against an antagonist who was drunk, as when he killed Joe Grant.

Ned Kelly did not live in a culture of violence comparable to Billy the Kid's. He resorted to violence only when he believed it justified.

Australia's citizens drank intoxicants, often excessively. Drunks were a common sight among the people. In every town, and scattered through the countryside, pubs did a rousing business. Ned Kelly's mother often conducted a "sly grog" business—selling liquor without a license. Drinking in northeast Victoria was not comparable to Billy the Kid's country, where as a matter of custom drinking occurred throughout the day—leading to constant inebriation. Ned himself drank, but never to the point of intoxication.

Northeast Victoria, with its sparse population, lived by two different cultures, that of the Squatters and that of the Selectors. Squatters, mostly English, arrived first and leased public lands from the government. Selectors, a large number Irish, took advantage of new land laws that permitted people to take out a selection of land and meet the legal requirements before acquiring title. Poverty afflicted most of the Selectors. Their rude habitations alone dictated a rough way of life: large families, closely tied together, bold in confronting adversity, struggling to keep food on the table, stealing cattle, sheep, and horses from the Squatters, confronting police harassment. Selectors believed that the Squatters, backed by the government, sought to oppress them at every opportunity, even obstructing them from meeting the terms of their selection and thus forcing them into default in their obligations. In these circumstances, Selectors clung together to fight off what they believed were the threats of the Squatters and the police.

Religion and ethnicity played a large part in the culture of northeastern Victoria. Most of the Squatters were English Protestants, the Selectors Irish Catholics. Not only profound doctrinal differences created tensions between the two. English Protestants regarded Irish Catholics as traitors to England and the queen. The Irish Catholics, having endured the queen's oppression in Ireland, regarded the Protestants with abhorrence. Contrasting doctrines inevitably poured over into the schools, creating further conflict. In northeast Victoria, the fondest dream of the Irish was to rid the land of the English and the queen's rule.

The lightly populated bush of Ned Kelly's time, both mountain and plain, produced a young man immensely different from his counterparts in urban Melbourne. He was free to roam a large countryside, unrestrained by any feature of bush landscape or culture. He did so, acquiring an intimate knowledge that served him well as he entered his outlaw years. In moving north to Avenel, Red Kelly ensured that his sons grew up products of the bush—and also retain their father's deep Irish roots. The bush and its Irish population created the stage and players on which Ned made his name known throughout Australia. In viewing Ned Kelly bush and Irish loom large.

The economy of Billy the Kid country relied on agriculture and livestock. Anglos and Hispanics practiced both. Corn, wheat, and beans were the principal crops. On the plains, cattle grazed on the abundant grass, leaving agriculture to the Hispanics living in villages farther up the Pecos River. Hispanics herded sheep instead of cattle.

American industrialization featured large corporations holding a corner on their products and services. Monopoly was common to the times. Lincoln County's economy was controlled by a monopoly—the "big store," better known simply as "The House," belonging to Lawrence G. Murphy. Murphy bought all the agricultural produce and much of the beef to fill contracts with the army at Fort Stanton and the Mescalero Apache Indian Agency. He set the price for what he bought and for what he sold. The people of the county had no choice on his terms. As one critic charged, "L. G. Murphy & Co. were absolute monarchs of Lincoln County and ruled their subjects (farmers & ranchers & others) with an oppressive iron heel."

The arrival of a competitor, John H. Tunstall, set off the Lincoln

County War of 1877–78. Murphy's successor, James J. Dolan, conducted the war and managed the store, which continued to control the economy until after the war.

Nationally, industrialization relied heavily on fraud and corruption. Reflecting the nation's "gilded age," on a smaller scale Murphy and Dolan manipulated Lincoln County's economy through fraudulent techniques in supplying contracts with the army and Indian agency. Corruption was rampant locally as it was nationally. Billy must have been aware of the corruption, but it touched him hardly at all.

In Ned Kelly country, the pastoral scene remained undisturbed. Wool from sheep and, where land was fertile, crops of wheat defined the economy. The railroad improved the economy by affording quick access to markets. Population increased slightly as new land laws allowed selection of parcels of limited acreage for agriculture. In addition to sheep, cattle and horses grazed the land. Horses were prized possessions and the object of widespread theft.

The economy of both Victoria and New South Wales still retained its heritage of the great gold rush that began in 1851 at Bathurst in New South Wales and followed at Ballarat and Bendigo in Victoria. The gold rush was a defining moment for the people of Australia. By Kelly's time, gold had trickled as an export, but "diggers" could still find enough gold to make it profitable. In Kelly country, gold deposits surrounded Beechworth, and diggers frequently exploited them. In his refuge high in the Wombat Ranges, Ned and his companions, when in residence, dug for gold, but the returns were seldom rewarding.

Unlike Billy the Kid country, mercantile corruption was not an important issue in Kelly country. Corruption was confined to the police, who often, in the name of official harassment, simply removed from a residence whatever they fancied. The Irish in particular were targeted by the police, none more so than the Kellys. Although the force contained some Irish police officers, most were English with their traditional contempt for the Irish. Officers brought false charges and perjured themselves on the witness stand. Some were not immune from bribery. Confined largely to the police, corruption in Kelly country never attained the huge scale of Billy the Kid country.

For both Billy and Ned, early manhood involved them in criminal activities and prepared them for the outlaw life that followed. For Billy, early manhood never led to manhood. By the time of his death, he was still essentially a youth, but a youth capable of committing crime. For Ned, outlaw life began when he was still a youth and continued until outlawry became an enforced way of life.

In October 1878, Ned Kelly collided once more with the police, this time with deadly consequences. A corrupt policeman created an incident that led to the charge of attempting to murder a policeman, leveled at Ned, his brother Dan, and their mother. Ned and Dan took refuge in the mountains while their mother was convicted and jailed. Police roamed the ranges looking for Ned and Dan. On October 25, 1878, with two comrades, Joe Byrne and Steve Hart, Ned and Dan ambushed a police party at Stringybark Creek and killed three. When they later failed to surrender as ordered, by a rare act of the Legislative Assembly the four were outlawed. Such was the rest of Ned Kelly's life. He was a month shy of twenty-four.

Earlier in the same year, 1878, a grand jury in Lincoln indicted a host of participants in the Lincoln Country War, including Billy Bonney. Like Ned Kelly but under the contrasting American judicial system, Billy was outlawed—but not until he could stand trial. Before that could take place, the law had to catch him. In the next two years, Billy participated in several gun battles and killings. Highlight was the siege of the McSween house in Lincoln in July 1878, in which Billy first asserted leadership, which led ultimately to his captaincy of the McSween army. In December 1880, however, a gun fight with a sheriff's posse at Stinking Springs finally led to Billy's arrest.

Legislatively outlawed after Stringybark, Ned took charge of what was styled the "Kelly Gang." Under his leadership, the gang cleverly eluded the scores of police seeking them. Whereas Billy sought to elude the law, Ned Kelly took the initiative: robbing the bank at Euroa. He and his comrades staged the robbery on December 10, 1878. At the same time, after a period of simply drifting, Billy returned to Lincoln to try to clear himself of the murder indictment. He failed.

When the government outlawed Ned and the rest of the Kelly Gang in November 1878, Ned clearly established his leadership, although he sought the counsel of his mates. They would be no ordinary bushrangers, as the police expected. They were outlaws committed to elaborate deeds of outlawry. Robbing the bank at Euroa was the first. It unfolded not only as a bank robbery but as a clever theatrical production. Much of the proceeds were distributed to his Irish sympathizers.

Billy lacked Ned's imagination, his ability to set goals, work toward them, and if possible carry them out. Billy's outlaw life after the murder indictment was more proactive than reactive. When the law got too close in Lincoln, Billy headed east for Fort Sumner, noted for its distance from lawmen. He teamed up with several nasty outlaws, but he devoted his life mainly to having a good time at the dances and the town's two saloons. In one, in January 1880, he killed a Texas bully in the second killing credited to him alone. He shrugged it off with a cocky remark.

Beginning with Euroa, Ned Kelly also demonstrated an increasing cockiness absent previously. Whenever he had an audience, he now played the brash showman. Likewise, when Billy had an audience, he displayed similar behavior. After his arrest following the shootout at Stinking Springs, he had such an audience in the people of Las Vegas and the newspaper reporters who interviewed him.

During the two outlaw years, Ned Kelly constantly tried to tell his side of the story. In the Cameron and Jerilderie letters, he used grandiloquent language to tell of police harassment and the iniquities of the courts, especially in confining his mother in jail for attempting to murder a policeman. These letters also contained threats of unspecified penalties if his side of the story were not credited. Although neither letter achieved much publicity, they reveal Ned's thinking.

By contrast, Billy came across as a witty braggart, proud of the effect his crimes had produced. Like Ned, Billy had his own justifying story to tell, growing out of a supposed bargain with territorial governor Lew Wallace. Three times he wrote letters to the governor, but they had no effect on the law's determination to try him for the murder of Sheriff Brady. His brash commentary ceased when he found himself behind the bars of the Santa Fe jail.

Ned Kelly planned another bank holdup, this one in New South Wales. Like the first, the robbery of the bank in Jerilderie followed the pattern of Euroa, accompanied by an extravagant display of exhibitionism.

Billy was taken to Mesilla and stood trial for murder. He was convicted and sentenced to be hanged. But his outlaw life had not ended, in fact grew more deadly. His breakout from confinement in Lincoln cost the lives of two lawmen, his third and fourth killings. Now he had to escape. Advised to seek refuge in Mexico, which he should have done, he demonstrated his impulsive thinking by returning to Fort Sumner.

Billy expressed remorse for having killed one of his two guards, but said he had to do it. Ned waved his pistol and threatened to shoot people. But he never intended to shoot anyone. He prized life and took it only in the one instance when he believed his own life depended on it. After Stringybark, Ned repeatedly insisted that he did not want to shoot the police but only to get them to surrender. Moreover, unlike Billy, Ned cleverly avoided the scores of police chasing him.

From robbing banks, Ned moved on to more grandiose plans: inspire an uprising of Irish sympathizers and establish a republic in northeastern Victoria. The shootout with the police at Glenrowan enhanced Ned's reputation but ended his outlaw life. For Billy, his main purpose was to elude the law, which was closing in on his haunts around Fort Sumner. His failure cost him his life. After protracted trial, Ned Kelly was hanged in the Melbourne jail on November 11, 1880. Billy grew careless and was shot and killed by Sheriff Pat Garrett on July 14, 1881.

Two short and violent lives that began four years apart had ended nine months apart. But their outlaw lives ensured that their names would live on in the folklore of their respective countries.

* * *

Against this background, who can we conclude Billy the Kid and New Kelly really were? English historian Eric Hobsbawm put forth a definition in his 1959 book, *Primitive Rebels*. He labeled them "social bandits." Social bandits, he wrote, "are considered by their people as heroes, as champions, avengers, fighters for justice, perhaps even leaders of liberation, and in any case as men to be admired, helped and supported. . . . Social banditry of this kind is one of the most universal social phenomena known to history." Among many characters Hobsbawm cites, besides Robin Hood, are Ned Kelly and Billy the Kid. Ned Kelly fits the definition of social bandit as hero to his people. On this basis Ned Kelly flourished through the decades as Australian hero.

Australian historian Manning Clark echoed Hobsbawm with more specificity:

> The memory of [Ned] lived on. The squatters and the bourgeoisie attributed the Kellys and their outrages to the selection acts, which had afforded opportunities for people to take up land in remote districts where religious and educational influences could not penetrate. The result was a race of godless, lawless men and women, half bandits, half cattle stealers, and wholly vicious. But to the dispossessed in both town and country Ned was a hero. In an age in which the gods of the old religions were toppling to their ruins, Ned, or the idea of Ned, was an image in which men could believe, because his life and death symbolized the experience of the native-born, their unwillingness to accept the morality of the English, and their groping for a new morality and a new way of life.

Why did two such national celebrities in their respective countries arise at the same time? One answer may lie in the fact that both the United States and Australia experienced a period of transition and uncertainty during and after the lives of Billy the Kid and Ned Kelly—periods when their fame was taking root.

Billy still roamed an essentially frontier environment, but it was rapidly disappearing. Only nine years after his death, the census revealed that a definable edge of settlement no longer existed. From Atlantic to Pacific, the United States emerged as one unbroken nation —one, furthermore, undergoing momentous transformation from an agricultural realm to an industrial nation.

Paradoxically, Billy's fame lurched erratically for nearly half a century until it rose in fictional form to become what people believed to be the real Billy the Kid. In 1926, Walter Noble Burns's *Saga of Billy the Kid* created a fictional character masquerading as the real Billy that immediately grasped the public imagination. Ironically, this transformation occurred on the edge of another great epoch in American history—the Great Depression of 1929 to World War II in the 1940s. The notoriety of the young hero strengthened during those dark years and never dimmed.

Australia experienced its own transformation, both during and after Ned Kelly's time. In 1883, the railway linking Melbourne to Sydney was completed, which inspired a banquet oration calling for the union of the colonies. Such sentiments were expressed when the railway between Victoria and South Australia was finished in 1887, and between New South Wales and Queensland in 1888. With the telegraph already in place, telephone exchanges burgeoning throughout the colonies, immigrant population exceeding native-born population, and industry, commerce, agriculture, and foreign trade flourishing, the 1880s, after Ned's death, reconfigured the Australian polity and kept alive the idea of federation. A financial collapse in the 1890s further strengthened the call for federation of the colonies into an Australian nation within the British Commonwealth. "The old order was dying at the moment when bourgeois statesmanship and civilization reached their apogee in Australia," writes historian Manning Clark. A convention in 1897–98 sanctioned confederation, and a huge celebration in Sydney in January 1901 proclaimed the Commonwealth of Australia.

Ned Kelly had been long dead during the culmination of these developments, but his memory lived through them as a constant, in contrast to Billy the Kid. Had Ned lived to experience them, he is unlikely to have attained the legendary character that enduringly marked his memory. The environment of Kelly country changed together with the rest of the colonies, hampering his ability to function as he had in the 1860s and 1870s.

* * *

And so, both countries in the twenty-first century possess national icons. Not all Americans or Australians approve of their lives and exploits. In fact, American academic historians scorn Billy the Kid and ridicule historians who devote time to him, as this author can attest. Billy the Kid, however, appeals to a large swath of the American public, no matter how distorted his life and exploits. His admirers revel in the distortions and entertain only scorn for professionals who try to tamper with them. For these Americans, Billy the Kid is an immortal symbol of the Old West.

Not all Australians see Ned Kelly as a great man. Although a traveler to Australia repeatedly hears Ned characterized as the nation's only hero, many Australians regard him as a murderer of policemen and attribute nothing positive to his life and persona. Yet, whatever their true sentiments, Australians flaunt Ned Kelly at every Kelly site and in a continuing stream of literature. From the viewpoint of the professional historian, Ned personifies important strains of Australian history, a virtue Billy the Kid cannot claim. Whether scorning or uplifting Ned, no Australian can deny his immortality.

Billy the Kid and Ned Kelly symbolize significant strands of their nations' folklore, if not their history. From the perspective of history, neither are heroes. The passage of time colored them, and writers and filmmakers dramatized them in unhistorical ways for audiences that did not particularly care so long as they were entertained. From the perspective of folklore, Billy and Ned have been treasured for more than a century. But were they truly national icons? If not, they were two young men whose deeds entitle them to be remembered for what they contributed to their nations' heritage.

BIBLIOGRAPHIC ESSAY

Both Billy the Kid and Ned Kelly have been exhaustively researched, and reliable, documented books have been published on both. I have relied on these books because they have plumbed the original sources and presented accurate interpretations. I saw no need to repeat the process. So this book rests on those previous authoritative books. It is not documented with footnotes or endnotes. I have told the stories as they were presented by the authors I judged most reliable. For Billy the Kid the author is myself. For Ned Kelly the author is Ian Jones.

Billy the Kid

Most of what I have written here has been drawn from my own biography: *Billy the Kid: A Short and Violent Life* (Lincoln: University of Nebraska Press, 1989); and its predecessor, *High Noon in Lincoln: Violence on the Western Frontier* (Albuquerque: University of New Mexico Press, 1987). The prime authority on Billy the Kid, however, is Frederick Nolan. With *The Life and Death of John Henry Tunstall* (Albuquerque: University of New Mexico Press, 1965), he laid the basis for a series of books that he continues to produce. Among those I have found most useful are *The Lincoln County War: A Documentary History* (Norman: University of Oklahoma Press, 1992); *The West of Billy the Kid* (Norman: University of Oklahoma Press, 1998); and *The Billy the Kid Reader* (Norman: University of Oklahoma Press, 2007). In addition, I have used Stephen Tatum, *Inventing Billy the Kid: Visions of the Outlaw in America, 1881–1981* (Albuquerque: University of New Mexico Press, 1982);

Jon Tuska, *Billy the Kid: A Bio-Bibliography* (Westport, CT: Greenwood Press, 1983); and Joel Jacobsen, *Such Men as Billy the Kid: The Lincoln County War Reconsidered* (Lincoln: University of Nebraska Press, 1994).

Ned Kelly

For Ned Kelly, the preeminent source is Ian Jones, *Ned Kelly: A Short Life,* 2nd ed. (Melbourne: Lothian Press, 2003). Jones's other valuable book is *The Friendship that Destroyed Ned Kelly: Joe Byrne and Aaron Sherritt* (Melbourne: Lothian Press, 1992). Extremely valuable if not indispensable is Justin Cornfield, *The Ned Kelly Encyclopedia* (Melbourne: Lothian Press, 2003). Alex C. Castles, *Ned Kelly's Last Days: Setting the Record Straight on the Death of an Outlaw* (Crows Nest, NSW: Allen and Unwin, 2005), authoritatively and with some revisionism, treats Ned Kelly's life after Glenrowan until his hanging. Other books from which I have drawn include the following: Paul Terry, *The True Story of Ned Kelly's Last Stand: New Revelations Unearthed about the Bloody Siege at Glenrowan [archeological projects]* (Crows Nest, New South Wales: Allen and Unwin, 2012); Graham Jones, *Ned Kelly: The Larrikin Years, The Rise and Fall of the Prince of Larrikins* (Wangaratta, Victoria: Charquin Hills, 1990); John McQuilton, *The Kelly Outbreak, 1878–1880: The Geographical Dimension of Social Banditry* (Melbourne: Melbourne University Press, 1979); Charles Osborne, *Ned Kelly* (London: Anthony Bond, 1970); John Molony, *Ned Kelly* (Ringwood, Victoria: Penguin Books, 1982); Graham Seal, *Ned Kelly in Popular Tradition* (Melbourne: Highland House, 1980); Graham Seal, *The Outlaw Legend: A Cultural Tradition in Britain, America, and Australia* (Cambridge: Cambridge University Press, 1996); Keith Dunstan, *Saint Ned: The Story of the Near Sanctification of an Australian Outlaw* (Sydney: Methuen of Australia, 1980); Manning Clark, *A Short History of Australia* (Ringwood, Victoria: Penguin Books, 1963); and Robert Haldane, *The People's Force: A History of the Victoria Police,* 2nd ed. (Melbourne: Melbourne University Press, 1995).

Three additional books belong here: Ian Macfarland, *The Kelly Gang Unmasked* (Melbourne: Oxford University Press, 2012), Peter FitzSimons, *Ned Kelly: The Story of Australia's Most Notorious Legend* (Sydney: William Heinemann, 2013), and a Booker Prize–winning novel, Peter Carey's *True History of the Kelly Gang* (New York: Alfred A. Knopf, 2000). Although fiction, Carey's novel captures the spirit of the story and sets forth many valuable insights. Macfarland consistently excoriates the Kelly Gang and exonerates the police of all misbehavior. FitzSimons is strictly narrative, with little attempt at interpretation.

INDEX

Aboriginal Mounted Police, 154

Aborigines, 118, 154, 184

Ah Fook, 124–25

Alabama, 24

Albury, Australia, 115

Anglos, 18, 19, 26, 47, 62, 95, 97, 199, 201, 202, 203

Anton Chico, New Mexico, 64, 76

Antrim, Catherine McCarty, 8, 193, 194, 196, *plates*

Antrim, Joe, 8

Antrim, William H. H., 8, 194

Apache Indians, 19, 63

Arizona, 4, 19, 20, 194, 195, 196, 197

armor, vii, 157–58, 162, 165, 167, 168, 188, 193, *plates*

Atchison, Topeka, and Santa Fe Railroad, 3

Atkins, George, 10

Australia, vii, viii–ix, 111, 112, 118, 121, 122, 123, 129, 136, 139, 149, 150, 184, 187, 196, 197, 202–4, 208–9

Authentic Life of Billy the Kid (Garrett), 102, 106

Avenel, Australia, 111, 115, 116–17, 118–19, 154, 168, 188, 203

Axtell, Samuel B., 38, 41, 51

Baca, José Chavez y, 52, 61

Baker, Frank, 27, 29, 37, 41, 106

ballads, 153, 171, 185–86

Ballarat, Australia, 204

Bank of New South Wales, 150

Barry, Ellen, 157

Barry, Redmond, 132–33, 176–77, 178, 179, 180

Bathurst, Australia, 204

Battle of Lincoln, 49, 50, 53, 176

Beckwith, Robert, 60, 90

Beechworth, Australia, vii, 115, 120, 127, 132, 156, 161, 162, 163, 173, 174–75, 176, 180, 188, 204

Beechworth gaol, 127, 132, 133, 148, 174

Beery, Wallace, 103

Bell, James W., 91–93, 94, 96, 106

Benalla, Australia, 115, 125, 130, 131, 133, 134, 154, 155, 159, 161–64 passim, 166, 169, 171, 172, 185, 188

Bendigo, Australia, 204

Ben-Hur (Wallace), 66, 72, 88

Bernstein, Morris, 63–64

Berry, Graham, 137, 143, 147

Beveridge, Australia, 111, 112, 115, 116, 174, 188

Billy the Kid (aka William H. Bonney, aka Kid, aka Henry McCarty, aka Henry Antrim), vii–viii, 6, 19, 21, 48, 50, 62, 63, 64, 65, 66, 67–68, 73, 80, 82, 87, 88, 89, 90–91, 138, *plates;* in Arizona, 9–11; and Blazer's Mill fight, 43, 44, 46; with The Boys, 13–16; and Brady assassination, 39–40; compared with Ned Kelly, 191–207 passim; and conspiracy theories, 104–5; country of, 5, 16–19, 203; described, 5, 11–12, 19, 20, 65, 69, 76, 84–85; escapes Grant County jail, 7; escapes Lincoln, 91–95; in five-day battle, 54, 55, 59, 60, 61; in fight at Greathouse Ranch, 79; at Fort Sumner, 75–78, 80, 97–99; and guns, 19, 28, 77; Hispanics on, 5–6; indicted for murder, 48, 205; kills Joe Grant, 77; and Lew Wallace, 69–72, 88; and Martínez posse, 34–36; myths of, 106–7; names of, 4, 7, 12, 70; pact with Evans, 67–68; photos of, 104; in print and film, 103–4; in raid on Dolan cow camp, 51; as Regulator, 36–40 passim, 41, 51; and Sallie Chisum, 53, 63–64, 65; at Stinking Springs, 82–83, 85–86; at Tunstall ranch, 22–24; and Tunstall's death, 29, 30–34; youth of, 8–9

Billy the Kid (ballet), 104

Billy the Kid (film), 103

Billy the Kid National Scenic Highway, viii, 105

Billy the Kid Outlaw Gang, viii, 105

Billy the Kid Returns (film), 103

Bindon, Henry, 177, 178

black trackers, 118, 154

Blazer, Joseph H., 42, 43, 46, 47

Blazer's Mill, New Mexico, 18, 42–45 passim, 50, 61, 62

Boer War, viii, 189

Book-of-the-Month Club, 102

Bosque Grande, New Mexico, 63

Bowdre, Charley, 24, 43, 44, 48, 49, 50–51, 52, 62, 64, 75, 78, 80–83, 86, 100, *plates*

Bowdre, Manuela, 24, 81, *plates*

Boys, The, 13–16, 19, 20, 27, 198

Bracken, Hugh, 164, 165, 168, 172, 174, *plates*

Brady, William, 27, 28–29, 30, 34, 35, 36, 37, 38, 40, 48, 49, 200, *plates;* assassination of, 39–40, 43, 45, 46, 47, 48, 61, 63, 66, 72, 77, 89, 90, 106, 207

Brazil, Manuel, 81–82, 84

Brewer, Richard, 22, 24, 28, 30, 31, 36–38, 40–41, 42–45 passim, 62, 199, *plates;* death of, 45, 48

Bristol, Warren, 27, 28, 36, 38, 47, 72, 87, 88–89, 90, 107

British Commonwealth, 209

British Empire, 187

Brown, Henry N., 24, 65

Brown, Johnny Mack, 103
Bullock Creek, Australia, 132, 133
Bureau of Indian Affairs, 5
Burns, Walter Noble, 102–3, 104, 107, 209
bush, Australian, 115, 117, 129, 136, 195, 197, 203
bushranger, 122, 139, 145, 146, 184, 196, 200, 206
Byrne, Joe, 132, 133, 135–38, 142, 143, 145, 155–58, 161–65 passim; killed, 167, 205
Byrne, Kate, 156

Cahill, Francis P., 10, 11, 77, 106, 195
Cameron, Donald, 143
Cameron letter, 143–44, 145, 147, 150, 151, 170, 175, 179, 206
Camp Grant, Arizona, 9, 11, 77
Campbell, Billy, 67, 68, 69, 71, 72
Canberra, Australia, 187
Capitan Mountains, New Mexico, 5, 17, 69, 94
Carey, Peter, 183–84
Carlyle, Jimmy, 79, 91, 106
Carroll, Henry, 69
Cass, Godfrey, 185
Castieau, John, 172, 173, 179, 180
Catholic Church, 111, 112, 116, 117, 179, 196, 202
Catron, Thomas B., 48, 51, 52
Chapman, Arthur, 107
Chapman, Huston, 65–66, 68, 69, 70, 71, 87
Chavez, Josefita, 51
Chavez, Martín, 54
Chavez y Baca, José, 52, 61
Chickasaw Indians, 23
Chisum, James, 63, 77

Chisum, John Simpson, 13, 18–19, 27, 38, 48, 52, 63, 77, 78, 107
Chisum, Pitzer, 63
Chisum, Sallie, 53, 63–64, 65, 192
Chisum, William, 77
Chitty, Bob, 185
Church of England, 117
Civil War, 3, 8, 18, 24, 28, 42, 45, 66, 199, 201
Clark, Manning, 208, 209
Coburn, James, 104
Coe, Frank, 20–24, 34, 40, 43, 44, 53, 63, 64
Coe, George, 20, 22, 43, 44, 49, 52, 55, 60–63
Colfax County War (New Mexico), 22
Colorado, 64
Commonwealth of Australia, 209
convicts, 112, 113, 184
Cooke's Canyon, New Mexico, 14
Copeland, Aaron, 104
Copeland, John N., 47, 48, 49, 50, 51, 52
Crabb, Buster, 103
Crimean War, 142
Curnow, Thomas, 163, 164, 165, 170
Custer, George A., 107

Davis, George, 27, 29
Death Valley Days (TV series), 104
Declaration of Outlawry, 137
Denver, Colorado, 8
Devine, George, 149, 153
Dirty Little Billy (film), 103
Discovery Channel, 104
Dolan, James J., 24, 26, 28–31, 34, 36, 38, 40–42, 48, 49, 51, 52, 66–70, 72, 90, 204, *plates*; described, 25; and five-day battle, 54, 61

Dolan & Co., 27, 28, 35, 36, 39, 40, 91

Doña Ana County, New Mexico, 72, 73

Dudley, Nathan A. M., 50, 51, 62, 63, 64, 66, 68, 69, 72–73, *plates;* in five-day battle, 55–56, 57–58, 59, 61, 72–73

Ealy, Mary, 48

Ealy, Taylor, 40

Ellis, Isaac, 40, 54, 55, 58, 61, 65

England, 107, 112, 184, 203

Estevez, Emilio, 104

Etulain, Richard, ix

Euroa, Australia, 115, 144–46 passim, 147, 150, 151, 153, 155, 174–76, 188, 205–7

Evans, Jesse, 13–16, 21, 24, 27, 29, 30, 31, 35–37, 41, 52, 54, 66–72

Faithfull's Creek Homestead, Australia, 144

Felons Apprehension Act, 137, 148, 170, 173, 177

Fifteen-Mile Creek, Australia, 120

First Presbyterian Church of Santa Fe, 8

Fitzpatrick, Alexander, 128, 130–31, 138, 143–44, 170

Ford, Thomas, 120

Fort Cummings, New Mexico, 14

Fort Stanton, New Mexico, 5, 18, 25, 35, 40, 49, 50, 62, 67–71 passim, 73, 199, 203

Fort Sumner, New Mexico, 4, 19, 64, 71, 75–79 passim, 81, 84, 94–95, 97, 105, 107, 192, 198, 199, 206, 207

Fort Union, New Mexico, 50

Foster, William, 175, 176

Fountain, Albert J., 14–15

French, Jim, 39–40, 43, 55, 60, 61, 62

Fritz, Emil, 28

Frost, Bill, 125, 128

Garfield, James, 88

Garrett, Patrick F., 78, 80, 81, 82–86, 91, 95, 96, 97–100, 102, 104–6, 207, *plates; Authentic Life of Billy the Kid,* 102, 106

Gatling Gun, 55, 58, 61

Gaunson, David, 174–75, 177, 179

Gauss, Godfrey, 92

Germany, 28

Geronimo (Apache), vii, ix

Gibney, Matthew, 169

Gill, Samuel, 151

Glenmore, Australia, 124

Glenrowan, Australia, vii, 115, 159, 161, 171, 174, 176, *plates*; battle of, 161–170, 175, 187–88, 192, 207

Glenrowan Inn, 162–63 passim

Gloster, George, 144, 145

Godfroy, Frederick C., 43, 46, 62, 63

Goulburn, Australia, 156

Grant, Joe, 77, 80, 106, 202, 206

Grant County, New Mexico, 7

Great Depression, 209

Great Sebastopol Raid, 142, 155

Greathouse, "Whiskey Jim," 79

Greathouse Ranch, New Mexico, 80, 81, 91

Greta, Australia, 120, 121, 124, 125, 126, 128, 130–32 passim, 134, 136, 140, 169, 182, 188

Greta Mob, 122, 132, 136

Guadalupe Mountains, New Mexico, 3, 5, 15

Gunn, Alex, 126
Gunn, Annie, 125
Gurner, Henry, 173, 176, 177
Gutierrez, Celsa, 96

Hall, Ben, 137
Hall, Edward, 126–127, 129
Hare, Francis, 147, 155–56, 158,
    165–66, 172
Hargrove, Bob, 76, 81
Hart, Steve, viii, 132, 133, 137, 138,
    145, 158, 161, 162, 167, 169, 188,
    205, *plates*
Hatch, Edward, 50, 69
Hayes, Rutherford B., 4
Herrerra, Antonia, 24
Hico, Texas, 105
High Noon in Lincoln (Utley), viii
Hill, Tom, 27, 29, 31–32, 37, 48
Hispanics, 5–6, 18, 19, 26, 36, 38, 47,
    51, 52, 54, 55, 60, 62–63, 94, 95,
    191, 199, 201, 203
History Channel, 104
History of Billy the Kid, The (Siringo),
    102
Hobsbawm, Eric, 208
Homestead Act, 8, 113
Hooker, Henry C., 9–10, 11
Horrell War, 201
Hough, Emerson, 106, 107
House, The, 17, 25, 26, 27, 28, 29, 33,
    36, 38
Hudgens, William H., 79
Hutton, Paul A., 107

Indianapolis, Indiana, 8
Ireland, 112, 115, 119, 129, 144, 150,
    196
Irish, 112, 116, 129, 138, 150, 196,
    202, 203, 204

Jagger, Mick, 185
Jerilderie, Australia, 149–53, 155,
    156, 175, 207
Jerilderie letter, 150, 151, 153, 158,
    170, 175, 179, 206
Johnston, Charles, 142, 169
Jones, Anne, 162, 163, 165, 166, 170,
    171, 174, 188
Jones, Barbara, 16
Jones, Heiskell, 15–16
Jones, Ian, ix, 159, 181
Jones, Jack, 164, 166

Kansas, 75
Kathner, Rupert, 185
Kelly, Anne "Annie" (sister), 115,
    116, 119
Kelly, Catherine "Kate" (sister), 116,
    131, 138, 169, 179, 180
Kelly, Daniel (brother), viii, 115, 130,
    131, 132, 134–35, 137–39, 145,
    158, 161, 185, 188, 205, *plates*
Kelly, Edward "Ned," vii, 111, 112,
    113, 115, 116, 120, 128, 132,
    137, 142, 157, 171–72, 179, 180,
    181–82, 187, 188, 203, 205,
    plates; and Aborigines, 118;
    and Ah Fook, 124–25; as Aus-
    tralian icon, 170, 171, 183, 189;
    awarded green sash, 118, 168;
    Beechworth committal hearing,
    174–76; as boxing champion, 128;
    as bushranger, 123–24, 125–26;
    compared with Billy the Kid,
    191–207 passim; described, 111,
    116, 117–18, 119, 122, 128–29,
    136, 139, 145, 146, 175–76, 204;
    education of, 116, 117; films on,
    184–85; and Fitzpatrick, 130–31;
    138; at Glenrowan, 161–70;

Kelly, Edward "Ned" (*continued*)
hanged, 179–81; imprisoned after
Glenrowan, 172; imprisoned for
three years, 127; as larrikin,
122–23, 128; literature on, 103–4,
183–84; murder trial of, 177–78,
plates; as outlaw, 137–38, 139,
143, 148 (map), 205; and republic, 158–59, 161; robs Euroa
bank, 144–46; robs Jerilderie
bank, 149–53; saves Richard
Shelton, 118; and Stringybark,
134–35, 138–39
Kelly, Ellen (mother), 111, 115–17,
121, 125, 128, 131, 132, 138, 195,
plates; described, 119–20; jailed,
132–33, 170, 172, 175, 176, 180,
205, 206
Kelly, Grace (sister), 116, 117, 169,
180
Kelly, James (brother), 115, 116,
121, 180
Kelly, John "Red" (father), 111–12,
115–18 passim, 194, 203
Kelly, Margaret "Maggie" (sister),
115, 116, 169, 173, 174, 177, 179
Kelly country, 113–15, 204
Kelly Gang, 136, 138, 140–45
passim, 146, 147, 156, 158, 187,
191, 206; and Euroa, 144–46; and
Glenrowan, 161–70; and Jerilderie, 149–54; and Stringybark,
138–39
Kelly Gang, The (film), 185
Kelly Gang Unmasked, The (Macfarland), 189–90
Kelly Irish sympathizers, 138, 146,
147–48, 153, 157, 161, 191, 192,
195, 206, 207; and Glenrowan,
163, 167, 169–70

Kennedy, Michael, 135, 176
Killmore, Australia, 115
Kimball, George, 67, 68, 71, 72, 73
King, George, 128, 132
King River, Australia, 124
Kinney, John, 14
Koogler, W. S., 3–4, 5, 6, 7, 79, 80,
93, 94
Kristofferson, Kris, 103–4
Kyneton, Australia, 126

larrikin, 121–22, 124, 132, 134, 139,
146, 200
Las Cruces, New Mexico, 14
Las Tablas, New Mexico, 69, 94
Las Vegas, Nevada, 3
Las Vegas, New Mexico, 3, 16, 55,
64, 73, 75, 76, 84–85, 87, 89, 93,
206
Las Vegas Gazette, 3, 80
Lawson, Henry, 115
Ledger, Heath, 185
Left-Handed Gun, The (film), 103
Lincoln, New Mexico, 5, 16, 17
(map), 20, 22, 24, 25, 28–30, 32,
36–38, 40, 47–51, 53, 55, 56–57
(map), 62, 64, 65, 69–74, 76, 80,
88–91, 93, 95, 96, 198, 205–7,
plates; described, 17–18, 39
Lincoln County, New Mexico, 5, 16,
26, 38, 45, 47, 66, 78, 81, 86, 105,
198, 199, 201–4
Lincoln County Bank, 27, 38
Lincoln County War, viii, 5, 20, 21,
28, 42, 50, 51, 53, 62, 70, 72, 89,
90, 107, 192, 199, 200, 201, 204;
five-day battle, 54–61; phase, 1,
24–33; as *war*, 41, 45–46, 52
Living, Edward, 151
Lloyd, Jack, 120, 124, 126, 166–67

Lloyd, Kate, 172, 177, 180, 192
Lloyd, Tom, 120, 124, 136, 167, 173, 174, 177, 180
Long, Jack, 52, 54, 55, 59, 60
Lonigan, William, 131, 134, 176, 178

Macfarland, Ian, 159–60, 212
Mackie, John R., 10
Mansfield, Australia, 124, 126, 134, 137
Martínez, Atanacio, 33, 34, 35, 40
Mathews, Jacob B., 29–31, 39–40, 42, 48, 49, 54, 67, 90, 91, *plates*
Maxwell, Deluvina, 99
Maxwell, Lucien, 19, 84
Maxwell, Paulita, 84
Maxwell, Pete, 19, 75, 98, 107
Maxwell House, 98–100, *plates*
Maxwell land grant, 19
McBean, Robert, 125
McCloskey, William, 37, 41, 106
McDonnell's Railway Tavern, 159, 162, 163
McInerny, David, 125
McIntyre, Thomas, 134–36, 174, 176
McKinney, Tom, 100
McNab, Frank, 48, 49, 50, 51
McSween, Alexander, 24, 27, 28, 32–33, 34, 36, 39, 40, 45, 47, 48, 49, 50, 52, 53, 64, 86, 199, 200, *plates;* Brady assassination plotted, 38–39; described, 26; in five-day battle, 58, 59, 60
McSween, Susan, 26, 27, 38, 48, 55, 58, 59, 65–66, 72, 106
McSween House, 55, 58, 59, 61, 90, 94, 96, 106, 191, 199, 205
Meadows, John, 94–95, 96, 100
Melbourne, Australia, vii, viii, 112, 113, 115–17, 120, 123, 126, 137, 143, 144, 147, 158, 168, 169, 171–73, 176, 179, 181, 188, 197, 203, 209
Melbourne City Court, 173
Melbourne Club, 123, 177
Melbourne Cup, 177
Mescalero Apache Indian Agency, New Mexico, 5, 18, 25, 203
Mescalero Apache Indian Reservation, New Mexico, 43
Mescalero Apache Indians, 13, 63
Mesilla, New Mexico, 14, 15, 18, 27, 28, 29, 87, 88, 90, 207
Mesilla Valley Independent, 13, 14–15
Mexicans, 18, 106, 199. *See also* Hispanics
Mexico, 12, 82, 94, 100, 192, 207
Middleton, John, 22, 31, 38, 40, 43, 44, 48, 49, 50–51, 62, 65
Miller, John, 104
Mississippi, 24
Mogollon Mountains, New Mexico, 14
Montaño, Juan, 54
Montaño store, 54, 55, 58, 69, 71
Mortimer, David, 163, 165
Morton, William S., 27, 30, 31–32, 36–37, 41, 48, 77, 106
Mount Graham, Arizona, 9
Murphy, Lawrence G., 17, 24–25, 28, 43, 69, 203, 204, *plates*
Murray River, Australia, 115, 137, 140, 149, 152, 156

National Gallery of Australia, 187
Navajo Indians, 19
Ned Kelly (1970 film), 185
Ned Kelly (2003 film), 185
Ned Kelly: A Short Life (Jones), 159
Ned Kelly Fan Club, viii, 188

Ned Kelly Trail, viii, 188
New Mexico, 3, 5, 12, 13, 20, 23 (map), 24, 36, 48, 52, 65, 72, 75, 78, 80, 85, 88, 93, 94, 96, 105, 195, 197, 198
New Mexico Volunteers, 24
New South Wales, Australia, 115, 136, 137, 140, 149, 153, 156, 204, 207, 209
New York City, 8, 193, 196
New York Sun, 101
New Zealand, vii
Newman, Paul, 103
Newmarket Railway Station, 174
Nicholson, John, 168
Nicolson, Charles, 140, 142, 143, 147, 156–58
Ninth Cavalry, 50
Nolan, Frederick, 8
Nolan, Sydney, 187, 193
Norris, Tom, 94–95
North Melbourne Railway Station, 172
Northeast Police District, 140

O'Connor, Stanhope, 154
O'Folliard, Tom, 53, 55, 60, 61, 65–69, 72, 75, 78, 80–82, 86, 100, *plates*
O'Hea, Charles, 111, 180, 181
Ohio, 76
Old Melbourne Gaol, vii, 133, 171, 172, 176, 182, 188, 191, 207
Olinger, Bob "Pecos Bob," 90–93, 94, 96, 106, *plates*
Organ Mountains, New Mexico Stockman's Association, 78, 82

Pat Garrett and Billy the Kid (film), 103
Patrón house, 58, 71
Peckinpah, Sam, 103

Pecos River, New Mexico, 3, 4, 13, 15, 16, 18, 20, 37, 49, 63, 64, 75, 76, 198, 199, 201, 203
Pentridge gaol, 120, 123, 124, 127, 128, 182
Peppin, George "Dad," 40, 48–49, 51–52, 53, 62; in five-day battle, 54, 58, 59, 61, 67
Pickett, Tom, 75, 76, 81, 82, 87
Poe, John, 100, *plates*
Power, Harry, 123–24, 125–26, 200
Primitive Rebels (Hobsbawm), 208
Proclamation of Outlawry, 137, 138, 140, 146
Protestant churches, 112, 123, 155, 196, 202, 203
Puerto de Luna, New Mexico, 64, 76

Queen Victoria, 116, 119, 122, 150, 157, 196, 203
Queensland, Australia, 154, 155, 209
Queensland Police, 154
Quinn, James, 115, 116, 124

Rama, New Mexico, 104
Ramsay, Robert, 171, 173
Regulators, 36–39 passim, 40, 43, 45, 48–53, 63–65, 67, 199, 200; in five-day battle, 54–61
Republic of Northeastern Victoria, 158, 159, 192, 207
Richards, Henry, 149, 151–52, 153
Richardson, Bill, 105
Río Bonito, New Mexico, 17, 18, 20, 30, 38, 60, 61, 73
Río Feliz, New Mexico, 22, 23
Rio Grande, 5, 8, 14, 15, 16, 88
Río Hondo, New Mexico, 18, 20, 52
Río Peñasco, New Mexico, 23, 30, 65, 66, 94

Río Ruidoso, New Mexico, 16, 18, 20, 22, 24, 30, 31, 32, 42, 44, 94

Roberts, Andrew L. "Buckshot," 42–45, 47, 48, 49, 52, 66

Roberts, "Brushy Bill," viii, 105

Robin Hood, 208

Rogers, Christopher, vii–viii, ix

Rogers, Roy, 103

Romero, Desiderio, 64

Ross, Thom, 193

Roswell, New Mexico, 75, 78

Rowe, J. P., 124

Royal Mail Hotel (Avenel), 117, 118

Royal Mail Hotel (Jerilderie), 150, 151

Rudabaugh, Dave, 75, 78, 81, 82, 83, 84, 87

Ryan, Charles, 172

Rynerson, William L., 27, 36, 47, 52, 71, 72, 73, 89

Sadleir, John, 140, 142, 143, 145, 147, 156, 166, 168, 169

Saga of Billy the Kid, The (Burns), 102, 103, 107, 209

Saint Louis, Missouri, 19

Salazar, Yginio, 60, 94, 100

San Augustine Pass, New Mexico, 15

San Miguel County, New Mexico, 64, 75, 81

San Patricio, New Mexico, 18, 38, 49, 50, 52, 53, 54, 55, 69, 71, 94, 199

Sanchez, Manuel

Sangre de Cristo Mountains (New Mexico), 16

Santa Barbara, New Mexico, 14

Santa Fe, New Mexico, 3, 8, 26, 27, 29, 48, 66, 72, 85, 87, 89, 193, 200, 207

Santa Fe New Mexican, 97, 102

Santa Fe Ring, 48

Santa Fe Trail, 85

Santa Rosa, New Mexico, 76

Saunders, Ab, 49

Scanlan, Michael, 135, 176

Scott, Robert, 145, 146

Scurlock, Josiah "Doc," 24, 51, 52, 55, 61, 62, 64, 71, 73, 75

Sebastopol, Australia, 142

Segovia, Manuel "Indian," 51, 106

Selectors, 113, 121, 124, 157, 158, 202

Seven Rivers, New Mexico, 15, 16, 18, 19, 20, 27, 31, 37, 49, 51, 60, 64, 90

Seven Rivers posse, 30, 31, 49, 50, 51, 53, 54

Sherritt, Aaron, 136, 137, 155, 157, 158, 163, 165, *plates;* murder of, 161–62, 170

Shield, David, 55, 58, 59

Shields, John, 172, 173

Sierra Blanca, New Mexico, 3, 5, 15, 18

Silver City, New Mexico, 7–11, 13, 14, 73, 105, 193–97

Siringo, Charlie, 102, 106

Skilling, William, 132, 173

Smith, Alexander Brooke, 142–43

Smith, Beaver, 76, 81

Smyth, Charles, 173, 176, 177

social bandits, 208

Sombrero Jack, 7

South Africa, 189

South Australia, 209

South Spring Ranch, New Mexico, 38, 52–53

Southwell, Henry, 185

Spencer Street Railway Station, 172, 174

Squatters, 113, 125, 138, 157, 202

Staked Plains, Texas, 3, 5, 64

Standish, Frederick, 123, 126, 142, 143, 147, 148, 154, 155, 156, 157, 158, 168, 171, 172, 175

Stanistreet, John, 162, 163, 164, 165, 169

State Library of Victoria, 188

Steele, Arthur, 167–68, 172, 173–74, *plates*

Steele, Bob, 103

Stewart, Frank, 78

Stinking Springs, New Mexico, 82–84, 85, 87, 89, 94, 205, 206

Story of the Kelly Gang, The (film), 184

Strathbogie Ranges, Australia, 115, 125, 174

Stringybark Creek, Australia, 134, 188

Stringybark murders, 134–36, 137–40, 143, 145, 146, 151, 175, 176, 205, 207, *plates*

Sulphur Springs Valley, Arizona, 9

Sydney, Australia, 115, 209

Sylvester, 15

Tarleton, John, 151

Tascosa, Texas, 65

Tasmania, Australia, 112

Taylor, Robert, 103

Texas, 13, 16, 18, 19, 22, 24, 45, 53, 64, 67, 71, 72, 75, 199, 201, 206

Texas Cowboy, A: Or, Fifteen Years on the Hurricane Deck of a Spanish Pony (Siringo), 102, 106

Texas Panhandle, 3, 4, 64, 65, 78

Tingwell, Charles, 185

torreon, 18, 54, 55, 59, 61

transport, 112, 115, 184, 196

True History of the Kelly Gang (Carey), 183

Trujillo, Francisco, 51

Tularosa, New Mexico, 15, 21, 78

Tularosa River, New Mexico, 42

Tunstall, John H., 22, 28, 36; death of, 31–32, 37, 39, 42, 46, 48, 49, 67, 86, 90, 106, 203, *plates;* described, 25–26; in Lincoln County War, 24–32

Tunstall Ranch, 22, 24, 29–31, 36, 39, 92, 199, 200

Tunstall Store, 24, 26, 29, 32, 35, 39, 54, 55, 60, 61

United States Congress, 137–38

United States of America, viii–ix, 107, 137, 201, 208–9

United States Secret Service, 78

University of New Mexico, ix

Upjohn, Elijah, 179, 180

Upson, Marshall Ashman, 102, 106

Van Dieman's Land, Australia, 112, 115

Victoria, Australia, 113, 114 (map), 115, 129, 138, 141 (map), 146, 153, 161, 170, 198, 202, 204, 209

Victoria Chief Justice, 137

Victoria Executive Council, 178, 179

Victoria Lands Department, 157

Victoria Legislative Assembly, 137, 143, 170, 205

Victoria Legislative Council, 137

Victoria Parliament, 137, 147, 173

Victoria Police Force, 119, 122, 123, 124–25, 127, 134–35, 140–43, 147–48, 149–51, 153, 161–70 passim, 187, *plates*

Victoria Supreme Court, 176, 177
Vidal, Gore, 103
Vidor, King, 103

Waite, Fred, 22–23, 30, 31, 35, 36,
    38–40, 43, 48, 52, 53, 62, 65,
    plates
Wallace, Lew, 3–4, 66, 68–72, 73–74,
    80, 85, 87, 89, 93, 200, 206–7,
    plates; Ben-Hur, 66, 72, 88
Wallan, Australia, 115
Wangaratta, Australia, 115, 121,
    126, 127, 140–41, 143, 166
Warby Ranges, Australia, 113, 136,
    140, 142–43, 159, 162, 166
Washington, DC, 87, 88
"Wearing of the Green, The," 164–65
Webb, Melody, vii, ix
Whelan, James, 125, 130
When the Kellys Rode (film), 185
When the Kellys Were Out (film), 185
White Oaks, New Mexico, 78, 79, 91,
    96
White Sands, New Mexico, 5
Whitehill, Harvey, 7, 11, 69, 193,
    196–97

Wichita, Kansas, 8
Widenmann, Rob, 29, 30, 31, 35
Wild Colonial Boy, 122, 164
Williams, Henry, 174
Williamson, Brickey, 132
Wilson, Billy, 75, 76, 81, 82, 83, 87, 88
Wilson, John B., 18, 34, 35, 36, 37,
    38, 41, 47, 51, 69, 70, 71, 73
Winchester rifle, 14, 29, 35, 36,
    39–40, 71, 86, 201, 202
Wombat Ranges, Australia, 115, 120,
    124, 132, 133, 134, 139, 204
Woolshed Valley, Australia, 115,
    136, 142, 155, 156, 157, 161
World War II, 209
Wortley, Sam, 18
Wortley Hotel, 18, 54, 55, 91–93
Wright, Isaiah "Wild," 126, 127–28
Wyatt, Alfred, 133

Yale University Press, vii, ix
Yerby, Thomas G., 81
Young Guns (film), 104
Young Guns 2 (film), 104

Zincke, William, 173, 174